VIEW FROM THE SECOND ROW

Winning a lineout against France at the 2011 Rugby World Cup, Eden Park. *(Tim Clayton/Corbis Sport via Getty Images)*

SAMUEL
WHITELOCK

VIEW FROM THE SECOND ROW

with Dylan Cleaver

HarperCollins*Publishers*

HarperCollins*Publishers*
Australia • Brazil • Canada • France • Germany • Holland • India
Italy • Japan • Mexico • New Zealand • Poland • Spain • Sweden
Switzerland • United Kingdom • United States of America

First published in 2024
by HarperCollins*Publishers* (New Zealand) Limited
Unit D1, 63 Apollo Drive, Rosedale, Auckland 0632, New Zealand
harpercollins.co.nz

A catalogue record for this book is available from the National Library of New Zealand

ISBN 978 1 7755 4250 6 (hardback)
ISBN 978 1 7754 9281 8 (ebook)

Cover design by Luke Causby, Blue Cork
Front cover image: Hannah Peters/Getty Images
Back cover image: Final game in black. The Rugby World Cup Final, 2023.
Adam Pretty/World Rugby via Getty Images
Back endpaper image: Holding aloft the Super Rugby trophy in 2019.
Phil Walter/Getty Images
Front endpaper image: First start for the All Blacks, 2010, vs England.
All internal images courtesy of Samuel Whitelock or the Whitelock family archive,
unless otherwise noted
Samuel Whitelock statistics provided by New Zealand Rugby allblacks.com
Typeset in Adobe Garamond Pro by Kirby Jones
Printed and bound in Australia by McPherson's Printing Group

For my family

Player of the Day, under-7s, Palmerston North High School Old Boys' Junior Rugby Club.

CONTENTS

FOREWORD

Scott 'Razor' Robertson, 2023

I SHOULD START BY saying that as much as I like and admire Samuel, he is not my favourite Whitelock. That honour belongs to his mother, Caroline, who stayed true to her Culverden roots by creating and feeding an incredible supply chain of talent into Canterbury, Crusaders and New Zealand rugby.

Samuel is a product of his environment. He has a father, Braeden, who dedicated himself to coaching the boys to be men first and players second, and a set of brothers who all enjoy each other's company immensely while tacitly holding each other to account in the best kind of way.

Being brought up on a farm taught Samuel about hard work and maintaining high standards, about putting in to getting back. That playtime with his brothers taught him that bumps and bruises heal, but loyalty and resilience lasts a lifetime.

It's been one of the great privileges of my life to coach the four Whitelock brothers. All of them – George, Adam, Samuel and Luke – have in their own way coached me as well. They're their own men and have unique characteristics, but approach rugby with the same simple philosophy that remains timeless, no matter which way the winds of the sport are blowing: 'Everything is earned; nothing is given.'

The Whitelocks embraced the daily grind like few others I've seen. They refused to be bored and never skipped over the little things that others might find less important. They knew that if you took care of those one-percenters, bigger things would follow.

I first met Samuel in 2008, when he was coming back from a gap year in Australia and I was assistant coach for Canterbury. I met him at the airport and was blown away by his physical presence for someone so young, and by the size of his hands when we shook. He was both humble and full of self-assurance. He wasn't timid. He knew he had some natural physical gifts that would hold him in good stead if he stayed fit and worked hard.

In time, Samuel became my captain, but before that he was still a leader. I call him a general commander. He's a person who, when he speaks, demands your immediate attention, because you know what he has to say will be meaningful. He is not one to waste words on or off the field, and has a gift for identifying what the team needs and the best way to go about it.

That being said, Samuel could be pretty brutal, particularly in his early days of captaincy. He saw the world and the game in pretty black-and-white terms. You didn't have to guess what he was feeling about anything. If he approached me and said, 'Look, Razor, can we have a chat?', I knew full well that there was something I was doing that he wasn't happy with.

But I never minded, because I knew it came from a place of care. He cared about the team and he cared about me, and the way he showed that was to be direct and to the point. It was never personal.

Initially, when he captained the Crusaders, the younger players, particularly the Pasifika boys, could be a bit fearful of his presence, and perhaps even went into their shells a bit around him. To his immense credit, Samuel knew he had to work on his softer skills. He knew they weren't a strong point, and that at times his language had to subtly change. He could still be commanding and demanding, but do it in a way that made everyone around him grow in confidence, not shrink. He definitely got better with the empathetic side of his leadership as he got older, and I think in a quiet moment he would tell you that he got a kick out of seeing the way some of those younger guys, who might once have been wary of him, now had the confidence to give him a bit of good-natured grief from time to time.

Samuel has a sense of humour that might not be obvious to outsiders, but in a team environment shows itself more often than you'd think. When he's on, he's really on. He also has an incredible memory and can reference specific incidents from games long past to make a point or add to the analysis. That really keeps me on my toes.

As a captain, Samuel learned to toggle between being a rooster and a sheepdog. A rooster leads from the front with his chest puffed out. He's always first in, knowing others will follow. A sheepdog will watch and observe and guide his flock to where they need to go. He can identify the alphas in his flock and give them the responsibility of leading the rest. In the early days, you might need to tell Samuel when to be a bit less of a rooster and a bit more of a sheepdog, but it didn't take long before he intuitively knew when to switch between the two.

In short, Samuel went from a very good captain to a brilliant leader, one who, for me, transcended age, ethnicity and gender within the Crusaders environment. He was instrumental in bringing the partners into the fold in a meaningful way and having them more involved in the off-field life of the club.

His respect is earned. You can see that in the way he approaches every training. To stay at the top for such a long period of time is the very definition of physical and mental toughness. The difference between his best performances and his worst are minimal, which speaks to his preparation and consistency.

I can't begin to tell you how highly I rate the guy as a player and leader. He's a pragmatic, thoughtful, intelligent man. He's played more than 300 first-class games of rugby. He's got a degree. He has a beautiful wife and children. Samuel and Hannah have achieved a great balance in their lives, and I know that will continue when his playing days are over.

If I had to sum up Samuel Whitelock in a few words it would be this: he's the ultimate winner.

Celebrating after the 2023 Super Rugby Final against the Chiefs, our 7th consecutive championship. I discovered later that of the nine Super Rugby finals I'd started, I'd played every minute.
(Phil Walter/Getty Images)

THE BEGINNING OF THE END

AS A DIRECT RESULT of playing rugby, I have had scrum toe; a broken little toe; multiple ankle and high-ankle sprains; a broken ankle and torn ankle tendons; a torn Achilles tendon, twice; torn calf muscles; a partial tear of a posterior cruciate ligament; a pulled quadricep; a pulled hamstring; a torn adductor (groin); athletic pubalgia (sports hernia); snapping hip syndrome; multiple cracked ribs; broken fingers, thumb and hand; hyperextended fingers; torn ligaments in a wrist; hyperextended elbows; a torn labrum in the left shoulder; disc bulges in the thoracic spine; stress fractures in the thoracic spine; infected wisdom teeth; multiple broken noses; a blood clot in my nasal passage; multiple cuts on my brow; an eyelid sliced open; a hole torn in my ear; multiple cuts to my head, and multiple concussions and delayed concussions. As a result of some of these injuries, all the direct result of playing rugby, I have endured five surgeries under general anaesthetic.

Perhaps the best illustration of the rigours I've put my body through to keep playing professional rugby deep into my 30s is the fact that many of my thoughts for this book were taken down while I was propped up in a hyperbaric chamber that I borrowed from Owen Franks, a player who also benefited from that intrinsic brotherly competition that I thrived upon too.

I was using his chamber, a tent-like contraption, in a bid to play in the 2023 Super Rugby Pacific final – an issue that became political, as the wishes of the team I had at that stage played 179 games with, the Crusaders, and the team I had played 143 Tests for, the All Blacks, did not necessarily align.

I had seen the issue percolating from a long way out, knew all the different angles that various interested parties were coming from and sympathised with all of them. Yes, trying to rush back from a partially torn Achilles tendon was a risk. Yes, if it went wrong, my playing year would be over and my dream of playing in a fourth and final World Cup would be gone. No, I was not ignorant of how that might be perceived by those All Blacks fans who couldn't have cared less if the Crusaders won or lost another Super Rugby title.

I was thinking about the final, the Crusaders were thinking about the final and the All Blacks were thinking a few months further ahead.

It doesn't matter who I'm playing for – whether it's High School Old Boys juniors, Feilding High School, Lincoln, the Panasonic Wild Knights, Section Paloise, Canterbury, the Crusaders, South Island or the All Blacks – I've always played as hard as I can and I've always played when I can. If I'm fit,

I'm available, if I'm not, I'm not. I know that sounds simple but sometimes people overcomplicate matters. I've played this game long enough to trust myself. But at the same time, I knew that by playing, I was setting my timetable for full fitness back a couple of weeks.

Written goals have been a huge motivating force in my life. Every year I get an exercise book, write my goals in the front – where I can't ignore them – and work towards them. My primary goal for 2023 was to win the William Webb Ellis Cup for the third time. My secondary goal was to reach 150 Test caps. The third was to win a seventh Super Rugby title.

Was my bull-headed pursuit of my tertiary goal going to affect my ability to achieve my primary and secondary goals? Was I sacrificing one for the others? It almost felt like I was being forced to choose, and that was an awful feeling because I wanted to achieve them all. In my mind, it wasn't a simple calculation of whether I valued playing for the Crusaders or the All Blacks more. It was more personal than that. The best way I can explain it is that I wanted to finish playing in New Zealand on my terms, not somebody else's.

I talked to the All Blacks' physios, doctors and coaches, and did the same with the Crusaders' staff. I made sure those conversations were open and honest. There was added intrigue in that my Crusaders coach, Scott Robertson, had been named as the next All Blacks coach. I didn't take any of that lightly, so the very least I could do was be transparent. Yes, I wanted to play this game. Yes, there was probably a selfish, emotional reason for that. Yes, I knew there was risk involved.

There were two scenarios. I could go out there and snap my Achilles in half, and that would be my career in New Zealand done. Or I could manage myself, get through the game and then get back on the rehab program. The less time I was out there, the better it would be for my body – but I also had to be prepared for the possibility that somebody else might get injured early and I would have to play the full 80 minutes. It wasn't possible to commit to bringing me off after 50 minutes. Rugby doesn't always end with neat and tidy resolutions.

Between the first and second tweaks of the Achilles that bothered me that campaign, the tear had grown, but it was up and down the tendon, rather than across it. That was a less common injury and was making the prognosis quite difficult. I was also probably hearing what I wanted to hear. I was told that the likelihood of snapping it was reduced when it was grumbly like mine was, because your pain receptors and protective instincts take over. You naturally avoid doing things on that leg that require elasticity in the tendon. Subconsciously, you don't accelerate or bounce off that leg as much as you normally would or should. If you played like that for any length of time, you would likely develop muscle or ligament problems in your other leg, as it would literally be doing too much of the heavy lifting. But by that stage of my career, there were not that many parts of me that were not grumbling.

If it was a round-robin game, there was no way I would have played. Quarter-final? Definitely not. Even a semi-final would have been a no-go. Truth be told, if it hadn't been my last year, I probably wouldn't have played in the final either. The fact that it was almost certainly my last game in Crusaders colours was tipping the balance.

My greatest strength and weakness as a rugby player is being in the now. I don't often have regrets unless they help me to understand moments in the present, and I'm hopeless at projecting ahead and saying, 'Okay, if I do this now, what is going to happen in three weeks' time?' It can frustrate coaches, but that is who I am.

I knew this was almost certainly my last chance to play for the Crusaders, and it was against a team we had really struggled against, not just in 2023 but right back to 2012 and 2013, when the Chiefs won back-to-back titles. The Chiefs were the favourites to win. They were the season's top-performing team, and with the final in their home stadium, the odds were stacked in their favour. But we had won the last six titles. We knew how to win when it counted the most. I spent a lot of time thinking about what those words 'last match' meant. If I missed this match, that was it – I wouldn't be pulling on the red-and-black jumper ever again.

So that was why I was hunkered down in my chamber, hoping that the increase in air pressure would help my lungs collect more oxygen, which in turn would get more red blood cells around the tear to reduce swelling and heal it faster. According to a few people I talked to, the efficacy of the treatment was not necessarily scientifically robust, but Owie swore by it. My thinking was that even if it only helped a couple of per cent, that was better than nothing.

So, against the advice of All Blacks management, I made the trip to Hamilton for the final, although my place in the 23 was in doubt right up until the final warm-up. I had a checklist of targets I had to reach before making the decision, from a light run and some gym work on the Monday, through to full involvement in the final warm-ups on game night.

I don't reckon I went a waking hour without somebody asking me how I felt and whether I thought I was going to be fit. I was joking with my teammates that I was going to get a T-shirt that read, 'I don't know – it will be a game-day decision.'

If I didn't feel good during the warm-ups, I wasn't going to play. I knew I had to be at a certain level, that I couldn't go out there and cruise and still expect to be involved.

After successfully managing myself through a few exercises, we made the call that I would play. It was time to switch on. I put on some headphones and tried to push away the negative thoughts. I knew I was playing and I knew it was going to hurt. I was going to wake up the next morning very sore. Now it was time to shelve those thoughts and figure out how I could affect the game in a positive way.

My uncle Reece flicked me a message to wish me luck and ask me how I was. I'm usually pretty slack about responding to messages on game day but I used this one to start getting my head around my job. I replied, telling him I was going to have to use all my game smarts, knowing when to push things and when to dial back. I was moving into game mode.

The Chiefs' game plan suited me. With Shaun Stevenson and Damian McKenzie, two excellent long kickers of the ball, they tried to apply pressure by kicking deep out of their half and squeezing teams in their own 30- to 40-metre zone, forcing penalties, kicking to the corner and using strike moves. I knew that if I could get to halfway, I would be close enough, if our back three ran it back, to clean out the ruck or be ready for a carry. I could also preserve my energy and give my grumbling Achilles a rest.

These were the pictures I started painting in my head, using all the mental skills I had accumulated over a decade and a half of professional rugby. I had to trust myself, trust my instincts.

Our captain, Scott 'Scooter' Barrett, won the toss and decided to kick off. That was good, because Richie Mo'unga would be kicking to my side and it was my job to try to control the kick-off. I didn't have to be right there, but I had to be close enough. I would be involved from the start. The second time I tweaked my Achilles was while I was chasing a kick-off, so there were nerves, but once I got through that, I knew the adrenaline and my competitive edge would take over.

Despite everything that had happened in the lead-up, my only focus now was rugby. I didn't know how to be a doctor, a physio or a diplomat between two camps that had different opinions on what I should do, but I did know how to play rugby.

After what seemed like a few minutes of play, I looked up at the clock and got a shock to see it was showing 20. I was feeling good. I didn't have to run too fast. Everything apart from top-end speed was feeling great, and – thanks to the way the game was being played – I'd barely had to sprint. That was a nice feeling. We were a quarter of the match down, I was feeling good and, most importantly, we were right in this match. My worst-case scenario – snap my Achilles in the first ten minutes, ending my year and putting my team under incredible pressure – had passed.

The game was playing out pretty much as I'd hoped. It felt like we had a lot of the ball. There were plenty of lineouts and I won a few. There are games when everything seems slightly slowed down, when you take a ball and it feels like you have that split second of time to execute your skills and present the ball cleanly and crisply. This wasn't one of those games. The moment you won possession, there was an opposition hand on the ball, there was pressure. Your skills had to be top-drawer to get any sort of fluidity.

It was, in other words, a final.

There was never any hint either team was about to crack, never any passive periods of play. That was a defining trait of the Chiefs under Clayton McMillan, and it was something Razor had rebuilt in us. By the time the first half came to an end, we had been able to impose our style on the game without ever gaining control of the match. They'd scored a great try off a strike move, and we'd replied with a lineout-drive try and fantastic five-pointer from Richie to lead 15–10. I don't know what it was like to watch because I'm a terrible rugby spectator, but it was the sort of game you love to play in.

Tendons, when they cool down quickly, tend to stiffen up – a little bit like a cold piece of gum that isn't being chewed – so I went straight from the field at half-time and onto a stationary bike. I noticed that one of my boots was missing a sprig. It had ripped out and taken the thread lining with it. This might sound like a minor irritation, but that part of my boot was critical to me digging in with my big toe at scrum time. The Chiefs had a big scrum and had used it as a weapon against us during the season. I had two choices: change into a pair of boots that I hadn't broken in properly, or wear one that could cost us a scrum penalty if I slipped. In the end I opted to stay with the pair I had on, because the risk of everything cooling down if I got off the bike felt greater.

I told the doctor that my tendon was starting to get pretty sore and, because the crowd was so loud and it was impossible to communicate verbally with the sideline, that I'd scratch my nose when it got too painful and they could drag my carcass off. The flaw in that plan was evident when the Chiefs scored straight after half-time with a well-worked scrum move and we were back under the posts. I flicked some sweat off my nose, the doctor saw it and I had to hurriedly get the picture across that I wasn't sending the bail-out signal. A subsequent penalty pushed the Chiefs out to a five-point lead.

We needed to grab the momentum back. This was something we trained for all the time. It gave me great encouragement to hear our leaders talk so calmly about what we needed to do next. There wasn't a hint of panic; there was no sense that scoreboard pressure would hinder our decision-making.

We were soon huddling under our sticks again, however. Damian McKenzie had caught an overthrown lineout that we had competed on, burst through a gap and put Emoni Narawa in for what looked like a devastating try. That would have put them out by more than seven, but Damian was called back for offside and we kicked for the corner and mauled.

It was a huge moment in the game. We didn't score immediately, but we never really relinquished control of the match from that moment on – though I did give our team a huge scare in the dying minutes. We had most of the territory and we could smell blood in the water. We'd scored a try off the maul in the first half and did so again immediately after Sam Cane had been put in the bin for what ref Ben O'Keeffe called a 'cynical' foul. It was a shot to their heart. There really is nothing to sap an opposition's spirits like scoring a maul try against a team that prides itself on its forward play.

It had been a long time coming, because the Chiefs had shown incredible grit to turn us back time and again. There was a period of ten to 15 minutes where we were in the right zone, the right areas and were squeezing them slowly but surely out of the game. The scoreline might have been close, but we were soaking up their last remaining energy and taking time off the clock. It was a thoroughly professional execution of a plan.

Our lineout attack was the key element of that game. Ever since 2017, our whole attitude around mauling had changed, whether it was with the ball or defending. It used to be our soft underbelly but we turned it into our strength.

Jason Ryan and Luke Romano had been key in instigating themes around our lineout defence. In years past we called it 'the vault'. It was up to other teams to try to crack the vault, and our pride in that concept helped us defend lineout drives successfully over a long period. I can't remember exactly how many we repelled, but we're talking whole seasons. I can remember as clear as day exactly when we lost it: a penalty try against the Waratahs in April 2022 that haunts me to this day. The Waratahs cracking the vault literally brought me to my knees.

The vault was exactly what our team needed. The backs loved challenging us to keep it locked. We'd always had the ability to score tries, but prior to 2017 we might play great rugby and have teams under the pump, but one penalty and they'd kick to the corner and take seven off us as easy as you like. Then we got this theme, this mantra, and everything changed. The more we trained it, the better we got and the more tangible the vault became. Guys from other teams knew about it, which meant we were challenged less on the lineout drive. Teams still tried to take us on there but we definitely had the sense that they were resigned to it failing.

That was why it was such a dark day when we finally buckled. We haven't given up a lineout maul try since then. We don't talk about the vault as often as we once did, but we're still bloody proud of it.

After we punched the Chiefs in the face with our second maul try, my legs were starting to feel like jelly. The easiest way to describe mauling for someone who has never been involved in it is to imagine walking up a steep hill. Your legs are getting tired and the lactic acid is kicking in, but once you hit flat ground you have to immediately start running. When you're mauling and scrummaging, you're stressing your calves and quads, then all of a sudden you're being asked to tackle a back who has great feet. Forwards are at their most vulnerable on defence immediately after a maul. That's when teams want a player like Damian McKenzie running at them.

We got back to the halfway line after the try and gathered around as Richie lined up the kick. We talked about how these were the moments we trained for, that we wanted to be part of. Right back to the era of Wayne Smith, the Crusaders had been schooled on the simple philosophy that defence wins championships.

The Chiefs were going to be desperate to get themselves back into the game, but we knew we could execute our skills and plans under the most intense duress. Securing the kick-off was vital, and playing the game in their half was also important. We knew the Chiefs were programmed to kick the ball back from deep in their half, and with Richie, Will Jordan, Leicester Fainga'anuku and Braydon Ennor, we had great counter-attackers. If the Chiefs tried to run the ball, they'd be out of their comfort zone and we liked our chances of squeezing them with our defence. As we hoped, the Chiefs tried to play with the ball in hand and we were penning them in.

Then, with a few minutes to go, I gave them a massive get-out-of-jail-free card. I tackled Damian, tried to roll out of the way but hit a leg. I thought, 'I can't go that way,' so I rolled the other way and got trapped. It was just on their side of halfway, and I knew Damian would have a crack at goal. I also knew it was right at the limit of his range.

Willi Heinz, our veteran reserve halfback, had visions of 2014 racing through his mind. Back then, Bernard Foley of the New South Wales Waratahs had kicked a goal after Richie McCaw was penalised, wrongly, in that year's final. I had the same image in my mind. I felt terrible but Scooter helped settle me down. He walked past, slapped me on the arse and told me not to worry, just to get the next one. It was what I needed to hear, because it made me realise that this wasn't the end of the game – there was still time on the clock.

It was a timely reversal of roles. Early in his career, Scooter's enthusiasm could get the better of him and I had developed a couple of techniques to help him get his head back in the game. One of them, believe it or not, was to ask him a simple maths question that had nothing to do with rugby. That would snap him out of his white-line fever or whatever it was that was clouding his judgement.

Scott has always been a great player. He's got all the attributes to be a world-class lock and he's getting better all the time. On this occasion it wasn't his skills I needed but a few calming words to get me out of the 'I've just cost us the game' headspace I was in.

We were under the sticks. I told Willi that if it was short, he was to catch it. If it hit the post or the crossbar, I'd regather. From the moment he hit the ball it seemed to take an age to get to us. My initial thought was that he'd under-hit it – that he had too much elevation. Take my words with a pinch of salt, however, as I'd never place-kicked a ball in my life. I'd seen a few travel through the air, though, and although Damian's radar was true, I was right about him under-hitting it.

Willi caught it just short of our try line, ran it towards the touchline and punted it out. We got into their lineout, turned the ball over and kicked deep, and just like that we were back playing the game at the right end of the field. Because Damian had taken the full allotted time for his shot at goal – one thing I love about kickers is they always back themselves – it had taken 90 seconds off the clock. Now they had to keep the ball in hand.

There was no way I or anyone on our side was going to give them another sniff. We held true. We were disciplined and smart, and Leicester got over the ball and with 40 seconds left won a kickable penalty.

It always amazes me how quickly rugby can turn. It was not long ago that I was despairing about having cost us the final, and now we had a chance to seal it. On the flipside, Damian was probably feeling the opposite range of emotions. But that's why we love sport and occasionally hate it, right?

This was a scenario we'd spent time talking about in preparation. If we were less than a score ahead and got a late penalty, what would we do? Kick to touch and keep the ball out of their hands? Kick for goal? There was no time for a restart, but what if the kick missed and didn't go dead? Could it lead to an incredible break-out try? According to the laws of the game, Richie's kick at goal had to be an honest attempt, but I wouldn't mind if he missed it as long as it went dead.

We talked it over and decided to take a genuine shot at goal. We were ready to chase hard in case the ball hit the bar, but Richie knocked it over. I was standing right behind him and felt great for the guy. He was also playing his last game for the Crusaders (for the foreseeable future, at least), and it solidified what he'd brought to the club.

It was an amazing moment. It took a while for the victory to sink in, but then I realised that I'd just played the full 80 minutes. Later I would discover that, of the nine Super Rugby finals I'd started, I played every minute. That's 720 minutes plus add-ons of finals footy.

There was a time early in my career when if you would have offered me the chance to win one final – we lost the first two I played – I would have ripped your arm off, but here I was in Hamilton with a seventh title. It was surreal.

Razor watched the replay of the game on Monday, and at Tuesday's team function he showed me a screenshot he had taken of a graphic the broadcasters had discussed. That final was the 24th playoff game I had played for the Crusaders. Richie Mo'unga had played 23. Everyone else on the leaderboard was a Crusader too.

*

Those few weeks leading up to the final painted a picture of where my rugby and body were at during the latter portion of my career. You could probably count on one hand the number of professional games I played free from knocks and niggles. Playing at 100 per cent fit – it just doesn't happen. The deeper you get into your career, the more damage stacks up, until you realise you've become an expert on pain management. I take great pride in the way I prepare myself, the way I manage pain and injuries, and the way I ensure I'm able to front up for whatever jersey it is that I'm required to wear. In 2023, I was faster in testing than I had ever been before, but then I broke my hand, did my Achilles and was in and out of rugby, so I lost a bit of condition. Still, to be doing PBs well into my 30s showed me that while arthritis is going to play a big part in my future, there's still plenty of life left in these old bones yet.

I was talking to Grandad one day at the beach. He loved saltwater swims because they relieved his pain, particularly in the eye he lost as a kid. 'Getting old is no fun,' he would tell me as he hobbled along on a 20-minute walk that should have taken five. I had a vision of the future then and could see myself as a grandfather, walking that same path, hoping one of my grandkids stayed back with me to chat.

I could well end up like Grandad, feeling the pain of all the punishment I've put myself through. You know what, though, I reckon I'd have more regrets if I went to the grave with my body in great nick. That would tell me I hadn't given it a decent crack.

And if there's one thing I'd like to be remembered for, it's this: I gave it a decent crack.

FIRST
HALF

1
THE OPENING WHISTLE

LET'S GET THE BASICS out of the way.

I was born on 12 October 1988, in Palmerston North.

I'm the third of four boys born to Caroline and Braeden Whitelock, the younger brother of George and Adam, and older brother of Luke, who, the rest of us boys are pretty sure, is Mum's favourite child. I'm a husband to Hannah, whom I met on my first day at Lincoln University, and father to Fred, Iris and Penelope.

My friends call me Sam. Most of my family prefer Samuel. No shortcuts around home.

You may know the bare bones of the family story: four boys, all born within 1770 days of each other, all playing rugby for New Zealand in either sevens or 15s.

George is All Black number 1093, I'm 1104 and Luke is 1129. Adam is All Blacks Sevens number 252, the only back among us. He played more than 50 games for Canterbury and the Crusaders before taking up a contract at Bayonne.

The family connections to rugby and the All Blacks run even deeper than that. My maternal grandfather, Nelson Dalzell, was All Black number 553, while my great-uncle Allan Elsom was number 538. Another uncle, Graeme Higginson, who is married to Mum's sister Jo, was All Black number 808.

Hannah also has an All Black in the family. Her great-great-grandfather, Hubert 'Jum' Turtill, All Black number 139, played one Test against Australia in 1905 before joining the 'professional' New Zealand team, which would become known as rugby league pioneers the All Golds. Hubert died in the Great War at the Battle of Givenchy, part of the attritional and extraordinarily bloody Ypres campaigns.

The Barrett boys might have us covered for sheer number of All Blacks Tests, but if you cast the net a bit wider, I'm not sure there is any other extended family that has had the intergenerational reach into the All Blacks as ours. I love the connection the wider Whitelock and Dalzell clans have to such a cherished part of our national fabric. I take an enormous amount of pride in that because family has played an integral part in the successes I've enjoyed. If you could sum my life up in a tidy catchphrase, you couldn't go wrong with family, footy and farming.

I'm not a complicated guy, nor am I vulnerable to wild swings of emotion. Some might say that's a weakness, others a strength. That's just who I am. Those three Fs, though – I care more deeply about them than you can imagine. They're central to my life, and intertwined. I could not have become the footy player I did without family, certainly, and probably not without the bedrock of my rural upbringing and everything it taught me about hard work and sacrifice.

My directness and my willingness to engage with people of all walks of life and treat them the same – I get that from Dad. My inner strength – that's Mum. That willingness to claw for every advantage, the refusal to yield – that's what living with three tight-knit, sports-mad brothers does for you.

This is my story, for sure, but it is also the story of my family.

In keeping with that, I suppose we should get this out of the way early: I was meant to be the girl. Mum was apparently convinced I was going to be a little sister to the two older boys. As you can imagine, George gets a bit of mileage out of that one. I was, however, later to be joined by a fourth brother.

If there's one place you can get away with four growing boys in one place, it's a farm. We weren't lacking for space. When you grow up on a farm, surrounded by other farmers, you can take for granted some of the special opportunities you have and, without being too poetic about it, the sheer majesty of your surroundings.

Our Linton dairy farm was large, at about 850 hectares of owned and leased land. The farm is flat – as you'd expect, since it's on the Manawatū Plains – but our view was framed to the east by the Tararua Ranges, which stretch north to the Manawatū Gorge. Look the other way and you'll see the stopbanks of the Manawatū River, which provides the natural border to our farm.

The river was an extension of our childhood playground, providing fishing and recreational opportunities, but it also came with an ever-present threat. In 2004, flooding devastated the region, but thanks to the help of 50 volunteers – who Dad reckoned put in close to 50 hours each – more than 50,000 sandbags were added to stop the water breaching its stopbanks. Dad says it's the river that helps provide such rich, grass-growing soil, so you can't complain if it occasionally plays up. In the south they have to worry about snow, in the east it might be drought. You're always battling the elements. 'It's just farming,' he says.

In between the river and the hills it's mostly cows. On our farm that meant Friesian and Friesian crosses. Twice a day they would be put through two 80-bale rotary sheds. It's a state-of-the-art operation now but it wasn't always like that. Over the course of buying 27 farms in 37 years, Mum and Dad have run up to five sheds at a time, and some fairly rustic operations at that.

I'm just old enough to remember living at the old farmhouse, which is only a couple of hundred metres from the newly built home we moved into in 1995.

Our first home ground was the family tennis court at the old farmhouse. Mum and Dad loved playing tennis, and Mum in particular was a very good player, as was her sister, Aunty Jo, who is still winning masters tournaments well into her 60s. I'd love to tell you we followed in their footsteps and became talented players ourselves, but by the time I was old enough to hold a racquet, George and Adam had annoyed the local coach enough that I was never offered lessons.

The standing joke was that Mum wanted to lock us in the tennis court so that we couldn't get out, and within two days we'd learned to climb up and over the chain-link fence. Pretty soon the tennis court was being commandeered for our games of rugby. There's a family video of my third birthday, with Dad and me versus Adam and George. Eventually, three out of the four players ended up in tears. Adam went to score a try and accidentally fended me in the face, so I started crying. Adam was crying because his hand went into my mouth and I bit him, while George ran away to score. Maybe he ended up crying because the video ref called him back for a knock-on.

Dad, who was a bloody good player, having played five years for Manawatū when they were a provincial powerhouse and also for the New Zealand Colts, would play on his knees, but before long it was George and Luke, the oldest and youngest, against Adam and me.

My introduction to a more organised form of rugby was much the same. George and Adam would travel into town to play for Dad's club, Palmerston North High School Old Boys Junior Rugby Club. I just wanted to do what they were doing, and Dad had to hold me back to stop me running on. By the time the second half rolled around, he would get sick of holding me back and just let me go. George and Adam were fast, and were invariably the best players, so they would run the length of the field, get to the line and then pass me the ball so I could catch it and fall over for a try. Quite nice of them, when you think about it. At home they loved nothing more than scrapping with me and putting me in my place, but in public they made sure I was looked after, even if I spent a fair bit of the game jumping in puddles and attempting cartwheels.

I knew rugby had been a big part of Dad's life, but in those amateur days the demands of a young family and a large farm took precedence. He was still playing club rugby when I came

Dad with the ball for Manawatū.

along, but I'm too young to remember the highs and lows that go along with being a club player who lives for Saturday afternoons. There was at least one occasion when the game had to be stopped when George and Adam ran onto the field to try to do their thing. Dad reckons that was one of the reasons his career was nipped in the bud, because Mum couldn't control us 'three little shits' on the sidelines.

Dad made his Manawatū debut the year after they had the Ranfurly Shield, and I think one of his regrets is never having the chance to defend it. Manawatū won its first and only National Provincial Championship in 1981, his first year in the squad, but he never really talked about that when we were boys. Typical Kiwi – he played down his own achievements. The rugby stories he told always tended to be about 'good buggers' he played with and against, rather than anything he might have done on the field.

At Old Boys, for example, Dad played with the fine All Blacks prop Gary Knight, one of his good mates, who had a farm not far from ours. Gary is one of the greatest examples of how dramatically rugby has changed. He played for the All Blacks for a decade, but missed three tours to Europe because of farm commitments. While he is remembered for being felled by a flour bomb dropped from a low-flying Cessna in the third Test against the Springboks at the conclusion of the controversial 1981 tour, not so well known is that he had to miss the second Test because of farming duties.

Old Boys also had a young wing who apparently was pretty windy, or non-committal, when it came to the contact side of the game. He went by the name Joe Schmidt. The first time I met Joe was when we'd played Ireland in Dublin, and I didn't know the connection that well. I had no idea, for example, that he'd been to Mum and Dad's wedding, and they to his. I asked him if he had a story about Dad from their club rugby days that I might be able to use against the old man at a later date.

He stood back with a big smirk on his face. 'Yeah, alright, I'll tell you one story,' he said. 'Your father is the only person I was scared to play against, and the only problem with that was that he was on my own team.'

Apparently, Dad and Gary Knight liked to perform a chest punch on the outside backs just to remind them where their hearts were. That was my first introduction to what Dad must have been like as a player and a teammate. Dad was an enforcer, rough and raw. I think he and Gary got along well because Gary was a very good wrestler, winning a Commonwealth Games medal in the super-heavyweight class in 1974. Much like Joe Moody – another wrestler – and me later on, Dad and Gary loved to grapple and wind each other up.

Growing up, I never thought becoming an All Black was possible. I knew my maternal grandfather was an All Black, but he'd passed away when I was six months old so I never had the chance to hear about his adventures directly. Gary was a good family friend, as was Mark 'Cowboy' Shaw. Dad played with a few All Blacks from that Ranfurly Shield era, like Frank Oliver (Anton's father), Mark Donaldson and Geoff Old. As a boy, I never saw these guys as All Blacks, just as Dad's mates. I was oblivious to the fact they were outstanding players who had taken on the world in what was then a very different rugby environment.

Sometimes I wonder how Mum managed with us all demanding food and attention!

The history of our farm goes back some time on my paternal grandmother's side of the family. The land was sectioned up after the world wars and intended in part for returned servicemen for what they called 'rehab farms', but it wasn't particularly attractive land. My great-grandfather, Loyal Craw, better known as Roy, cleared the properties, many of which were initially just swamp or flaxy wetlands. They then underwent significant stumping, before being converted to grass and dairy pasture. He was a pioneering type and at one point ran ten dairy herds with various sharemilkers, and he started and operated his own cheese factory under the Galaxy brand.

My grandfather John grew up on a farm in Newbury, between Palmerston North and Feilding. He married Roy's daughter Lyndall – she is Nanna to me – and they looked to buy their own farm. His father wanted him to stay on the Newbury farm, but Roy was looking to leave the industry. It made sense for Grandad to buy the Linton farm.

His eldest son, Dad, took on the farm and grew it further still, and now George and Kayla have leased-to-buy half of the 400-odd hectares, so the property will remain under the Whitelock name for some time yet.

Grandad was a traditional family patriarch and an impressive man who rose to the chairmanship of the Tui milk company, which was later folded into the giant Fonterra cooperative. He was made an Officer of the Order of the British Empire (OBE) for his services to the dairy industry. John was instantly recognisable by his eyepatch, which he wore after losing an eye at the age of 17. He was a spectator at the speedway in Palmerston North in 1948 when a car crashed through the fence and threw parts into the crowd. One struck Grandad in the face and he woke up three weeks later in Wellington Hospital with terrible facial injuries that necessitated an operation to remove his left eye. He was lucky to be alive.

Grandad was a fastidious student of family history, compiling two books, *John's Journey* and *Before & Beyond: The Family of Lyndall & John*. Pretty much everything you need to know about our family tree or the history of the farm is in those two books. He was also a wise man and very good company. Grandad died aged 91 in 2022 and is missed.

*

My brothers and I enjoyed an upbringing that I imagine was pretty typical for kids growing up on a farm. When we were little, Mum would take us out for a walk to get us some fresh air, but the ulterior motive was always to tire us out. Mum used to put Luke in the pram and start walking down the road. Us older ones would be on our bikes, but we'd soon get tired and try to jump in with Luke on the pram to get a lift. Dad would have to retrace our steps later and pick up all the bikes and toys left behind. When we got a bit older we'd be let loose on our bikes. The family was completed when Uncle Dave rescued a fox terrier that was left at the pound because it had too much energy.

That was pretty much our childhood right there. Jimmy the fox terrier chased, caught and killed possums, rats, rabbits and probably a few things he wasn't meant to as well. So when we were testing Mum or Dad's patience, or they just wanted a bit of space, they'd send us out to walk Jimmy, or later Joy, Adam's foxy, and we'd head down to the river to cause a bit of carnage there. We were never given pocket money – we had to earn it by killing possums. The dogs would find the possums, we'd climb the willow trees to shake them out and the dogs would be waiting at the bottom. It was pretty brutal, but the possums had it coming. They have a voracious appetite, kill the native birds and trees, and carry bovine tuberculosis on them. On a farm, the only good possum is a dead possum.

Which is probably a good time to tell you I'm a little bit scared of the creatures.

We used to push all the hay bales out of the shed in winter to remove all the possums who would move in because it was warm and dry. When I was about seven or eight, my job was to stand at the entrance of the hay shed to stop the possums running out to freedom. Adam and George started rocking a bale that was high up in the shed. When they eventually tipped it over, all these possums started running everywhere. One possum ran to the edge of the bales and jumped. I was standing at the entrance of the hay shed and the possum was flying through the air like a sugar glider. I backed up as quickly as possible, but not quickly enough. The possum landed flat on my chest and dug in while I froze with fear. Enter Jimmy, who had run to my rescue. He leapt up, grabbed it by the tail, ripped it off me and was killing it right there in front of me, while I remained paralysed by fear.

That became known among the family as the day Jimmy saved me from a possum that was going to eat me alive. I ended up with a few scratches but nothing too bad. What was worse was that I started having nightmares about the incident, and that my brothers now knew I was scared of possums and weren't going to let me forget.

Fast forward to my 21st birthday, which coincided with the first time I took Hannah home to the farm. I had my flatmate Rigg, Luke and a couple of other mates on the back of the truck, with Hannah and I in the cab as we went out for a night of possum shooting. Hannah's a city girl from Auckland's North Shore, so this was a novelty for her. Luke, on the other hand, is an old hand at possum hunting. He'd been in the United Kingdom, working at a school in Loughborough, so this was his first time meeting my future wife.

As we drove, I was explaining to Hannah why this was necessary and the damage possums did to flora and fauna. I had the whole biodiversity spiel going to make sure she didn't just think we were bloodthirsty savages. Finally, we saw a possum at the top of a dead tree. There was nothing in the line of sight, so this was Hannah's big chance to bag her first. Everyone was egging her on: 'Come on, Hannah, this is your big test to see if you've got what it takes.'

She got out, lined up this possum and – *bang!* – she missed. That was alright; she was nervous, it happens. *Bang!* – she fired again but missed by even more. I realised Hannah was doing it on purpose. She was not ready to be a possum hunter. The animal scurried away and ended up on a fencepost next to the gate. Hannah and I jumped back in the truck, but Luke wasn't done. He saw his chance to revisit my childhood nightmares and grabbed the possum. I could see what he was up to and tried to get the window up as quickly as I could, but Hannah had no idea what was coming.

I got the window about a possum's width from the top but Luke's form was spot on and the pest came flying in. I instinctively ducked and it went over the top of my head and landed right next to Hannah. She panicked, but displayed incredible athleticism to get herself out the window *Dukes of Hazzard* style. Within a few seconds she was half a paddock away and Luke was wetting himself laughing. Meanwhile, I'm trapped in the cab with a possum and can't get out, because as Hannah had slid out the window she'd hit the lock button.

Eventually I escaped, and would have liked nothing better than to give Luke a slap and a few choice words, but my mates – and, more importantly, my girlfriend – were there so I had to play it cool. Luke had a smirk a mile wide on his face and another possum story for the collection.

Welcome to the farm, Hannah.

My love of the outdoors and of hunting all stems from growing up on the farm. We'd fish for trout in the Manawatū River and hunt rabbits. As we got older we were introduced to pig hunting, and then it was time to shoot your first deer. It's been a way for George and me, in particular, to stay connected as we've got older. He'll spend hours planning our hunts and even the worst ones are great fun. As it turned out, hunting was the focal point for the biggest controversy of my career, but we'll get to that in good time.

We had about 2600 cows on the farm, but also the odd pet lamb. We had a pony for a while and I had Mary the pig.

Mary was pretty much like a dog, and she was all mine. She'd follow me everywhere, eat out of my hand and when I gave her a scratch she'd roll over and let me pet her. For a while there she was my best mate. At the same time, we had all these chooks. We'd go to the AMP shows, wait until the end and buy the last of the silly things for about 50 cents each. Mary started to turn a bit feral in the presence of chooks and ducks, and when she started catching and eating a few, she was put in a sty pretty quickly. We were trying to get piglets out of her but for whatever reason we couldn't get her in pig, and as I went off to boarding school Dad gave me the news that we were going to have to sell Mary. A beautiful friendship was coming to an end.

A few weeks later, I was home and giving Luke grief about something, being a typical older brother and pushing him too far. This time he had something to fire back at me. 'By the way,' he said nonchalantly, 'you ate Mary last night.' I turned around and Mum just put her head down and couldn't look me in the eye.

As much as it pains me to say it, Mary made beautiful eating.

I'm appreciative of the upbringing I had. I love the farming life because it forces self-reliance. Mum and Dad weren't just farmers, they were plumbers, electricians, builders, butchers, cooks, everything. They had to be able to drive the tractor, the motorbike, the truck and all those things. We have family videos of George being five in the old Commer truck, letting it self-rev as he steered it around the paddock as Dad would be forking the silage off it with the tractor. I hate to think what would happen with health and safety if you tried that now, but that's just what we did.

Sometimes that self-reliance can bite you on the bum if you don't make sure you stay connected with the outside world. That's where my work with Farmstrong comes in. I'm proud to be an ambassador for the rural wellbeing initiative, because while I love the farming life, it does come with unique pressures.

There's a lot of research to show that many farmers are great at looking after their equipment and stock, but they can neglect their own wellbeing. The rate of depression among farming folk is far too high. Farmstrong is a great way of connecting people in the sector, to share ideas and concepts that help farmers not only with productivity, but also with coping with the inevitable ups and downs of the vocation.

One of the things I'm particularly focused on is spreading the message to farmers about how important it is to take breaks. I'm talking about building minibreaks into your day and rigidly sticking to them, because it boosts your performance when dealing with physically and mentally demanding jobs. Taking time off when you're busy sounds odd, but it helps a lot with decision-making. You're not tired and overthinking things.

Giving yourself longer breaks during the year is also critical. The key is to plan them, put them in the calendar and stick to it. I never used to do this, and the reality is there's always another task or a reason not to take a break. Farming and rugby are very similar in that you've got to operate to an unbending calendar. It's hard to take a lot of time off when you're shearing, calf-marking or docking, and it's the same with rugby. Rugby has taught me that I need to get away from things on a regular basis. I've learned to park everything and make taking a break a priority. I've got a lot better at that.

Finally, it's also knowing when to call it for the day. There is always the temptation to keep going when you're on task, and there's that old cliché that you don't leave for tomorrow what can be done today, but the reality is there are very few things that cannot wait. When you're fatigued, you're more likely to make bad decisions that can have a knock-on effect. Of all the things farmers could get better at, knowing when to press the pause button is the most critical.

Mum and Dad were practical people. Some of that practicality was on full display in 2013, when Mum said yes to an interview with the '12 Questions' column in *The New Zealand Herald*.

The first question was fairly harmless – or so it seemed: 'So what does a mum put in the pasta water to get four such supremely talented rugby players?'

Mum decided to take it into areas nobody really expected, not least our partners. 'Actually, the boys didn't have a lot of pasta when they were growing up,' she answered. 'It was a roast, spuds, veggies and fruit salad with ice cream most nights. Oh, they would eat a lot. I'd have to do two roasts to feed them all. Mainly mutton, it was. I remember going grocery shopping and I'd spend $70 to $90 just on fruit.'

That wasn't what caught everybody's attention, however. For reasons known only to Mum, she followed that up with: 'But I wormed them regularly. They were boys, you know, outside all the time, killing possums and that. I still worm them when they come home. They think it's a hell of a joke. Now I even worm their girlfriends.'

You can imagine what the talking point for our girlfriends was when they caught up with friends after that.

Mum crammed a lot of information into that article, which also informed the readers of the *Herald* that the moment she might have realised she had athletes on her hands was when she 'chased them with the strap' but couldn't catch us.

'Oh jeepers, you're probably not allowed to do that anymore,' Mum continued. 'We had Charlie, the leather strap, and the boys were very afraid of Charlie. There was more threatening going on than anything, slamming it on the table and that. He's still here, actually.'

There was even an inquiry about my gruts: 'I've noticed that Sam always seems to wear striped underwear when he's playing for the All Blacks. What's that about?'

'You and a lot of others have noticed that,' Mum replied. 'They're his lucky undies. He's got a long back and I think that's why you tend to see them a lot. All the boys went to boarding school and the laundry lady at the hostel told me she was watching Sam play one day and saw those and said to her friend, "I've washed those undies."'

Thanks, Mum!

*

Our Linton farm is not far from the army camp, just off State Highway 57, which links Ashurst to Levin while bypassing Palmerston North. The farm is also right on the boundary of Opiki, which sits on the other side of the Manawatū River. We went to the Opiki school because it was a bit bigger than Linton. There would have been 70 to 80 kids there, and more than ten of them would have been my brothers or cousins. I tended to find a bit of trouble, didn't listen to the teachers enough and followed around my older cousins, who were all heroes to me. I have nieces and nephews there now, and my cousins' kids attend as well, so history's repeating itself. The local Linton school, where Dad went, has recently closed. His school stories are a little bit different to ours, including the one where another kid chopped his finger off with an axe after a bit of misbehaviour. Dad would take his dubious behavioural record to high school, where he held the record for the most canings.

We went into town for intermediate school at Palmerston North Intermediate Normal. Aaron Cruden was there at the same time. He was special. Even then he played like he did as a professional. He was never a big guy but he had awesome feet and handling skills, which created so much time and space for him and his teammates.

One of the defining moments in my education occurred at intermediate. I was having one of those reading tests that were commonplace. I finished the test and the teacher, who would have been 22 or 23, straight out of teachers' college, said: 'Look, you have a reading age of eight. You're not going to get School C, you're not going to get to university.' I remember hearing that and thinking, 'Oh shit, this is no good.' I took it personally and was so embarrassed to take that report home to Mum and Dad. The way she said it was so final, like I was miles behind and there was no hope of catching up.

Mum enrolled me in a Kip McGrath tutoring course and we worked hard at it together. It's funny how the world works. Years later, when I'd just graduated from university with a science degree, I bumped into that same teacher. She remembered me. 'Oh, I was your teacher at intermediate,' she said proudly, but I didn't need reminding because I knew who she was straightaway. I doubt she recalled that conversation about my learning issues, but I remembered every single word – and how it had destroyed me at the time.

Part of me really wanted to give her a serve, and tell her that I'd proved her wrong and she'd had no right to make me feel the way I had that day, but overall I didn't want to create an awkward confrontation. The more I thought about it, too, the more sympathy I had for her plight – that maybe as a first-year teacher she was in a tough spot, and she'd probably had a bit of growing and learning to do herself. It ended up being a nice moment. Yes, she'd made me feel small and stupid all those years ago, but she'd also lit a fire under me. I began to understand that no matter how big the problem was, you can find ways to overcome it.

When it came to high school, there was no way I was doing anything other than following my brothers into boarding at Feilding High School. It might have been a decision for George, who was a standout age-group rugby player. The temptation must have been there for him to attend Palmerston North Boys' High, a more traditional school that enjoyed a number of high-profile First XV matches each year. It was known as a rugby school, and at that point Feilding wasn't, so in many ways it would have made sense to send George there. But Dad and Grandad had gone to Feilding, and both had played in the First XV there, so we could be the third generation of Whitelocks to achieve that feat.

There was another factor, too, which showed a bit of foresight on Mum's part. She was worried that growing up in a house full of boys and then going to a boys' school might mean we failed to knock a few rough edges off. She felt that a co-ed environment was a healthier social choice for us, and I'm glad they made that call as I loved my time at Feilding High. It might not have had the prestige of those big boys' schools, but it gave me everything I needed at that time: good teaching, great coaching, a lifetime of mateship, and the independence that boarding school creates in you.

I didn't have the greatest start there, though, and was possibly even looking at an early finish. I had a pretty rough first year. I think 22 kids went into the hostel with me in Year 9 and maybe three of us made it through to Year 13. Some were expelled; some jumped before they were pushed. I went in a bit overconfident because I had two older brothers there, and I fell in with a few who weren't the best role models and ended up with a suspension. Mum tells people it was for throwing eels into the girls' showers, and while that makes for a quirky story, I'm not sure she's got my timeline of trouble quite right there.

Mum reckoned that when she picked me up I looked devastated and couldn't look at her. That was because I thought I'd been expelled. It turned out it was only a yellow card, but I still wasn't popular at home. Actually, that's not quite true. Luke, who was still to experience the joys of boarding school, thought it was pretty funny and that it was about time I was taken down a peg or two.

Our principal, Roger Menzies, was a no-nonsense type of leader. He was great. He wasn't afraid to red-card kids – legend has it that for two years we had the highest suspension and expulsion rate in the country. What the experience taught me was that there was a line, and if I crossed it there were going to be consequences.

Those consequences extended to home as well. During my suspension, Dad made sure I worked every minute of it, and I was left with the worst chores on the farm. There was a tree-lined hole on the river where all the rubbish that floated down would collect among the branches. Dad made me go and clean that out. It's no fun dredging used nappies out of the river. Gary Knight drove past us one day and stopped to chat to

Dad, who told him why I was fishing crap out of the river. By this stage my bottom lip was dragging on the ground, and I heard Gary say: 'It looks like he's had enough.' When I got back to the hostel and the opportunity for mischief arrived, I thought, 'Bugger that – I'm not getting in trouble again.'

Over the years, a few of the rugby boys came to our farm to serve their suspensions, because in some cases their home lives were more problematic than their behaviour at school. Dad would put them to work, give them a bit of support and hopefully turn a negative situation into a positive experience.

It was around this time that I realised I had to put my excess energy to better use, and it was then that I fell in love with basketball. I still wasn't that much taller than everyone else in my junior high-school years. That big growth spurt came when I was 15. When you get taller in a hurry, you get a bit gangly and uncoordinated, and basketball was such a massive help to me at that time. Darron Larsen, who played a number of years for the Manawatū Jets in the National Basketball League, was my coach, and he was exactly the sort of man I needed in my life then. He was pretty hard and demanding when it came to the fundamentals of the game, but he also encouraged us to just play. We'd be in the gym all the time.

I was also making rep rugby teams, following in my brothers' footsteps, though there was a setback when I got to Manawatū under-16s. I trialled a year young, at the same time as Adam. I was playing blindside flanker and thought I had an awesome trial. It was one of those days when you just walk off the field and think, 'Yeah, I nailed that.' Adam made the team, as he should have, but the coach, who was also the selector, sat me down and told me that though I was good enough to make the team, they were going to overlook me in favour of an older player. I was heartbroken because I'd played really well, and although I was still a scrawny kid, all skin and bone, I'd outplayed and outmuscled these older kids.

The hardest thing about that conversation was that the coach was Dad.

He'd started coaching only out of frustration at watching other people not give kids opportunities or age-appropriate coaching. On this occasion, he knew I'd have other chances, but there might not be for the kid who was in his last year at that level. But to me at that time, that didn't make the news any easier to take. To rub salt in the wound, he and Adam headed off to the provincial tournament on the East Coast, with Mum, Luke and me tagging along to watch. I was miserable – especially when there were a couple of injuries but Dad was still saying no to me.

Later, I understood it was the right call. Dad saw something that was a bit self-destructive in me, and knew I needed to pull my head in a bit. He had my best interests at heart, but if you'd asked me back then whether I thought that was the case, I would have given you a very different answer.

As it turned out, Dad didn't coach me a whole lot through the age groups. He coached my brothers more than me – on the field at least. At home it was a different story. There would barely be a dinner-table discussion that didn't circle back to rugby – what we'd done, what we could have done, what we should have done. Those conversations fed into our knowledge of the game. Dad was coaching us without us realising it, because we all just loved the game and loved talking about it. We would have sat there all night discussing different aspects of the sport if Mum didn't step in to tell us to do some schoolwork. Even when we were playing Super Rugby and Test rugby, those conversations would continue whenever we went home.

At school, we'd be teased about being 'rugby heads' but I didn't mind that. There's worse things to be known for than loving sport. And sport was starting to take over my school life, especially when I made the First XV in Year 11, along with being in the premier basketball team. In my final two years, Monday was prefect duties at the hostel, Tuesday was rugby, Wednesday was basketball, Thursday rugby, Friday basketball game, Saturday rugby game, Sunday was either rep basketball or rep rugby. It was hard trying to fit everything in, especially when I started trialling for national squads in both sports. I was never going to be an A+ student – Adam was definitely the most book-smart of the four of us – but I did possess some street smarts and worked out what I needed to focus on and what to brush over as I tried to cram study in alongside sport.

I had played mostly No. 8 until then but when I got into the firsts we had George playing there, Nick Crosswell at blindside and Chris Walker, who played a lot of games for Taranaki, at openside. They were all future professional players so there wasn't much debate to be had. I was tall, so the logical landing spot was lock. I was pretty light, too, so my teammates didn't have to waste too much energy throwing me up in the lineouts. I'd hated playing lock in junior rugby, but once I made the First XV in the second row, I never really left.

We were a good team and won a lot of games. In Rick Francis and Dan Paki, we didn't just have excellent coaches but wonderful mentors. We even got to play Palmerston North Boys'

High in Year 11, but it was just the once. If you want to wind Dad up, the quickest way to do it is to ask him why Feilding High and Palmy Boys don't play. Dad hates the unfairness of the system that favours traditional schools over others. As it happens, Feilding has done pretty well in recent times. Aaron Smith and I have racked up 280 Tests between us, and Codie Taylor, who came to Feilding High from another state co-ed, Horowhenua College, is well on the way to 100 himself.

Darron had spotted my height pretty early on and convinced me to run with the basketball team. I didn't play in my first year, but he had me running and training with the team a bit. In my second year I started playing and getting meaningful minutes. I won the 'most improved' award, something I would do again in my third and fourth years, until Luke took that title in my final year at school.

Basketball was massive not just for my self-esteem, but also for my rugby career. I'm convinced about that. I was a tall, gumby kind of kid with no understanding of the nuances of the sport – my first attempt at a lay-up hit the backboard and never got close to touching the rim – but I fell in love with it almost instantly. Darron pretty quickly identified my strengths and told me, 'Sam, you're never to bounce the ball, and you're not to shoot from outside this circle.' He'd indicate a line on the court with his foot, and it was no more than a few feet from the hoop. 'We just want you to rebound.'

That was something I instantly understood. It was similar to rugby, in that it was a battle for possession. That battle was won by those who got their bodies into the best positions and, as often as not, by those who wanted the ball more. The basketballers were an awesome bunch. Down to earth. We had a committed spectator, too. Aaron Smith wasn't blessed with a basketballer's height, but he watched every game, and when we were feeling kind to the little fella we let him play with us at lunch.

Rugby was the family love, but one of the reasons I fell so hard for basketball was that it wasn't a sport George or Adam took seriously. It felt like my point of difference, even though it was only temporary. When Luke came along he became pretty keen on it as well, and pretty bloody handy too. We had a couple of great years playing together.

Towards the end of my school days, I was faced with a couple of decisions I knew would be pivotal for the rest of my sporting life. The first was the choice between rugby and basketball; the next was between staying in Manawatū or moving south, as George and Adam had done.

For a while I was thinking basketball was probably the way to go. You can't coach size, and there were potentially doors that might open for me in the US college system if I decided to go down that path. The thing that swayed my decision was that there were simply more opportunities in rugby. I was selected to participate in the New Zealand Under-19 trials for rugby at the same time I was invited to a New Zealand basketball camp. If I made the Under-19s, I'd be going on a tour, but all basketball could offer was camps. When you're that age, it doesn't take much to turn your head, but a trip overseas to play rugby was far more attractive than a local camp. Once I had committed to rugby, I threw myself into it, but I've always appreciated what basketball gave me.

Whether to uproot my life and move out of Manawatū was a far more challenging decision. I ummed and ahhed for a long time about that. I had rugby options at both academies, and Manawatū was where most of my mates were staying. Something was nagging away at me, though. It was time for me to stand on my own two feet.

Mum was a proud Cantab: she'd met Dad at the rugby club in Culverden and we still had a lot of family there and it felt like it was time to trade Dad's green and white for my Mum's red and black.

Mum running the ball for Culverden in the late 1970s.

2

'I'M NOT GOOD ENOUGH'

ONE OF THE DETERMINING factors for me choosing to move to Canterbury in 2007 was the knowledge that if I didn't like it, I could always hightail it back home, whereas if I didn't have a crack at it, part of me would have always wondered, 'What if?' That would have burned me up. It helped that Adam was enrolled at Canterbury University, while George was also in the South Island, studying at Telford, Otago.

I know it rankles with Mum and Dad when they hear people say we were abandoning our home province for a bigger program, with the implication being that they could have done more to keep their kids in Manawatū. It's understandable that smaller provinces are frustrated to lose talent to bigger teams, but it wasn't as if we chose Canterbury by throwing a dart at a map. The success and professionalism of Canterbury and the

Crusaders was certainly attractive, but this was never a move I made to spite my hometown.

I packed up my old Ford Telstar – it was a horrible red thing nicknamed Randy that had sun-damaged paintwork peeling off the bonnet – and drove to Wellington to catch the ferry. I was so nervous. I was 18 and had spent the past five years shuttling between Feilding and the farm. That was my comfort zone. I knew how everything worked there but had no idea about what I was about to step into and what the expectations would be.

Randy was a thirsty bugger. The petrol gauge started tilting down the moment you put your foot on the gas. I had to fill up in Kaikōura, and as I did so I noticed the nerves had kicked in and I hadn't even hit Christchurch yet.

In Christchurch, I moved into one of the Rugby Park flats with another couple of guys, but I knew I was only going to be there for a little bit before I went to Australia for a short, pre-arranged overseas experience, and then I would be returning to start a degree at Lincoln and, hopefully, a professional rugby career. There were guys I knew at my first Canterbury Academy training – Ash Dixon, Nasi Manu, Ryan Crotty, Mark Jackman and Rodney Ah You – who I played New Zealand schools and age-group rugby with. They were my first friends in the set-up, my backyard cricket buddies, but I also had Adam there to lean on, although he was ready to move on to the next stage.

I made an early connection with Luke Thornley, the trainer. A couple of years later he tragically died. That was a bloody hard time, and made me think about how easily some guys who are really bubbly on the outside can hide inner turmoil.

He had an energy and excitement that helped gel all the guys together, especially those who had come from out of town.

We hit it off as a group and learned to work hard. It was so different to anything I'd done before. We trained together and learned together but we weren't a team – we didn't play games. Up until then, all the training I had done was team-based, in preparation for a game, and now, all of a sudden, I was training with the sole intention of becoming a better player.

My first gym session was an interesting experience. Lukey told me to jump on the bench, saying that there were 60 kilograms on the bar and that I should do six or seven of those before working up to a one-rep max, which is putting the most you can lift on the bar and doing a single bench press. He'd asked me if I had done much gym work before and I said, 'Yeah, a bit.' What I should have said was that I'd mucked around a bit inside a gym, but had never lifted any serious weights. On the bench next to me, Nasi was pumping out 100-kilogram reps. I looked at him and thought, 'We're both strong guys – I should be fine.' By the time I had got to four lifts of 60 kilograms, my arms were shaking like jelly and I could barely get the fifth one back on the supports. Lukey saw me struggling and asked again: 'So, have you done a lot of weight training?'

'Nah, not a lot.'

'Right,' he said, 'we won't test you today.'

I'll always be grateful to him for that. Lukey knew I couldn't have done a lot more than 60 kilograms, and rather than embarrass me in front of everyone, he just adjusted my program there on the spot. He knew that if he tried to make me train like these guys, who had all been doing weights programs through school, he was going to break me. I was the skinny, tall, white kid who was beginning to understand how much work was required to make a life out of this sport.

We were terrible cooks in the rugby flats, but we did our best. Having never had to cook before, I was the worst of the lot. I began to understand some of the privileges I'd been lucky enough to grow up with. Food had always just been there for me when I needed it. Just looking after myself was a challenge. We played far too much backyard cricket and ate too much bad food – but that's what young men do, right?

Sean Maitland was in the flat next door, and although he was in the academy, he was getting fast-tracked into the Crusaders and Canterbury NPC environments because he was a lot more developed as a player than the rest of us. In 2007 they had the controversial All Blacks reconditioning window and Luke was in charge of the Canterbury-based guys. Instead of us training at 7 pm at night, he would get Sean and me to come over and train with the All Blacks. I rocked up five minutes before I needed to be there, and bumped straight into Chris Jack, Richie McCaw, Dan Carter and Andrew Hore. Before I knew it I was doing full-on intervals with these guys, my absolute heroes, who had been training flat-stick for the past couple of months.

It's funny the little things you remember. Because I only had to walk across the road to the training session, I hadn't even thought to bring a water bottle. It was a bit unprofessional, but I remember Richie seeing my tongue hanging out and saying, 'Do you want a drink?' He threw me his bottle and I dropped it and it spilled everywhere. That was my introduction to the Great McCaw. It wasn't an auspicious start, but here I was rubbing shoulders with these guys who had been at the top of their games for a number of years. It was only a couple of sessions, but it was clever on Luke's part – he wanted to expose Sean and me to guys who were at the top, to give us an insight to the sort of fitness levels we'd need if we ever wanted to get there ourselves.

A key part of my early time in Christchurch was getting ready for the Under-19 World Cup, which was to be in Belfast, Northern Ireland. I'd played a year in the New Zealand Under-17s, and two years for New Zealand Secondary Schools, so I knew I had a chance of making the team. I was ready in some ways, but although I was tall, I hadn't grown into my body. Those in charge kept drumming into me how I had to get more physical, because South Africa, England and Ireland had guys who had been in the gym since they were 15, whereas I'd been playing basketball and cruising.

We played the trial at North Harbour Stadium, and Wayne Smith, Graham Henry and Steve Hansen came along. I was the captain of one trial team. It was said that the selectors liked to make guys they were unsure of captain, to see how they dealt with responsibility, so I took this as a warning sign and tried to focus on what the coaches were asking for.

When the team was selected, I had made it. The coaches gathered everybody together and the three wise men talked. They said there were guys in our group who would end up playing in the 2011 World Cup. Some players thought they were talking rubbish, but I looked around and thought, 'That will be Israel Dagg and Zac Guildford.' Izzy had been playing for Hawke's Bay, and Zac was already on the scene at the Hurricanes. I'd watched Izzy play at age-group level and had been in awe. His game just felt so much more advanced than anybody else's. There was also Nasi, Sean and Kade Poki, who were part of the Crusaders environment, so I guessed they weren't far away either.

This was the last-ever Under-19 World Cup. The New Zealand set-up in those days was Under-17s, Under-19s and Under-21s. They were amalgamating the 19s and 21s into Under-20s the following year, so we knew that if we performed well in Belfast we might also get another crack.

Touring with a bunch of good mates at that age and playing a lot of hard rugby was an amazing experience. Izzy broke his collarbone at training after running into coach Kieran Crowley, so he watched the final in a sling, but Nasi was a key guy and Kade was awesome. We had a stacked team and nearly everyone went on to play Super Rugby:

Forwards	Backs
Ben Afeaki	Matthew Cameron
Rodney Ah You	Ryan Crotty
Nick Barrett	Israel Dagg
Luke Braid	Robert Fruean
Thomas Crowley	Zac Guildford
Ash Dixon	Daniel Kirkpatrick
Paea Fa'anunu	Sean Maitland
John Hardie	Wayne Ngaluafe
Quentin MacDonald	Kade Poki
Nasi Manu	Trent Renata
Peter Saili	Winston Stanley
Chris Smith	Jackson Willison
Josh Townsend	
Samuel Whitelock	

We were told to prepare for it to be wet, cold and generally awful. It rained the day we arrived and the day we left, but everything else in between was unseasonably warm and sunny. Everybody was like, 'This is awesome! I love Ireland and want to come and live here,' but even the locals were telling us this wasn't normal. I've seen the other side of that coin in the years since.

I had no awareness of the tortured history of Belfast and Northern Ireland. We went on a city tour one day, and when we arrived at a square we were confronted with a mural of a gunman. No matter where you were standing in the square, it appeared to be looking right at you. It was a little bit different to what I was used to in The Square at Palmerston North.

We played and beat Wales in the semi-final and destroyed South Africa 31–7 in the final. We were smoking hot by that stage, and it wouldn't have mattered who we met. It sounds cocky but it got to the point where we understood that if we played close to our potential, nobody could match us.

We played an expansive style that nobody else could. Our outsides were running amok, scoring tries at will. We played every four days, and with recovery time thrown in it meant our training was limited. Kieran gave us a few moves, but his main message was to express ourselves and move the ball. We knew we couldn't match some of the teams in a physical arm wrestle, but we didn't need to, because our ability to execute our skills at speed was light-years ahead of that of any other team. At lineouts we used a lot of quick throw-ins, and I was more than happy with that because I was lean and fast and could play like a loose forward.

It was nice to be champions of the world at something. I wasn't an Izzy Dagg with the world at my feet – I had no idea what the future held. For all I knew, this could be the high point of my career.

When we returned home, I was bloody lucky to be under the guidance of the forward-thinking Matt Sexton at the academy. Because I'd been pursuing two sports at school, by the time I left I was close to burnout. I was too lean and light for my height, meaning I needed to put on muscle, but because I was running on empty, I was starting to get crook all the time.

Matt said to me, 'Hey, why don't you get through the Under-19 World Cup and then have six months away from footy?' I looked at playing basketball in the United States or Canada, but in the end I decided to go to the Gold Coast to spend six months at The Southport School (TSS), where I would coach basketball and rugby but not play.

It was an amazing experience. There was a lot of money at that school. Some kids were getting dropped off in limousines, while others were boating to school. It was a little different from what I'd grown up with at Feilding High.

I lived with Tabai Matson and his wife, Nadia, for the first couple of weeks. He was coaching club footy and selling real estate, and they took me in and helped me get settled before I moved into the TSS hostel. I was a housemaster there, even though I was only a year older than some of the students. They had an amazing First XV with some seriously talented kids. Seven or eight of them went on to play for Australian Schools. When I moved back to New Zealand, it wasn't too long before I was playing against the likes of James Slipper and Ben Tapuai, who were TSS kids.

After six months I returned home to do some fitness testing with Canterbury. Although I was having time off playing, I was still required to keep fit and to get into the gym to try to put weight on. The thing was, I was no good at weight training. I didn't know my body well enough to get the most out of it.

While I was back, I was named in the New Zealand Under-20s for the World Championships in 2008, so it was time to move home again permanently. When I said my goodbyes to Tabs and Nadia on the Gold Coast, they had some advice for me.

'Mate, on your first day at Lincoln, only talk to hot girls,' Tabs said.

'What do you mean by that?'

Nadia told me that was how they'd met, and that they had heaps of other friends who got together in those first few days of uni and stayed together. 'So you've got to be very careful who you talk to.'

'Okay, sweet,' I replied, immediately putting it out of my mind.

A couple of months later I was at Lincoln. I was on a sports scholarship through the academy and had a two-day induction before everyone else arrived. When all the freshies arrived we were gathered into a hall. I was sitting with some of the other scholarship guys, and this girl sat down next to me. I was facing the other way, but I'd noticed she was wearing a dress – she might have been the only girl in the entire university wearing one – and Jandals. The talk started and we were told all the rules around noise and alcohol.

Then the hostel manager asked us to stand up and introduce ourselves to the closest person. 'You might be standing next to your new best friend for the rest of your life,' she said. 'Some might end up being your archenemy, or it could be your future husband or wife.'

I was playing it cool, but the words of Tabs and Nadia flashed through my mind. Did I really want to talk to my scholarship mate, who I already knew, or should I introduce myself to—

'Hi, I'm Hannah.'

We couldn't be more different. I'm tall, she's not. I grew up on a farm 35 kilometres from windswept Hīmatangi Beach, she grew up on the North Shore with the Waitematā Harbour on her doorstep. I was a rugby head way out of my academic comfort zone, she was a super-brain studying viticulture who didn't know a whole lot about rugby.

So here we are 16 years, a marriage and three kids later.

A few months later, Tabs rang me excitedly to tell me he had won the assistant coaching job at Canterbury and was coming home. He asked me if I'd taken his life advice and I just brushed it off, but Nadia caught on pretty quickly. 'Believe me, you two are going to end up getting married,' she said. 'It's fate.'

I truly believe that having a stable, loving relationship has played a big part in my success. I don't mean that in a patronising way, or to reduce Hannah to a cog in my high-performance wheel, but multiple coaches have pointed out to me that no matter how well young men think they hide it, trouble at home or lifestyle issues tend to bleed into their rugby. Sure, there might be a handful who thrive on chaos, but there are far fewer of them than you'd think.

I slotted into university life and played for a short-lived Merivale–Lincoln club merger called Merlins. The Under-20s worlds were the next big thing on my checklist and we went to Wales under the coaching of Dave Rennie and Russell Hilton-Jones. Perhaps unsurprisingly, with 18 players who had swept through the Under-19s the previous season, we made no race of it, thrashing hosts Wales 31–6 in the semi-final and England 38–3 in the final at Swansea's Liberty Stadium.

Again, we were playing rugby that other teams could only dream about. Our ability to execute skills at high pace probably gave us all a warped sense of what rugby was like – we thought we'd spend the rest of our playing lives turning up to grounds around the world and running the opposition off their feet. In Sean, Kade, Nasi and Zac, we had four guys already immersed in Super Rugby. There was also a little Māori halfback with a rocket pass, a kid I knew well through school and age-group rugby, who wasn't with us in Belfast but who had edged himself into the spotlight. Aaron 'Nuggy' Smith was starting to realise his enormous talent, but he couldn't muscle his way past future Scotland halfback Grayson Hart for the start in that team.

When we returned from Wales, I was expecting another campaign with Merlins, but Canterbury locks Michael Paterson and Isaac Ross both suffered concussions so NPC coach Rob Penney called me up for training. So it was that I made my first-class debut in the 2008 NPC preseason. I'm not sure why it was listed as a first-class match, but we played Wellington at the now defunct Queen Elizabeth II Park in Christchurch's north-eastern suburbs. It had rained all week – and when I say 'rained', what I really mean was that it absolutely hosed down for days on end. QEII Park was the greenest field in the city, but it was also known as the wettest, as that part of Christchurch was historically marshlands. Within the first five minutes the field was a mudpit. In fact, it was a Canterbury debut for both George and I, who had transferred north from Otago and was named on the bench. Because I started, my Canterbury number will forever come before his, though – and before Adam's, as he made his debut in the next match.

Rob Penney pulled me aside ahead of the game and said, 'Look, just hang out on the wing and don't get too involved.' I was nodding my head but knew I was going to ignore him and get stuck in. In those days, the trend was for locks to do a bit of seagulling out wide and receive cross-field kicks. I dutifully performed that role and should have probably scored, but when Stephen Brett sent a kick my way, it was so muddy I failed to get any traction when I tried to run after it. It was probably lucky the game wasn't televised because it would have looked like one of those cartoons where the legs are spinning but you're not going anywhere.

We lost. Cory Jane was on top of his game, having just returned from sevens, and I remember watching him and thinking, 'Wow, I hope I don't have to try to tackle this guy – he's playing a different sport to everybody else.' Reado (Kieran Read) was playing for us, along with a couple of other All Blacks, so both teams were strong. It was a big step up from age-group or club rugby, and despite the conditions I had a lot of fun. I caught myself thinking that I wouldn't mind playing more of this when the time was right. But, given where my body was at, the time wasn't quite right.

Best-laid plans and all that. Michael and Isaac were still out injured when the start of the 2008 NPC rolled around and I was picked to play against Manawatū, of all provinces. This was a game I knew I couldn't afford to slip up in, because of what it would mean on multiple levels, both for my own confidence within the Canterbury set-up and for all the shit I would get from my mates and others in Manawatū. On cue, Manawatū came down to our turf and beat a Canterbury team containing three Whitelocks. My old intermediate school buddy Aaron Cruden and my New Zealand Under-20s teammate Andre Taylor put on an absolute show and we had no answers. They beat us 25–24 at the old Lancaster Park. The worst thing about it was that it was the only game Manawatū won all year.

You can probably imagine how I felt. There I was, having chosen to start my career in Canterbury rather than my home province, having suited up twice and lost twice, including against the province I left, a team Canterbury would expect to beat nine times out of ten. A whole lot of my university mates had come to watch, too, which just added to my embarrassment.

There were a few dark thoughts racing around my head: 'This is all my fault … I'm not good enough.' These were genuine thoughts, not just self-pity. My disappointment was heightened by the fact we were playing against the team I probably could have been playing for, and I was questioning the wisdom of my decision. I had mates texting me and teasing me about me dragging Canterbury down to Manawatū's level, and although it was all meant in fun, it stung a bit because there was an element of truth. I never once thought I was too good for Manawatū but I had moved because I thought Canterbury would be a better environment for me to develop my game, and right then it didn't look that way.

A few of the senior boys got around me and told me it was nothing to do with me, that I was playing well. They meant well and I appreciated that, but all I could think of was how much better I had to get. I didn't play again that season as those injured boys recovered and duly took their spots back. That Manawatū misadventure was the last game Canterbury lost, as they eventually beat Wellington 7–6 in the final at the Cake Tin.

I continued training with the team all through the season but my confidence had taken a knock. For Canterbury, it was the first in a run of championship finals. My contribution: played two, lost two and a dubious place in the team photo.

3

IF YOU GET ONE, YOU GET ALL FOUR

GEORGE, ADAM AND I were at the races when I found out that I had made the Crusaders squad for 2010. It was a fitting enough venue. Mum and Dad have long owned Standardbreds, and pictures of their most successful horses take pride of place on the walls of the family home alongside their kids.

Canterbury had just won the 2009 NPC, beating Wellington in Christchurch in the final. My contribution to this title was more substantial than the previous year, my rookie year. After beating Wellington, we had a big night on the Saturday, kicked on again on Sunday and on Monday I did the traditional '12 Cans for Canterbury', which was a rite of passage after playing 12 games. I chewed my way through it, but wouldn't say I passed with flying colours.

The next day was the races at Addington, the New Zealand Trotting Cup, part of the wider Cup Week, the biggest and booziest week of the year in Christchurch. George's phone rang. Back in the day you used to get a phone call from the coach, not like it is now, when everyone knows beforehand who is contracted and who's not. George had a quick conversation with coach Todd Blackadder and then said, 'Yep, here's Adam.' Adam got the good news, then he passed the phone to me. Toddy thought it was too easy, killing three birds with one stone.

Everything was happening so quickly, but making the Crusaders was the logical next step on the journey. By 2009, I was in an apprentice role with the team, which essentially meant I did all the training but didn't get paid for it. The only reason I could do it was because I was on a sports scholarship at Lincoln. I'd get back to Lincoln after Crusaders or academy training and grab a late and reheated dinner. Driving back and forward from Lincoln to Christchurch every day was a bit of a pain, but it gave me an appreciation for time management. Studying at university while pursuing a professional rugby career had not been easy. In 2007, I didn't study at all, and the following year I think I did all of four papers, but by 2009 I was getting better at utilising my time effectively.

In my rugby life, I had little responsibility. Some days I'd be training at lock, other days I would be filling in at prop in team runs (not in scrums, obviously). Our role as apprentices was to mimic the teams the Crusaders would be playing. One week we'd be the Stormers, the next the Highlanders. Some days I would end up on the wing or at fullback. It was the perfect environment from which to grow my knowledge of what I had to do as a lock and how that flowed on to other parts of the field. Some days it felt hard not being part of the proper Crusaders team, but it was critical in my development. On a daily basis I got to rub shoulders with Ross Filipo, Brad Thorn, Chris Jack, Isaac Ross and James Broadhurst. All those guys were or would become All Blacks, and they all had elements of their game that I could try to emulate.

I'd look at Brad and think, 'Right, I want to steal his mentality and strength, his professionalism. Isaac, I want to steal his skill. Broady, I love his energy; Chris, his understanding of lineouts; Ross, his rawboned, rugged way of operating.'

That whole year, I spent each week watching those guys to understand what made them the players they were, then tried to use that knowledge when I went back to Lincoln for club footy. Everything started to click. In 2009, I was back in the Canterbury NPC squad and immediately got an opportunity when we travelled to Albany to play North Harbour, a team that, on paper, we should have been too strong for. We lost 19–22.

The familiar negative thoughts came back. 'This has to be me. It's my problem. Shit!'

Immediately, I started to wonder whether the pressure of trying to study full-time and forge a first-class career was too much, but the older heads in the Canterbury environment were great. They'd had slow starts before and never panicked. They just said, 'Keep doing what you're doing. You're playing good rugby – everything is going to be fine.'

And they were right. All of a sudden things flipped. In my fourth attempt I finally experienced a win. That it was against Auckland only made it better. We went on a run, including winning the Ranfurly Shield at Wellington. We had a hell of a team that day. All the All Blacks came back except Kieran Read, who had knocked himself out. Richie was at No. 8 because George was captain and openside. DC (Dan Carter) played at first five, Brad Thorn was at lock. Corey Flynn was playing off the bench. All the regulars, including me, got knocked to the bench to accommodate these guys who needed a bit of rugby.

We ran out of alcohol in the sheds after the game. That was my first introduction to being part of a senior team that had achieved something really significant. My eyes and ears were wide open. This was what it was like to win something big. Yes, there were plenty of beers drunk, but I was less into that than I was just soaking up the camaraderie. The senior All Blacks on our team were quite emotional, because it was the first chance they'd got to play for the Shield. They felt they could tick another thing off. The stories were flowing, which I loved. A year ago I was the shy kid being introduced to these guys at training, and now I was playing with them, sharing in their successes.

All those regrets and anxieties I had when my record stood at played three, lost three were replaced by a sense of satisfaction. This was the Canterbury I thought I was going to be part of. Beside me, too, were my two big brothers. I was in heaven.

*

It might have looked like the whole Whitelocks-invade-Canterbury thing was planned, but in fact we'd all taken

Winning the Ranfurly Shield from Wellington in 2009. We had some team for that game.

very different routes to get there. Adam was planning to go to Otago University before deciding to do an extra year at Feilding High because he was a year younger than his original class. By the time the next year rolled around, he decided to study engineering at the University of Canterbury, but he ended up doing accountancy.

George had left home to go to Telford, a historic rural education institution just south of Balclutha. He was playing his club footy for Alhambra-Union in Dunedin and had made the Otago squad as a No. 8 and was playing pretty well. In those days, you had to be in the provincial catchment area of a Super Rugby team to make the squad, and although George had done some training with the Highlanders, it was the Crusaders who chased him. Coach Robbie Deans rang him and said, 'Hey, I think you're a seven, not an eight. Do you want to come up here to play for Canterbury and I'll pick you in the Crusaders?'

That conversation happened when I was living in Australia in 2007. I knew I was heading home in a couple of months' time, and remember thinking how cool it would be if we all ended up in the same spot. George had already played ten games for Otago before he moved, and while my Canterbury number might have been called before his, the reality is that he was a lot more ready than I was – but I never let the truth get in the way of a good story. George switched his agriculture diploma from Telford to Lincoln.

After taking a gap year at Loughborough, in England, Luke followed us to Canterbury in 2011, enrolling at UC to get a business management degree.

While we four brothers all enjoyed each other's company, we weren't joined at the hip. George was a bit more settled.

He'd already been flatting for a few years, and the novelty of being away from home and outside of parental control had well and truly worn off. He's always had an older head on his shoulders.

I wouldn't describe us four as best mates, but we're very, very close. We all had our own groups of friends, but if you're mates with one of us, you tend to inherit the other three as well. Now I think about it, perhaps that does make us best mates.

At the Crusaders I got stuck into the preseason. The trainers were constantly saying, 'More weights, more weights, more weights.' I got comfortable with all the guys, learning the names of the new players, because I was one myself. Sonny Bill Williams came in that year. I had never watched much rugby league but I checked out his highlights and quickly came to the conclusion that he was a weapon.

I'm a goal-setter and a record keeper. I had a red book, and once I made the squad I made some goals for myself, each one more challenging than the last.

At school I'd been fortunate to come under the tutelage of hostel master Rick Francis, who was also First XV coach. He was massive on goal setting. In the hostel, we all had to get up in front of our peers and say what our goals were at the start of the year – two academic goals and one extracurricular. It didn't matter if you were in your first year or a senior. And you had to renew your goals each term. If one of your goals was irrelevant or not challenging enough, he would tell you to come up with a new one.

I applied Rick's method to my rugby. I have kept all my rugby notebooks, and in each of them, at the front, you will find my goals for the year. If you look at my book from

2010, you'll see it's set up to be a massive year, because it was my first year as a full-time pro and my first year with the Crusaders.

And of course I wanted to be an All Black, so I set some goals around that too.

Before the actual All Blacks came back from their break, we talked about challenging them in different ways. Brad Thorn and I ended up playing a preseason game together against the Hurricanes in Motueka in February 2010, and I took that instruction too literally, challenging him in a race to the next ruck. I'd only been on the field for about two minutes and he'd been on for an hour, so he gave me an absolute serve and told me to worry about my game, not his.

I'm not sure why I even said it. My whole mentality was just to shut up and get into it, work hard and not say too much. That incident confirmed that I was better off at that point in my career being seen, not heard. Brad checked in with me later to apologise and make sure I hadn't been affected by his censure. He knew I was excited to be playing at that level, whereas for him it was just another preseason hit-out. He didn't need some jumped-up rookie trying to impress the coaches at his expense. I learned my lesson.

The Crusaders team was named for our first game against the Highlanders, and I was selected to start alongside Isaac Ross, with Thorny on the bench. George was starting at openside and Adam was on the bench. I was not expecting to play at all, and suddenly I had this opportunity in front of me. That week flew by. I didn't have an opportunity to stop, take a breath and work out what was going on. It was just all hands to the pump, getting stuck in. The game was exactly the same.

I had set myself a goal of playing ten senior games that season, and I ticked it off quicker than I'd expected.

There are two things I remember about that first game: Jimmy Cowan starting a fight, and Zac Guildford, who had just come down from the Hurricanes, running around Izzy Dagg, who was still with the Highlanders. We won, too, which meant it was a much better feeling than my Canterbury debut.

Todd Blackadder was the right coach for that stage of my career. He was very much a mindset coach who encouraged you to back yourself. He never bogged me down in detail, and encouraged me to make on-field decisions, especially on defence. It was far better, he drilled into me, to make a poor decision than no decision. Things were moving so fast I didn't have time to stop and think about how lucky I was to have all these amazing people – including Crusaders legends Daryl Gibson and Mark Hammett – pushing my game forward.

I was excited to be going to South Africa for the first time. Going toe to toe with their big boys was such an invaluable part of my rugby education, and it pains me to think that young Super Rugby players coming through today don't get that same opportunity. I don't have any expertise in the financial and broadcast aspects of that decision, but from a playing perspective, and for the contrast in styles, Super Rugby is a lot weaker for the absence of the South Africans.

With Chris Jack out after wrist surgery and Thorny troubled by a calf problem, there were plenty of opportunities for me, but in week two I got a reality check in Brisbane. The Reds thumped us 41–20, giving me a crash course in how much tougher playing away from home was in Super Rugby. Through the rest of the season I toggled between starting and the bench, and we finished fourth, which meant going back to South Africa to play the Bulls in Soweto in the semi-final.

It was my first start against one of those big South African forward packs, and my first opportunity to have a real crack at two of the legends of the second row: Bakkies Botha and Victor Matfield. I don't remember much about the game. All week we had talked about them box-kicking, especially through Fourie du Preez and Morné Steyn, two of the best to have ever kicked a ball. As forwards, we spoke about checking their chasers and getting a couple of metres from our catcher; if we all got our timing right, we'd be the shield for them to get a free catch.

Early in the game, we won a defensive lineout and Andy Ellis launched a clearing kick. Fullback Zane Kirchner caught it around halfway and put up one of the biggest bombs you'd ever see. I did exactly what we had been training all week to do, running back in line with the flight of the ball and watching Dan Carter's eyes to try to get a sense of when he was jumping for the ball.

Dan went to jump alright, but he didn't get near the ball because it landed slap-bang on top of my head, sending me to the turf and propelling the ball towards our try line, where Kirchner followed up to score a try (fortuitously perhaps, as it looked like Pierre Spies spilled it forward before the try, not that I knew that at the time). It had been close until then, but they absolutely pumped us after that, winning 39–24. Our total included a consolation try for me when I got on the end of a DC cutout pass.

I don't remember any of that. In fact, I 'woke up' on the bus with a beer in my hand, as Chris Jack had invited all the rookies down the back to talk about their first-year experiences.

Apparently, there was a moment where I clicked that the game was over and said to Chris, 'Hey, did we just win?' He said no, and quickly alerted the medical staff that I might not be quite right.

The whole incident was the cause of much humour. My mates told me it made Australia's *Footy Show* as one of the top ten best falcons of all time, and took the number one slot for 2010. There was a serious side to it, though. Back in 2010 there was no real concussion protocol. We had a day to wait in Johannesburg before we flew home and went down to the training ground for a kick around. Someone suggested playing keepy-uppy with headers, but after one go I realised I was not well at all, as I instantly felt a wave of nausea and had a thumping headache.

As funny as the falcon might have looked, I quickly learned that messing around with head injuries was no laughing matter.

4

'TOO LIGHT, TOO FAT, TOO WEAK'

IN THE FIRST FEW minutes of his first preseason hit-out for the 2010 Super Rugby season, Ali Williams snapped his Achilles tendon. It was the second year running that this fragile area of the body – one I would get to know too well – had ruined his season.

Being a typical halfback, Andy Ellis was yapping away to me when he found out Williams' bad news, implying that I must be pumped up and excited. There was no way I was taking any pleasure in someone else's misfortune, but a bit later I did sit back and wonder if there was something to what he was saying: that I might be in line for an All Blacks call-up.

Ali was out, Jason Eaton had done his knee and Tom Donnelly at the Highlanders had broken his foot towards the end of the Super Rugby campaign, but there were still some experienced internationals out there like Thorny and Anthony Boric. Of course I was hoping I might be in the frame, but I never wanted to put it out there that I was thinking like that.

Outside noise was starting to seep in a little, though. Some pundits were saying I'd had a great season and was ready for the next step; others were saying I was not ready. All of a sudden there was a bit of extra heat around my name, and even if deep down I didn't think I deserved it yet, the prospect was kind of sitting there. Even my flatmates started teasing me about being the next All Blacks lock. Mum and Dad obviously thought nothing was going to happen, because they had gone to Argentina to watch Luke play for the Under-20s.

A couple of weeks later, the All Blacks team was named a bit earlier than normal. After we were beaten by the Bulls in the Super Rugby semi-final in Soweto, all New Zealand interest in the competition was over, so management decided to name the team and get everyone ready for the June Tests against Ireland and Wales. The announcement came midweek, and the Andy Ellises of the world were telling me to tune in. I would probably rather have not. Whether that was a defence mechanism to guard against embarrassment if I didn't make it, I'm not sure, but in the end my mates made me. The announcement was on the Rugby Channel, which you had to pay for, so we poor students didn't have it. Instead, my flatmate Hamish Wright found an old radio and we hooked it up and listened in the old-school way.

The team was announced alphabetically, so I faced a long wait. Eventually it got to the part that all my mates had tuned in for: 'Neemia Tialata, Wellington; Victor Vito, Wellington; Piri Weepu, Wellington; Tony Woodcock, North Harbour.'

They announced four debutants – my old Palmy Intermediate mate Aaron Cruden, Benson Stanley, Victor Vito and Israel Dagg – but I wasn't one of them.

I felt nothing. There was no real disappointment because I hadn't expected to be named. My flatmates were gutted, so we turned off the radio and the mundanities of everyday life kicked back into gear. We went to the mall to get a feed and do some grocery shopping. My phone was in my pocket and I could feel it vibrating. I assumed it was a couple of messages of commiseration, so I didn't bother checking it. The vibrations kept coming, and I soon realised I didn't know enough people to get so many messages.

I had a bunch of missed calls from a random number, but being a lazy student I couldn't be bothered checking my voicemail. Eventually a text message popped up: 'Hey, it's Darren Shand here, can you give me a call?' Even that didn't move me into action until I scrolled down and saw that Darren Shand was 'All Blacks manager'.

Oh shit! I ditched my flatmates and hit the call button as fast as I could. The conversation was quick. I was wanted in Auckland for two days as injury cover for Donnelly. They wanted a few extra people there to look after some guys returning from injury.

I didn't have to be asked twice. I went home, found my rugby boots and a few clean pairs of socks and undies, and flew up the next day. Life comes at you fast, right?

Everyone else had flown in the day before, so when I arrived at the Heritage Hotel lobby I was looking around and wondering what I was meant to do. Pete Gallagher, the team physio, came up to me and just started chatting like we were old mates. I had never met Pete before but he's a true character and an absolute champion of a man. I admitted that I didn't really know what I was doing here, and his questions just kept coming, most of them straight out of left field.

'Your hair is like Conrad Smith – are you related to Conrad Smith? You guys are from the same part of the country, aren't you?'

'Well, not really.'

I immediately took a shine to Pete. Stuff was just falling out of his mouth at a rate I couldn't keep up with, but it immediately put me at ease and made me feel part of something, even if I wasn't officially part of the team. From that moment I knew that if I ever needed to have a yarn, I could go to Pete – but I'd have to be prepared to do a lot of listening as well.

Anthony Boric was my roommate. AB made me aware that this was an environment with different, more intense expectations. He'd tell me where the next meeting was and how many minutes it took to walk there so I'd arrive with plenty of time to spare. He told me what kit to wear for what activity.

My first day there coincided with a fitness test, and I'd done nothing for a couple of weeks. I wasn't very fit, fast or strong – I was also still a little bit skinny. Brad Thorn was fit and strong. He won the fitness test as a lock, smoking everyone else on the yo-yo, which was the new test on the scene. I tested pretty poorly. The inevitable follow-up conversation came when we trained at the gym.

Nic Gill, who these days is a good friend of mine, had a well-rehearsed speech that he gave to the young guys: 'You're too light, you're too fat, you're too weak, you're fit enough-ish, you're too slow …' He would go on like this for a bit before he said, 'For a 28-year-old, you're not where we need you.' I told him I'd only just turned 21, so he made this big show of tearing up the training program he'd devised for me. We laugh about it now, but there was an edge to his performance. It was my introduction to the fact that this environment expects so much more from you than you thought possible. It was Nic's way of saying that what I thought was acceptable wasn't, and that everybody in camp – teammates, coaches and management – would challenge me. I couldn't be late for meetings, I couldn't turn up to an activity in the wrong kit, I couldn't get away with being 'fit enough-ish'.

Those two days were so full on, but I loved every minute. I was both disappointed and excited that they were coming to an end and I would be flying home to Christchurch. I wanted more, but I was also looking forward to getting stuck into my work-ons, areas of my game and training coaches had identified that needed to improve, and there were plenty of them.

I never ended up catching that flight. Shandy told me I was heading in a different direction, to New Plymouth, where I was still required as injury cover for Tom, whose foot was taking a bit longer to heal than was hoped. Off I went to New Plymouth with the team, this time rooming with the ultimate professional in Thorny and wondering how I was going to make my three T-shirts and three pairs of undies last. I didn't have any black shoes or anything resembling smart casual.

We got straight into some promotional work in the community, but it was a strange experience for me: I was involved in the promotions, wearing the kit, but I was not actually part of the squad. I was an extra, a bag holder. I wasn't complaining – I was almost living the dream – but at the same time I felt like a bit of a fraud.

As the week progressed, Graham Henry – known as 'Ted' – was divvying up the workloads and the training groups. I found myself doing a bit of scrummaging work while paired with Thorny, and then I was doing other drills with AB. I found myself thinking, 'What's going on here? There are a few superstars by my side here.' I hadn't been fully immersed into the training but the work I was doing was making me wonder what the coaches had in mind.

Mum and Dad got in contact. They were having a great time in Argentina. There was no way I was going to suggest they come back on the off chance I was added to the squad, but I'd be lying if I said that thought hadn't crossed my mind.

The team was named with Thorny and AB as the locks. That was a given. I was thinking they were going to pick a blindside flanker who could play lock in the reserves, when all of a sudden my name got read out. 'Holy shit,' I thought. 'What just happened there?' Had I misheard? There were a lot of young guys named. Izzy was picked to start, as were Benson Stanley and Ben Franks, who had played against Munster in 2008, but this was his first Test. Aaron Cruden was on the bench with Victor and me. There were still a bunch of old heads, but with a few of us young guys sprinkled in.

Some of the events of the week started to make sense. Two days before the team was named, Shag Hansen had come into the room I was sharing with Thorny. There didn't seem to be any reason for it. He just walked around the room and talked to Thorny. I was sitting there as Shag was asking Brad, 'How's the kid going?' It was like I wasn't there. Thorny was like, 'Yeah, he's ready,' while I was just sitting on the bed awkwardly, trying to pretend I was minding my own business. He was scoping me out to see how I would react. When you're the assistant coach you can do that.

Once the team was named, I bombarded Thorny with questions. The poor bugger was asked whether I should fly Hannah up for the game, and whether I should ring my parents and tell them. My many questions must have seemed so mundane to him, but he was never anything but helpful. He knew I had so much information and emotion to process.

The rain was relentless that week. As bleak as anything I can recall before or since. Training would move from field to field. Halfway through a session we would up sticks and move to another field because we were ripping the ground to shreds. By the end of the week I had convinced myself that there was no way they'd put me on against a team like Ireland, in what was likely to be a close-fought mudfight. Maybe that was partly wishful thinking. Mum and Dad couldn't get here, and although I was glad they were following Luke, as they had when I was in the Under-20s, part of me knew it wouldn't quite be the same without them. They'd been pitchside for most of my big moments, and this would definitely be a big moment.

The family was still well represented. My aunty Debbie and uncle Reece came across from Hawke's Bay, Hannah flew up and George made sure he was there. I warned them that there was a good chance I wouldn't see the field – this was only at the start of the era when all the subs started getting used – but really I didn't have a clue. There were no pre-game instructions that suggested I would be put on at any given time, and I wouldn't have dared to ask.

I took my place for the anthem snuggled in between Thorny and Cruds, and was in the back row, far right, for 'Ka Mate'. I was so nervous about the haka. Derek Lardelli, composer of 'Kapa o Pango' and our cultural adviser, had drummed into us how important it was, and I got through it without any stuff-ups and took my place on the bench.

Rather than a forward-dominated game in the wet, the weather cleared and as early as the quarter-hour mark it was obvious the game was going to be looser than expected when Jamie Heaslip got caught kneeing Richie in the head – twice. He saw a red card from referee Wayne Barnes and the score started to get comfortable. It occurred to me that I was going to get a run at some point. That point was in the tenth minute of the second half. 'You're on for Brad when you're ready,' was the instruction.

I took my jacket off – no warm-up – and said, 'Yep, I'm ready.'

I ran straight out there for a scrum, but not before Thorny stopped me to shake my hand and say congratulations. I didn't even get a chance to shunt in my first international set piece because Ireland had gone early and we got a free kick. Kieran Read tapped and ran, and made good ground before he was dragged down. We got a super-quick ball and Piri Weepu had a quick dart before putting my locking partner, AB, into a hole. He drew the cover defender, halfback Tomás O'Leary, before passing back inside to Piri. I remember all this because I was charging up in support, but I thought it was going to be in vain as Piri was looking inside again to pass. Just as he got to the last man, however, he flicked a no-look pass to his right and all I had to do was catch it and gallop the last ten metres to fall over the line for a try.

A few seconds earlier, I was pumped to be engaging in my first Test scrum, and now I was being mobbed by my teammates, some of the best players in the world, after dotting down with my first touch of the ball. Talk about emotion. I had a smile as wide as the Tasman Sea! Was I about to wake up and discover I'd just had the best dream ever? This was what my brothers and I had always talked about, getting out there and having an awesome game and an awesome moment, and it had happened. It actually bloody happened.

On the match broadcast, the cameras panned to the coaches' box, and while Shag was clapping and seemed happy enough, Ted looked like he'd been sucking on lemons. Smithy looked gutted about something. I was smiling enough to make up for both of them, though.

The game swung a little after that. We had been up by heaps, but they found some fight and scored a few tries themselves. The weather deteriorated, but I was still running around on a massive high. No matter what happened from here, I was All Black number 1104 – which, by some incredible fluke, was Mum and Dad's room number at their hotel in Argentina – and I had five points next to my name that nobody could take away from me.

I didn't want the game to end, and luckily there was a bit of time left. I won a lineout and fed Weepu, who brought Zac Guildford, another sub, off the wing for a hit-up that got us over the advantage line. From the ruck I went into first receiver. Weepu's pass hit me on the run and I brushed off a couple of weak tackle attempts and crashed over in the tackle of Tommy Bowe. What was going on? I'd only gone and scored two tries. This was ridiculous. I spared a thought for George. He'd scored on his All Blacks debut and now I'd gone and doubled his tally. The dream just kept giving.

The game ended and I couldn't have been happier. It wasn't just the tries. I was just as proud of the fact that I'd made a heap of tackles, particularly when the game was starting to run Ireland's way, and secured some good lineout possession. I felt like I had constant involvement, which is pretty rare. I couldn't have been any more chuffed, but I quickly learned that it pays not to get too high on success. I picked up the paper the next morning and stupidly looked at the player ratings. Truth be told, I was probably expecting to read an 8/10, or something like that, followed by a few glowing words. Instead the number was a six, followed by a pithy note that everything was on a plate for me and Test matches weren't usually that easy. Okay, then. If nothing else, it brought me back down off Cloud Nine.

The debutants gathered for an informal photo and the capping ceremony. We went in order of the people who got on, so the starters Izzy, Ben Franks and Benson Stanley spoke first. By the time it got to me, everyone had said the stock-standard: 'Thanks to the family, thanks to the teammates.' I felt under a bit of pressure to deliver something a bit more entertaining for the masses. I moved through my thank-yous pretty quickly, but then I decided to go off script and give Mum and Dad some grief, telling the audience they clearly loved Luke more than me because they'd chosen to watch him play Under-20s rather than my Test debut.

Those gathered, including my aunt, uncle and George, seemed to lap that up, so I felt a bit of confidence I hadn't enjoyed before. I thought a bit about George and how the first All Blacks Test I'd attended was to watch his debut against

My family connections to rugby run deep. My maternal grandfather, Nelson Dalzell, was All Black number 553. Despite injuring a leg in World War II, he played 22 matches at lock from 1953 to 1954. He was also a sheep and beef farmer, from Culverden, and played for Canterbury at provincial level.

Nelson (fourth from the right) played every All Blacks Test on the tour of Great Britain and France in 1953 to 1954. All we know about this photo is that it was taken in France. Apparently, he was the biggest man in the team and also a second-rower, like myself.

New Zealand Rugby Representatives
TOURING TEAM 1953-54

Frank Thompson, Crown Studios, Wellington, Photo Copyright

Back Row—
C. J. Loader   A. E. G. Elsom   J. W. Kelly   W. A. McCaw   K. L. Skinner   R. C. Hemi   J. M. Tanner   I. J. Clarke
Second Row—
C. A. Woods   H. L. White   R. A. White   P. F. H. Jones   K. P. Bagley   R. J. O'Dea   D. O. Oliver   G. N. Dalzell   W. H. Clark
Sitting—
R. A. Jarden   J. T. Fitzgerald   D. D. Wilson   R. C. Stuart (*Captain*)   J. N. Millard (*Manager*)   A. E. Marslin (*Assistant Manager*)
L. S. Haig (*Vice Captain*)   R. W. H. Scott   B. P. Eastgate   V. D. Bevan
In Front—
B. B. J. Fitzpatrick   R. G. Bowers   K. Davis   M. J. Dixon   W. S. S. Freebairn

My great-uncle Allan Elsom was All Black number 538. He is pictured here in the back row, second from left, along with Nelson in the second row, second from the right.

My dad, Braeden, with a horrendous mullet. He must have been cutting it himself. Dad was a bloody good player; he was in age-group games for the Colts and then played five years for Manawatū when they were a provincial powerhouse.

Dad with the ball, playing for Manawatū. I love this photo; it shows it was a different game back then. Dad was an enforcer, rough and raw.

My mum, Caroline, as a young shepherd in Canterbury. My inner strength comes from her.

If there's one place you can manage four growing boys at once, it's a farm. My brothers and I enjoyed an upbringing that I imagine was pretty typical for kids growing up in rural New Zealand. Left to right: George, Adam, me and Luke.

Our Linton dairy farm was large at about 850 hectares. Left to right: Luke, me, Adam and George.

Me with my champion calf, Mary.

The Whitelock fishermen. We'd caught one trout; the rest are carp. That's Grandad John Whitelock at the back, instantly recognisable by his eyepatch, which he wore after losing an eye at the age of 17.

My love of the outdoors and of hunting all stems from growing up on the farm. When we were young, we'd fish for trout and hunt rabbits. As we got older, we were introduced to pig hunting, and then it was time to shoot your first deer.

Mum and Dad have long owned Standardbreds, and pictures of their most successful horses take pride of place on the walls of the family home alongside photos of us.

A typical kids' party spread, complete with brandy snaps and jolly fizzy. I used to devour food as a kid, especially oranges ... as the peels on my plate suggest.

Left to right: me, George and Adam. This photo was taken in our original home. Rugby was all barefoot at that age in those days. Our first club was Palmerston North High School Old Boys' Junior Rugby Club.

Playing against Te Kawau Rugby Club for High School Old Boys. Look at all the knobbly knees. Unbeknown to him, I was wearing my older brother George's shorts. They were a little bit big, but I wanted to be just like him!

Under-11s, for Manawatū.
I hadn't grown into my ears
just yet!

Bumping off a player from Whanganui for the Manawatū under-11s.

Playing for Palmerston North Intermediate Normal School at an under-13s rugby sevens tournament, Rathkeale College, Masterton. Aaron Cruden (top left) was there at the same time. Even then, the future All Blacks star played like he did later as a professional. I'm in the front row, second from left, with my High School Old Boys' club socks, and boots strapped with insulation tape from the back of Dad's farm truck.

Awaiting the lineout throw for the High School Old Boys' under-13s. This ground was on the old state highway going toward Bulls.

Manawatū under-16s vs Hawke's Bay, 2004. This was at a tournament in Upper Hutt. I'm pretty sure we got pumped in this game! The Hawke's Bay side would have included the likes of Zac Guildford and Izzy Dagg. Nevertheless, I went on to make the New Zealand under-17s after the tournament.

Going up for the ball in a lineout for Feilding High School's first XV against Palmy Boys, 2004. We won the match 31–25. A big part of my success can be put down to the excellent coaches and mentors we had at Feilding High.

I was selected to play in a New Zealand Under-19s trial at the same time as I was invited to a New Zealand basketball camp. I would end up choosing rugby, mostly because of the opportunities available. Here my lucky undies are on show! It was difficult to find jerseys that fully fitted.

Playing basketball for Feilding High School. Rugby was the family love, but one of the reasons I fell so hard for basketball was that it wasn't a sport George or Adam took seriously. It felt like my point of difference, even though it was only temporary. Basketball wasn't just massive for my self-esteem, but also for my rugby career. I'm convinced about that.

The Hurricanes schools team in 2006. Left to right: me, Lewis Marshall, Mitchell Crosswell, Aaron Smith, Kurt Baker and Andre Taylor.

Rugby Division 1 2009

Winners CBS Canterbury Bowl

Winners Press Trophy (Referee's Trophy awarded for Good Conduct – to a Division One Side)

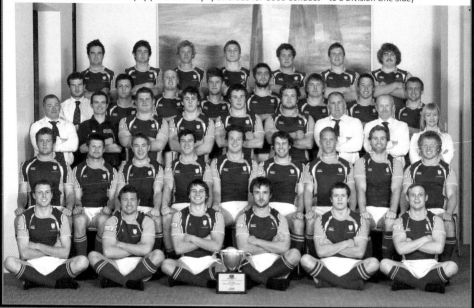

The team photo for Lincoln University, 2009. I'm in the centre, second row down, fourth from the right. Three along to the right is another player earning his stripes, and someone I'd play a lot of footy with: Joe Moody, who would go on to become All Black number 1134. *(Courtesy of Lincoln University)*

Luke's 21st birthday. At the time, Mum said, 'Mark my words, these couples will all be married one day!' And she was dead right.

Running the ball for Canterbury against Bay of Plenty, September 2010. Mum was a proud Cantab: she'd met Dad at the rugby club in Culverden and we still had a lot of family there, so it felt like a natural move to trade Dad's green and white for Mum's red and black. *(Photosport)*

Master and apprentice. Thorny set my career up – I can't put it any more simply than that. This was my first game for the All Blacks, vs Ireland, Yarrow Stadium, New Plymouth. I was 21 years old. (Photosport)

I scored two tries during my All Blacks debut. Maybe thanks to my lucky striped undies? Thirteen years later it would be Ireland who had us on the back foot.

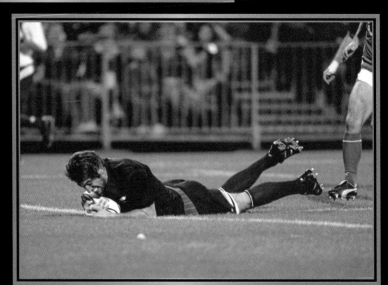

Regaining the Tri Nations trophy, in Johannesburg, 2010. The previous year, South Africa had won all three Tests against the All Blacks. Back left to right: Tony Woodcock, Ma'a Nonu, Richie McCaw, me; Keven Mealamu at the front. (David Rogers/Getty Images)

France at the Cake Tin in 2009. I'd played club footy for Lincoln that afternoon, so had to shower quickly and jump on a plane to Wellington. Everything seemed to be going smoothly, as my tickets were waiting for me at the gate, but as soon as I sat down Mum mentioned that my ears were still caked in mud. God knows what those sat next to me on the plane must have thought. As it turned out, George was an unused sub, so had to wait another week for his debut.

But back to my sparkling speech. Hannah had flown up for my debut. We'd been dating for a couple of years now, so she was a big part of my life. I knew she was 'the one'. That didn't mean I found room for her in my speech, though. Because I'd been so keen to avoid the standard clichés, and because I'd got a laugh with my line about Luke, I'd decided to end my little spiel while I had the crowd in my hand. It wasn't till I sat down that I glanced at her and realised I had left out a Very Important Person. I felt terrible. Aaron Cruden was speaking straight after me and I didn't hear a word. All I was thinking was, 'Shit, I can't really stop him mid-flight to get back up there to thank my girlfriend.'

Hannah has never really let me live that one down.

Following a capping ceremony, the tradition is that if somebody comes up to you with a drink, you have one with them – it doesn't matter if it's a player, a supporter or anybody else. I definitely enjoyed a beer or two and enjoyed spending time with my family, but it was actually a pretty low-key night because we had two big Tests against Wales coming up.

A day or two before my debut, one of the management team had walked up to my room, dropped a whole lot of gear off, said, 'You're going to be here a while,' and walked out.

What did that mean? Would I be here for the next week, the next month, or just the next couple of days? As a newcomer, I didn't want to ask the sort of questions that might make me seem presumptuous. Instead, I saved them up and bombarded Thorny, my very patient roommate.

Our next Test, at Carisbrook in Dunedin, was meant to be the last played there, but there ended up being another one because of an earthquake that was at that time brewing under Canterbury. It would have been a normal week for most of those in the squad, but I was still on a massive high from my two-try debut. My phone blew up all week. I was named on the bench again and it was a totally different Test match to the first one. I got out there about the same time and managed to steal a lineout ball early, but that was about it. The play refused to come my way, and the only thing of note from my perspective was that Anthony Boric broke his cheekbone. I couldn't help but wonder if the stars were aligning for me to make my starting debut.

As nondescript as the night was for me, the atmosphere at the 'Brook was amazing. The terraces were packed and after the game the students were throwing all sorts of stuff around because it was supposedly the last Test there. Photos after the game showed rubbish strewn across the ground, and students and locals stayed on the terraces long after the final whistle. We had a ceremony where we took some dirt and turf from Carisbrook to the site of what is now Forsyth Barr Stadium. I was pleased to have had the opportunity to play a Test at such a famous venue before it was bowled over for good.

It was a week for farewells. As a team we went down to the Gardies, the old student pub in the heart of North Dunedin. I didn't know it at the time but it was closing for good. I'd heard all these stories about the Gardies, which was one of three famous student pubs, along with the Cook and the Bowler. Like Carisbrook, all those pubs are gone now.

From Dunedin we headed north to Hamilton for the second Test against Wales. I was still with the squad, which was a good sign, because the team for the Rugby Championship – known back then as the Tri Nations – was being named after the game. I was on the bench again and was getting really excited about coming on. The guys were playing pretty well – not outstandingly, but in control. Darren Shand came over to me and said, 'Hey, we're going to put Jerome to lock to see if that's a position he can cover.' Adam Thomson was also on the bench and could shift into Jerome's position, so I sat there thinking, 'Damn, they're not putting me out there.' Shandy reassured me that they were happy with how I was going. I was nodding my head, but inside I was screaming: 'Just get me out there, I want to play!' There was an added incentive for me as well, because Mum and Dad were finally back from Argentina and had driven five hours to watch me play.

Eventually I got out there with about 15 minutes to go. Wales had been effective at holding us in the breakdown and slowing our ball down, so as I ran out, Shag sent down a message: I was not to put up with any shit; I was to clean out hard and make sure they didn't hold me in. I listened to every word and was also running out with a bit of frustration rattling around in my brain, because it felt like I'd been shunted down the pecking order. Within the first few minutes I cleaned out a ruck, and my Welsh opposite, veteran flanker Gavin Thomas, held on to me and pushed me off the ball. He might have taken a swing at me, but I know for sure I didn't, but it didn't matter. The ref, Jonathan Kaplan, had taken us off to the side and given us yellow cards.

What a come-down. A couple of weeks earlier I didn't think life could get much better after scoring two tries on debut. Now, in front of my parents, I'd been sent to the naughty corner after contributing one cleanout to a Test match.

It was still a Test cap, but it's not one I look back on with any fondness. Honestly, I don't think I did anything particularly wrong, and even now, when cards are far more prevalent, I think people were scratching their heads wondering what it was for. I reckon Kaplan thought he needed to do something to show he was in control and came in far too hot, but I was inconsolable. I stayed out on the field after the game to do some running in front of the trainers, as I hadn't got to do a whole lot of it during the game. All the time I was wondering if I'd blown my Tri Nations chances.

In the sheds at the end of the game, Shag walked up to me and I thought, 'Here we go.' He looked at me and said, 'If you're going to get yellow-carded, at least throw a decent punch,' and started laughing. In some ways it was worse than getting a huge serve. I was sitting there really confused, thinking, 'What's going on here? Am I in trouble or what?'

It hit home the most when I caught up with Mum and Dad after the game. Dad shook my hand and said, 'Well done, you're an All Black now.' He then quietly leaned in and whispered: 'Don't you ever get yellow-carded after we've driven five hours to watch you play two minutes.' That little square-up was probably what I was expecting in one form or another from my coaches, but I got it instead from Dad.

5

THE SLAM

THAT FIRST YEAR IN the All Blacks went by in a blur.

I had my first meetings with the Springboks, a team I had always admired from a distance. The previous year they had won all three Tests against the All Blacks with a simple game plan based around an aerial attack, the lineout and maul. We weren't good enough to deal with it. The guys who played in 2009 openly admitted that.

The first 2010 meeting was at Eden Park in front of 25,000, and if that sounds a bit light it's because they had torn down the old South Stand to rebuild it for the 2011 World Cup. Ali Williams was starting to get healthy again so they'd brought him into camp, providing another awesome resource for me to tap into. When I went on, we had them under a bit of pressure and Ali kept yelling at me. Because there was no crowd on that side of the ground, I could hear him crystal-clear. He'd be shouting out that Victor Matfield was going to call the lineout to himself. He was right.

That week had been so different to the previous Tests I'd played because it had a genuine edge. We hadn't been successful against the Boks, who were world champions. They played a type of rugby that was so hard to stop, as we'd experienced against the Bulls in Super Rugby.

We won 32–12 but I remember the Test most clearly for Bakkies Botha getting a yellow card for headbutting Jimmy Cowan from behind. Bakkies had charged down Jimmy's kick and was winning the race to the ball when he felt a tug on his jersey. Bakkies decided to seek redress in his own way. He copped a nine-week ban for it, and a few years later gave an interview to a French magazine that indicated he wasn't that sorry: 'He pulled me by the shirt to slow me down. When I caught up with him I made him understand that I hadn't liked it … I hate injustice.'

They're pretty uncompromising boys, those Boks.

The next Test was another comfortable win, this time in Wellington. Izzy, who came off the bench at the same time as me, scored an unbelievable try from nothing. He took the ball at first receiver and beat Francois Louw on the outside, Schalk Burger on the inside, brushed off Gio Aplon, swerved to beat Zane Kirchner and went over in the tackle of Andries Bekker. In scoring he also dummied to Owen Franks; he said at training later that he was never going to give it to him.

I was on the bench again in Melbourne, where we kicked off a Bledisloe Cup campaign with a win at Docklands Stadium, a massive AFL ground with a roof. I found myself out wide for some reason, probably shouldn't have been there, but I jammed in on defence and collected Adam Ashley-Cooper. I didn't pick him up but the tackle was a bit awkward and he landed on his shoulder. We played on until play stopped a couple of phases later. Craig Joubert, the ref, called Richie McCaw over, and I was close enough to hear it: 'If I had got the number of the player who made that tackle, he'd be in the bin.' It wasn't long since I had been binned and I didn't want it to happen again, so I put my head down and hid.

The next Bledisloe Test, in Christchurch, provided a different type of learning experience. Mum and Dad had flown down to watch the Test and were staying in the same hotel as the Aussies. Nathan Sharpe, the outstanding 100-Test lock, and the owner of one of rugby's most unstoppable lineout moves, was in the lobby of the Crowne Plaza, which like Lancaster Park has gone now. He walked up to me and said, 'What the f*** are you doing here?'

I was totally thrown, wondering if I'd broken a serious unwritten rule. I stuttered away about being there to see my parents, who were sitting in the corner. Always hide behind your Mum. Sharpe started laughing straightaway and a wave of relief washed over me, but not before I'd absolutely jacked myself. I could tell he was pretty pleased with himself for winding me up. When I'd regained my equilibrium, I reflected that it was nice to know that even legends of the game were fairly normal human beings.

The Test wasn't anything like the Melbourne match. I ran out to a packed house, with the new Paul Kelly Stand in place for the World Cup, and thought it was awesome to be playing a Test on my home ground in front of all my uni mates. It would be the first and last Test I played at Lancaster Park.

Because I wasn't starting, management was allowing me to go back and play for Canterbury to keep getting minutes in my legs. A week later I played an NPC game at the same ground, and we'd have been lucky if there were a couple of thousand people there. This alerted me to the fact that there was a finite amount of rugby people would pay to watch; unfortunately, provincial rugby was surplus for all but the hardiest fans.

What atmosphere was lacking there was made up for in Soweto in August, when we played the Boks on the same ground that had hosted the FIFA World Cup final between Spain and the Netherlands earlier that year. Everyone still seemed to have their vuvuzelas. The crowd was fizzing and the Boks were out for blood. It was John Smit's 100th Test, and they were determined to win it for the great hooker and skipper.

We were struggling badly, behind 17–22, and Dan Carter, who is normally money for us in big games, was having one of those days where the harder he tried, the worse he got. When I say 'one of those days', what I really mean is I've never seen him have a day like that. He dropped a ball under no pressure in front of our sticks and then missed a penalty from in front at the other end.

We had spent a lot of time talking about trusting ourselves when we were behind or in close games. It didn't matter if we had to go the full 80 minutes or beyond. This game was a good example of that. Richie scored a try in the corner with a few minutes to go that was about as close as you can get to being out, but DC miskicked his conversion from the sideline. You might have thought that drawing a game against a team that had beaten us three times the previous year would have been a great result, but we weren't thinking like that.

The Boks did us a favour when they won the kick-off and had the ball deep in our half with a minute to go, looking to set up a drop goal. It meant we didn't have the opportunity to run the clock out. We had to be proactive. We tackled Jean de Villiers well behind our 40-metre line and blew them off the ball at the breakdown. We attacked left and Ma'a Nonu got the ball. I was outside him and shouted for him to carry into contact, because there was nothing on and he was a much better ball carrier than me. I anticipated him taking the tackle and me blowing over in the cleanout to recycle quick ball. Instead, he took off with Mils Muliaina and Izzy in tow and burst through the line. Ma'a put Izzy in unopposed, although he got a bit of a bollocking afterwards for showboating before he put the ball down. That was Izzy, though – it didn't matter whether he was playing touch with his mates at the beach or a Test match in front of 60,000 screaming fans, he lived to have fun.

*

It was between our return from South Africa and our departure for the United Kingdom – via Hong Kong and a third Test against the Wallabies – that I was put on the intensive eight-week training block with Brad Thorn that changed my physique and set me up for the rest of my career.

I went back to play for Canterbury to keep myself match-fit. I'd been typically playing 20 minutes off the bench, and at the same time Nic Gill, the All Blacks' trainer, had me on five protein shakes a day to try to get me bulked up. I was playing at 105 or 106 kilograms and they needed me to get to 114 kilograms.

I'd have breakfast and a shake, I'd have a shake at training and a shake at lunch. I'd have a shake with my gym session and a shake with dinner before I went to bed. It wasn't just a shake with some powder and milk, either. We were doing anything to shove calories in there. There were a couple of yoghurts, some Weet-Bix and fruit. Honestly, I can't think of many things I've done that have made me feel as uncomfortable as forcing down food when I was already full.

I was now at 112 or 113 kilograms but I was only playing 20 minutes. The trainers kept telling me to keep eating, keep training and I'd be fine; I'd grow into the bulk sooner or later. The team to go north hadn't been named yet but they said they didn't want me to play any rugby. Instead I was to team up with Thorny and we would go to the gym together. Brad made it clear that he wasn't going running with me as he needed to run alone to mentally recharge. But in the gym he would teach me everything he'd learned.

I've always liked to surround myself with people who know more than I do. It's a trait I picked up from Mum and Dad, who in their social and work lives tended to gravitate towards older farmers, the ones who had lived through more winters. George and Adam had already blazed the trail in rugby that I followed, so I could lean on them for advice and pick up a lot of the stuff that had worked well for them, but I was also lucky to run into good people at the right time in my career – like Brad. He was a guy who didn't simply say his body was a temple, he lived that idea fully. He set a great example that I tried to follow.

Brad was in charge of my program in those couple of months and I soaked up so much knowledge. There was a lot of core work. He tested me on my one-rep max on the squat, the chin and the bench. This was not about skill development, it was about getting me bigger and stronger, and building up my physical defences so I could go out and try to dominate the best and biggest players on the planet.

Thorny worked to a fixed, unbending timetable. He'd take his kids to school and go straight to the gym. It was clear my uni classes were going to have to be put on hold, so I got a lot of notes from classmates during this time. It wasn't long before I was piling on weight and size. When I first walked into the Canterbury Academy, I could barely lift 60 kilograms on the bench. Under Brad's tutelage I managed to get to 140 kilograms. I was on an enormous adrenaline high, too, training with a guy who had been a professional athlete for almost as long as I'd been alive. I was learning about stretching, recovery, the mental game, these little tricks and shortcuts that should have taken a whole career to learn. He was giving me all this IP he had gathered over decades, and I was a sponge. I was loving every minute of it. In fact, I was so enamoured of the bloke that when I'd get home, I'd roll out my Brad Thorn impressions, complete with the croaky voice, to get a few laughs out of my flatmates.

Thorny set my career up. I can't put it any more simply than that.

It was during this time that the first of the two big quakes hit. The shake in the early hours of 4 September was centred at Darfield. It was the university holidays, so I just had one flatmate, Brendon Ridgen, in residence. 'Rigger' had a few drinks that night out on the Strip. I was in the doorway while the building was rocking and rolling. I don't know how long it went for but it felt like ages. I yelled out to him and he didn't reply, so I ran down to his room to see if he was okay. He slept through the whole thing. There were car alarms going off, house alarms, and the place was shaking like a fairground ride, but his experience of it was totally different to mine. When he finally woke up, his first thought was that the night was kicking off again and I was waking him up for a beer. 'No, Rigger, we've just had a massive earthquake,' I told him. I could tell he'd had a skinful but managed to talk some sense into him.

As we got closer to the Hong Kong match, I was starting to get nervous. I hadn't played a big chunk of rugby for a long time. Yes, I was getting fitter and stronger, but I needed to play. Thorny suggested I should ask for a clearance to play a game for Canterbury. The timing was perfect because we had a Ranfurly Shield challenge in Invercargill against Southland.

The All Blacks coaches had a chat about it with Canterbury coach Rob Penney and decided I could play, but I had to play lock – that was the only condition they put on my clearance.

At Canterbury training, the team was named and I was selected to play at blindside flanker. That was awkward. I decided to stay quiet and say nothing. This was between the two sets of coaches, I figured, and I wasn't yet confident enough in my own skin to get involved in arguments that seemed to be above my station.

George had tweaked his knee and couldn't play, so the loose forwards were Matt Todd at seven, Nasi Manu at eight and me at six. Andy Ellis was captain and Sonny Bill Williams, fresh from playing in France, was second five-eighth. It was a real mix-and-match team. We'd been playing pretty well that year but hadn't been outstanding. If I may say so, I was awesome in my first professional game in that position. I made a heap of tackles, carried well and was heavily involved against a team that did not want to give an inch.

In Hong Kong, I was named on the bench again. Brad and Tom Donnelly were named to start. We were in a huddle at training, it was stinking hot and I was sweating profusely. Shag was giving Owen Franks a tickle-up about how he could be more physical as a tighthead prop. I must have wiped a drip of sweat off my nose or looked at the wrong thing in the wrong way, and he just rounded on me. 'AND YOU ...'

For the next minute Shag tore strips off me in front of everybody. I was a big-headed so-and-so, and a number of other unpleasant things. I couldn't believe it. What had I done except everything they'd asked of me? I'd missed all this rugby to get myself to the size they needed, and here I was being scolded like a naughty schoolkid. What the hell was this all about?

Apparently, a reporter had written a glowing story about me and Shag had read it. He read everything because he thought it was what players did, and he hated that somebody was pumping me up. He sure as hell also hated me playing blindside flanker for Canterbury when he had expressly dictated that I was to play lock and lock alone.

It rattled my cage a bit, but that was fine – I needed that from time to time if it was for the right reasons. I'm not sure if somebody writing a positive story about me – one I hadn't even known existed – qualified as the right reason, but I guess Shag felt I needed cutting down to size. If that was his intention, he didn't miss.

As for the game, I came off the bench fairly late in the piece, just a few minutes after Stephen Donald had been brought on to replace DC. Australia was a different beast from what they had been in the first two Tests that year. They came to play from the opening whistle, shaping to kick one way and instead going to the unmanned side. I thought I did pretty well with my limited opportunities, but that match is known – for all the wrong reasons – as 'Beaver's Test', after a couple of wayward kicks, including one that didn't find touch, put us under pressure.

In my mind, you never blame one person. Losing is just as much a team effort as winning, and in the wash-up he made a couple of mistakes that we had every opportunity to recover from. The reaction was so over the top. A lot of people said Beaver would never play another Test match, but how wrong they were. When we needed him at our darkest hour, he fronted as he always did.

That was my first loss as an All Black, and it stung because the game was there for the taking. They scored, got the kick and celebrated as if they had won the World Cup, not a dead rubber. We stayed out on the field and did a lot of running. There were a few of us young guys out there and we didn't want to go back to the sheds because we didn't want to accept what had happened. We knew all the older guys would be grumpy so we stayed out longer, sweating some of that frustration out.

That loss set us up in some ways, because we were heading off on an end-of-year tour that was challenging. It was a rare Grand Slam opportunity. After years of trying and a lot of bad luck, including the brilliant 1967 touring squad being denied an opportunity due to a foot-and-mouth outbreak in Ireland, the All Blacks had finally won a Grand Slam in 1978. In the professional era, they won again in 2005 and 2008, and here we were just two years later with another opportunity. It was to be my first and last chance.

The first Test, against England at Twickenham, was potentially the most difficult, although I didn't know enough about the relative strengths of the Northern Hemisphere sides at that stage to make that call. Nor did I know much about the players I would be thrust into competition with. England had Tom Palmer and Courtney Lawes at lock, and the latter would become a great of the game, but I would have struggled to have picked either of them out of an identity parade prior to the Test. I was just worried about myself. I was more familiar with the guys I was playing against in the Tri Nations, because I'd seen them play Super Rugby, but I was in the dark about these guys from the north. That naivety meant I couldn't fear what I didn't know. All I knew was that they would be big and they would be good.

I'd been to Ireland with the Under-19s in 2007 and Wales the following year with the Under-20s, so I had experienced northern rugby culture, which was a lot different to ours, but I was still pretty green. Gary Knight had never been afraid to tell my brothers and me how much he hated the English, especially 'their' media. And Mark 'Cowboy' Shaw used to say that journalists were the fleas on the dog's back and they were just sucking juice out of us. I was inculcated to the idea that the media in general were best avoided, and the English media in particular. So I went with my guard fully up.

When we got there we were greeted with articles and headlines that pointed to the idea that this England team was awesome, while we were a poor All Blacks side that had massive challenges ahead. Gary and Cowboy were right, I thought.

I was named to start at Twickenham. My initial reaction was shock. To that point I had accumulated nine caps, every one of them off the bench. I was partnering Brad Thorn and the whole week he was talking about that first contact and how he couldn't wait to blow into it. He was so excited, and his energy was infectious. But even Thorny's enthusiasm couldn't stop me dakking myself.

Twickenham is an amazing stadium, where you feel like 80,000 people are sitting on top of you. For the first time I got to do the haka and stay out there. The atmosphere was everything I thought it would be. The occasion was special for a couple of reasons. Grandad Dalzell had played at Twickenham as an All Black, and it was where he'd scored his only Test try. The All Blacks had won and he was given a Cuban cigar for player of the day. It's still in its wooden box in a cabinet at home; as kids, we would carefully get it out, smell it and invariably go, 'Ew, gross.' Mum and Dad used to say that if any of us four boys became All Blacks, they'd smoke it. I'm glad they didn't. It's still at home in the trophy cabinet and it's one of the things we love to show people.

At the captain's run, the day before the Test, I shared a nice moment with Graham Henry. I brought up Grandad's try and he explained what end it was and what it would have looked like back in the day. He knew the history of the ground – the old Cabbage Patch, as it was known – and had been lucky enough to coach there several times. It was just nice to talk to the head coach without being worried that he was about to drop me or launch into a critique of my game.

That encounter humanised him in my eyes. Until then, he'd been a headmasterly figure, a man I had all the respect in the world for, but not someone I was comfortable starting a casual conversation with. I'd always assumed Ted liked to keep his distance from the players, especially relative nobodies like me, but in truth it was probably my shyness that prevented more moments like this.

Early on, I got to carry the ball and Thorny came in behind and cleaned it out, with Owie there on his shoulder. It was just as we'd talked about all week. It set the tone and helped me settle. Thorny was doing exactly what he'd said he was going to do. The Test went really, really quickly. I know it's a cliché but it honestly did. I came off late in the second half, so I still hadn't played a full 80, but it felt important for the team to get the job done after the missed opportunity in Hong Kong.

Was there any extra sense of satisfaction in winning after we had apparently been written off as a fairly average All Blacks team? I doubt it. The fact they were England was all the motivation we needed. In fact, it wasn't until I was doing some research for this book that I learned there had been some pointed criticism of me after the Test.

Whether the critics were right or wrong is almost immaterial. You can read into what you want with reviews. You can use it as fuel and energy if you want, or you can let it get on top of you. Either way, to me it is wasted emotion. As your career goes on, you work a few things out. One of them is whose opinions actually matter. It's not a matter of not caring. You're lying to yourself if you pretend you don't care about what other people think of you, but you need to identify the opinions you should take on board. Conversely, there are opinions that you might pretend to take in but you're really just fobbing them off, because you know they have little or no value. The more experienced you get, the more you understand that, in a high-performance sports environment, everyone has an opinion.

Early in my career, Richie was speaking to the group with a newspaper in his hands. He said, 'Boys, just don't pick it up. There's going to be an opinion in here that says you're playing outstandingly, or it'll say you're playing terribly – just don't pick it up. If you have to pick it up, just look at the photos and then put it down real quick. But if you've got to read it, just read the captions. If you've got to read the stories, just read the first paragraph …' This went on and on until we'd 'read' the paper from cover to cover. What he was trying to tell us was that it didn't matter. Treat the media speculation however you want, but never lose sight of what we're trying to achieve as a team. Richie knew there would be some guys in the team who read every word written about them and some who would read nothing. Most would be somewhere in between. The key message was to worry about yourself, but not the external noise.

It's the same today, but it's not a piece of paper, it's a phone. It's become even more important to know how to filter what's important from what's not, because it's not just journalists' and pundits' opinions that you have access to now, it's everybody. That's been a massive change since I started. It's social media posts, it's blogs, it's reels. I think back to the massive falcon I suffered in my first Super Rugby semi-final, and how that would have been treated in today's social media world. It would have been everywhere. I would have been a meme. For an old dog like me, it's exhausting trying to keep up, so I don't even try. Don't get me wrong, it's great that so many people have an opinion on the game we love, but as a player you can't let it dictate how you approach your job.

Regardless of what the papers said, I must have gone alright against England because I got another opportunity to start against Scotland, again alongside Brad.

All this was happening so fast that I didn't stop to think how cool it was. I was 21 and starting for the All Blacks in some of rugby's holiest cathedrals. The roller-coaster was moving and it wasn't slowing down for anybody.

Edinburgh was the first time I'd trained in snow. There had been a bunch of cold nights in Christchurch, but snow was never part of the equation. It was nice to get that classic Scottish stereotype out of the way early. What wasn't so postcard-perfect was the bog of a training ground. The mud was up around our ankles, and there was a fair bit of moaning from the older players. I found it quite enjoyable because it was different, but I didn't let on that I was getting a kick out of others' discomfort.

We expected Scotland to put up a good challenge but we ran away with it 49–3. I absolutely loved Murrayfield. Still do. There's something about that ground that gets me every time. Reado had talked to me beforehand, to give me some idea about what the pre-match would be like: the stadium shrouded in darkness, the lone bagpiper on the roof, 'Flower of Scotland', which is such a great anthem you feel like singing it yourself. His best advice, though, was to tell me about the little lip at the end of the tunnel as you enter the field. 'If you don't know it's there,' he said, 'you're going to trip over. No one will see it because it's dark, but you'll feel like an absolute dick.'

Sometimes the most practical advice is the best. There was no way I was going to fall over in front of 67,000 Scots, no matter how dark it was.

I didn't play as well as I would have liked at Murrayfield. It was a good win and I didn't do a whole lot wrong, but it did press home to me that just making the All Blacks wasn't enough. I was desperate to be a dominant contributor, and that Test was a perfect marker. I had played 11 and started two, and this was my first 80-minute match – and still I wasn't quite ready. I did some things well, the team was dominant, the Grand Slam was alive but I wasn't wholly satisfied.

Moving across to Dublin, I found myself back on the bench. Dropped. The coaches were saying all the right things – 'you're playing well, we just need to rest you up' – but in my mind I'd been axed from the starting XV, simple as that. I wasn't bitter about it, just disappointed in myself. I hadn't played well enough against Scotland, and Tom 'Sas' Donnelly deserved his chance.

My friends and family had been propping me up all week, telling me that I loved playing against Ireland and would come on and have an impact. Well, Sas ended up hurting himself just before half-time and I couldn't get onto Aviva Stadium quick enough. I was so pumped up and half-time seemed to last forever. The second half started with us clinging to a six-point lead. Soon after Reado had crossed on one touchline, I found myself seagulling on the other wing. I received an offload from Richie McCaw and stepped inside the cover defence to score. My friends were right – I did love playing Ireland! It was a satisfying result. We had been put under pressure and rallied to win comfortably. The Grand Slam was well and truly on.

It had been a real goal. Losing to Australia meant we couldn't enjoy an unbeaten season, but winning at Cardiff to complete a European clean sweep would be the next best thing.

I'd had a ball on my first big tour. I fell into a comfort zone that would serve me well throughout my career. I never wanted to be a grandstander or the public face of the team, but I loved standing at the back and watching what was going on. I loved reading people's body language. Part of that comes from having two older brothers and understanding if you read them wrong, you'll cop it. Later, if there was something I was passionate about, I'd put my two cents' worth in, but in that first year or two, I kept my head down and let my play do all the talking. I had Thorny there, so if I had any questions he'd be my sounding board, while I also spent a lot of time hanging out with the Franks brothers, with a bit of Johnny Afoa, Keven Mealamu and Daniel Braid thrown in.

Thorny was at a different part of his career. He was just dumping knowledge on me and I was soaking it up. He told me and Owie we could be 100-Test All Blacks, and outwardly I was like, 'Nah, I'm just happy playing a few here and there at the moment.' But that sort of endorsement from such a legend gave me a warm glow.

A couple of days before the Cardiff Test, the Pike River disaster hit the West Coast. Some 29 miners were trapped underground in the Pike River Mine after a methane explosion. When New Zealand Rugby president John Sturgeon, a proud Coaster who was travelling with the team, got in front of us to talk about what his community was going through – about how the last guy out had told those at the top that there were a few colleagues just behind him who would be out shortly –

well, that was enough to ensure there were a few eyes being rubbed in that room.

The Welsh public were incredibly considerate. They have a long and deep history with mining and have experienced tragedy themselves – more than 6000 Welsh men, women and children have been killed over the years in mining disasters. There was an incredible minute's silence before the game, which was touching. We could feel the crowd mourning those who were lost. It was a special moment for us Kiwis to have 80,000 Welsh fans show they were hurting just like we were.

I was disappointed that I couldn't match the moment with a good performance. I struggled to meet expectations and was deservedly taken off early in the second half. It was a tour of highs and lows. I hadn't grasped the opportunities I'd been given, and I was still getting used to my body and the way it reacted to certain situations.

Shag talked to the media afterwards and told them that I hadn't played the way they wanted me to, or the way that I expected to. I don't know how I felt about being publicly upbraided, but it was all part of the learning process. We'd pulled away late to win 37–25 and had won just the fourth Grand Slam in New Zealand history. It wasn't an opportunity that would come around again for me, yet I felt like I couldn't really enjoy the moment. It should have been cause for massive celebration but the performance nagged away at me.

I was young enough to put it aside and the team did enjoy a barnstorming night out in Cardiff. It was one of those pinch-yourself moments. Even though I'd been a part of the team for 13 Tests, it still felt like it was 'those guys over there' who deserved the title of All Black and I was just an interloper along for the ride. I didn't feel like I had done enough to be called an All Black.

Still, it had been a hell of a year. Incomprehensible in some ways. Super Rugby had gone well until the semi-finals, I'd had the high of my first Test quickly followed by the low of the yellow card against Wales. I'd been part of a Grand Slam tour and had played well enough to earn a couple of starts, and had also played poorly enough to be dropped and called out by the forwards coach.

I even had a chance to extend my season by a week and take Tom Donnelly's place in the Barbarians side, who were to meet South Africa at Twickenham. I had a good chat with Thorny about that. 'Put it this way,' he said, 'they've given you eight weeks off in the middle of the season to get big and strong, so to suddenly put an extra game on the end is probably not wise.' So I said no, and went and did some promotional work for Adidas instead. Ironically, I haven't had the opportunity to play for the Baa-baas since. That's definitely on my bucket list.

Thorny was right, though. I was knackered. I was full of resolve, too. The up-and-down nature of my performances in Europe ate away at me in the summer of 2010/11. I wanted to come back bigger, stronger and, most importantly, better.

6

THIS ONE FEELS DIFFERENT

IF I WERE TO view the 2011 Super Rugby season purely through the lens of my development as a player, I'd have to label it as one where I didn't nail my goals.

My coaches at international and Super Rugby level still needed me to add size, so they basically forbade me from doing any running. My tasks were to go to the gym and to eat. I did that, but instead of it translating into performance, I fell into the very common second-year syndrome.

The gym obsession was a perfect example. I listened to the coaches too literally. I went to the gym as much as possible. I ate as much as I could. The only person I'd stopped listening to was myself and my instincts. I knew I wasn't feeling great, but these were the smartest rugby guys in the room, so if they wanted me pushing huge weights and eating five meals a day, that's what I had to do. It didn't matter that my body was screaming to me that something wasn't right.

It came to a head when I did a fitness test for the Crusaders and was found to be slow and unfit. My body wasn't lying, and neither were the numbers. The trainer, Ash Jones, right there and then told me to go and run some laps and finish with a few shuttles.

It was almost a relief to be told that. As I became more experienced, I learned to trust myself more, to question everything, but just a couple of years into professional rugby I was still waiting for the 'experts' to tell me what to do and when. I'd doggedly stayed true to the gym-and-eat mantra, and while it was important to get big and strong, I'd forgotten that it was still my job to be a rugby player, not a powerlifter.

My fitness numbers were so poor that I was immediately on the back foot for 2011.

My problems, however, were trivial. My form at the start of the year might have been forgettable, but as a whole the season was the opposite of that. This was the year the Crusaders were a team without a home. Let me rephrase that – we were a team from a broken home.

It was the first year of the Super 15 system, where the competition was divided into three conferences – New Zealand, Australia and South Africa. It could be confusing, because the three conference leaders automatically took the first three places on the overall table, although at some stages one or two of those teams might have fewer points than teams below them. It was also imbalanced, because you played the teams within your conference, home and away, and then four teams from the other conferences away, and four teams at home. With all due respect to the other conferences, New Zealand's was broadly the strongest, so our opponents were much tougher than those of, say, the Reds, who had home-and-away matches against the newly created Rebels to look forward to.

We had played one game – a two-point loss to the Blues at Eden Park – when disaster struck on 22 February 2011. I still remember it like it was yesterday. We were at Rugby Park. I'd finished training, had taken a shower and had just wrapped a towel around me when it hit. I ran straight out the door and onto the ground. Luke Romano followed, looking like a drowned rat.

'What are you up to, mate?' I asked.

The cold bath he had been in had tsunami'd over the rim and the wash had tipped him onto the floor. Luke was in his undies, dripping wet, in the middle of the field. Everyone was giving him grief. Dan Carter was standing next to me and we were giving each other grief about who pushed who to get out of the building first. It was all a bit of a joke, because we'd all been through that first earthquake in the early hours of 4 September 2010. While that was massive and had done significant property damage, there had been no deaths directly attributed to it, so perhaps we'd become a bit blasé about it.

That experience framed our thinking while we were standing out on that field, the ground still grumbling beneath our feet. There was a lightness about it because we thought we'd been through the worst nature could throw at us and we'd come through relatively unscathed. That changed in an instant.

I can still see the look on Willi Heinz's face. It is seared into my memory in a way I don't think will ever leave. He had his phone on him, and someone he knew had sent him a message, because he looked up and simply said: 'The CTV Building has pancaked; people would have died.' Just like that, everything changed. Everyone went quiet.

Staff started coming down from the offices and you could tell how badly shaken they were. Guys were coming out of the gym, where weights had been flying around and machines falling over. In what felt like an instant, our attitude changed. 'This is different from the first time,' I remember thinking. 'I don't know how different, but it's different.'

I didn't have to look far to check that Adam and George were safe as they were out on the field with me. Older brothers have a different level of responsibility and common sense. Something told George that the cellular networks were about to crash, so he immediately texted Mum and Dad: 'We're all fine.' That allowed Mum and Dad to message all our partners and family. Hannah was working at a winery in Auckland, so she got a message from Mum telling her that I was safe.

We were allowed back into the building to get our valuables only, and then had to get out again. We didn't know much about what it looked like around the city. We got to our cars and began the journey home. It took some guys two hours to make what would normally have been a 15-minute drive. I was living two minutes down the road from Rugby Park, so I got home pretty quickly. I had a mate from uni staying with me for a couple of weeks. He was in shock. He couldn't actually stand up to walk outside, so I managed to get him on his feet and outside to try to get a few breaths of fresh air into him to calm him down. He had too much adrenaline coursing through his body.

I went next door because I knew the neighbours had a toddler. The wee boy was fine but the father was in much the same state as my mate, in shock and panicking. Outside, there was water and a strange grey sludge oozing out of the road and the ground. An old well was suddenly sticking a couple of feet out of the ground. Where had that come from? It was absolute chaos.

The shock was starting to wear off and was replaced by a sense of disorientation. 'Well, we're alive, so what do we do now?' Nobody knew what the process was or what to do. There was no power, no running water and the mobile networks were down. It was only a couple of hours after the big shake but as a community we were looking for answers that very few people had, and those who did had no way of getting them to us.

I went around to Adam's place nearby. It was dripping water from the ceilings because the hot-water cylinder had cracked and spilled. He decided he needed to get up there and turn the water off before the place became a write-off, but while he was up in the roof cavity one of the big aftershocks hit. The whole building was shaking again and people were running for the doorways while Adam was trapped up there. He got out so quickly through a small gap that he took all the skin off his shoulders.

The whole experience was chaotic and frightening, and yet what I experienced was mild compared to others. I talked to some guys who had been standing under a balcony when the quake hit at 12.51 pm. The balcony collapsed and the falling masonry had missed them by centimetres. That's how random it was: had those people been standing a metre to one side, they would have been instantly killed. It was unbelievable what people were going through.

How do you turn your thoughts to rugby after that?

The truth is you don't. Not for a while, anyway. All you're worried about is ascertaining whether all those you know who could potentially be in danger are safe. The people closest to me were fine, but there were guys like the great Chalky Carr – who would be the MC at my wedding and also the All Blacks' logistics manager – who were burrowing through the CTV Building, pulling people out and rescuing them. People were just in that mode: making sure neighbours, friends and family were okay and had access to the necessities.

I'd never heard the word *liquefaction* until the earthquake, and then a couple of days later we were around at Kieran Read's place, shovelling out as much mud and that strange grey sludge from around his house as possible. We had wheelbarrows, spades and shovels getting rid of this stuff, which was a couple of feet deep in places. Bridget, his wife, was feeding us potato-chip sandwiches because that was the only food they had left. The supermarkets were either closed or had been cleaned out. The message came pretty quickly from the senior players that we would not be travelling to play the Hurricanes that weekend. There was no way we could have played. Our city was broken, and even if it was logistically possible to get there for the match, we needed time to process what we had seen and heard, and to start getting our lives in order.

Our season restarted in Nelson. It was obvious that Lancaster Park was not going to be in working order for the rest of the season, and there was already talk that it was so badly damaged it might be gone for good. I'm not sure if irony is the right word, but the match against the Waratahs was already marked as a fundraiser for a tragedy – the previous year's Pike River disaster.

The West Coast was part of the Crusaders' territory and for this match we played in their red-and-white hooped jerseys. Graham Henry came down for the match, and despite his Blues background he wore a jersey for the night. All the jerseys were later sold or auctioned, with the funds going to the victims' families.

We won that match to kick-start our season, but there was so much uncertainty because we were now effectively a road team. We still had games within our region at Nelson and Timaru, but as we were all based in or near Christchurch, it felt like we were permanently travelling. The way we dealt with the situation would become a source of pride. We were determined not to make an excuse out of it, because there were plenty of our fans going through far greater hardships than us. We had rugby as an escape. Rugby Park became our fortress. When we rocked up to the gates every day for training, we had the luxury of leaving the troubles of the city behind for a few hours at a time. Others had to live with the aftereffects of the quake on a daily basis – they were living day by day.

We all wanted to help in different ways, but the senior players said the best way we could make a difference was by going out there and playing attractive rugby for our fans and the community. We were never going to be able to fix things, but we might be able to take their minds off the tragedy for 80 minutes each weekend.

We started to get on a roll. For the first time that year, I was starting to feel pretty good about my rugby as my aerobic fitness was finally catching up to the gains I had made in the gym. We hammered the Brumbies in Nelson, then headed south to beat the Highlanders at Carisbrook. We then travelled to play our next 'home' game against the Sharks at … Twickenham. The game was earmarked as a big money-spinner, and while there was a good crowd, the occasion was lost on me as I completely wrecked my ankle.

I remember the lead-up to the injury pretty clearly, but not the immediate aftermath. We broke from a scrum because we'd gone over the mark early and the Sharks were awarded a free kick. They tapped and ran, someone made a tackle and I rotated over to try to get over the ball all in one movement. My sprigs must have got caught in the ground because as I went over my toes touched my shin. George was right alongside me and reckons I was squealing like a baby. That bit I don't remember so well, but it's probably true.

It was a World Cup year. I had big hopes and dreams about what I wanted to achieve, and they all seemed poised to turn to dust on the hallowed turf of Twickenham during a game we should have been playing at Lancaster Park.

I was devastated. Scans showed that I had chipped the bottom of both my tibia and fibula, the two bones that make up the lower leg. I'd torn all the ligaments in the ankle. I flew home, had surgery and embarked on a race against time. I was out for ten weeks, meaning I'd miss eight games. It was bloody hard watching a team that was representing a city that was hurting, a region that was hurting, fans that were hurting, and yet here I was feeling sorry for myself. It didn't feel right.

The Crusaders were putting together a campaign that was capturing everyone's imagination, and there was also the small matter of a World Cup on home turf at the end of the year that I was pretty keen to be part of.

I had to quickly get over myself.

Getting taken off the field at Twickenham in 2011 … not ideal in a World Cup year. *(Matthew Impey/Photosport)*

7

BRING ON THE WORLD

TWO MONTHS WENT BY before I could test my ankle again in a game. I was pencilled in to play for Lincoln in June 2011, in what would turn out to be my last club game in New Zealand. They just needed me to get through 40 minutes and then I'd be considered for Super Rugby the following week. Scotland lock Grant Gilchrist, who I was doing some mentoring work with, was playing too, so it wasn't a bad second row we put on the field.

I was playing under the watchful eye of Mike Cron, who mentioned after the game that the best thing we could say about it was that it was a box ticked. My ankle wasn't where I needed it to be and my form was ordinary. If you were benchmarking yourself against me that day, you wouldn't have thought you needed to do much to become an All Black.

My first hit-out back for the Crusaders was a tight win against the Blues in Timaru, then the following week we squeaked another win, this time against the Hurricanes in Wellington. I went okay in the first game but was terrible against the Canes and had no trust in my ankle. I couldn't do everything I wanted to do. I was young and didn't know how to rehab properly. The physios had given me a list of stuff to do, but in truth I probably cut some corners.

Our 'home' qualifying final, against the Sharks, was to be played in Nelson. This match was a happier experience as we won 36–8. I was starting to feel more like myself, and the outside noise was starting to build around what a miracle it would be if the Crusaders could win a title despite what our city was going through. There was a sense of excitement as we got on the plane to face the Stormers, who had played great rugby to top the South African conference and had earned a bye before the semi-final.

We got to Cape Town with just four days to prepare after all the time-zone changes. Something about the adversity gelled us that day and we were awesome. Sean Maitland scored from an intercept, Sonny Bill offloaded to Robbie Fruean for a great try and DC kept nudging the scoreboard up in threes. We won 29–10, silencing a stunned Newlands crowd.

We'd talked about how we wanted to play and then gone out there and done it to a tee. Meanwhile, on a different continent, the Reds beat the Blues, and so we prepared to head to Queensland for the final. A couple of the boys mentioned that if we got the job done in Brisbane, there would be a documentary made about our season. It was a tantalising thought – but, not for the last time in my career, the scriptwriters weren't listening.

Before we left Cape Town, Luke Romano had come down with a brutal case of chickenpox. He smeared ointment all over his body but he had sores everywhere. The poor bugger was feeling sorry for himself, and it got worse when the airline decided he couldn't fly to Brisbane. He'd have to wait another day. His bags were on the plane and couldn't be removed, so he had to go back to his room with nothing but what he was wearing. He was insanely itchy and needed his pants and polo shirt washed, so somebody collected his washing and left him to sit in his room for hours in his undies, with nothing to do but try not to pick at his scabs.

When we caught up with him a couple of days later and he was telling us this tale of woe, he didn't get the outpouring of sympathy he was expecting. We thought it was hilarious.

I couldn't wait for the game to start. It was only year two for me, but this was where I expected the Crusaders to be. This was what I'd watched growing up – the Crusaders getting to finals, winning finals, hitting their straps at exactly the right time.

For me, the final is best summed up as an invaluable learning experience. I would love to have won it, but that didn't happen. In the first half, our lineout fell to pieces. I kept getting caught out and couldn't work out why. At half-time Chris Jack, who was not in the match-day squad, came into the sheds and said, 'They're defending a five-man lineout with six men. The ref hasn't seen it, you guys haven't seen it and they've won four or five lineouts in a row on our ball.' That might not have lost us the game, as we were still well and truly in the contest, leading 7–6, but it was the main reason we couldn't build any sustained pressure in the first half.

It was the last Super Rugby game Thorny and I were to play together. He was at home in Brisbane, where he had played all these massive NRL games for the Broncos, State of Origin matches for Queensland, league Tests for Australia and rugby Tests for the All Blacks. The coaches took him off with about ten minutes to go to bring on Luke. I was in disbelief. Surely they had called the wrong number and it should have been me, not Brad. I don't know why they did it and I know it hurt him. We were on his turf and he was being dragged while there was still a game to be won. It hurt us as a team, and it hurt me not to get the job done for him. We got so close but couldn't get that final try to bridge the four-point gap. Quade Cooper and Will Genia were brilliant. We'd talked all week about shutting them down, but we gave them two opportunities and they scored two tries. That was the game.

I was filthy. I couldn't process the result and put it in a wider context. To me, it was an opportunity for a title and we'd screwed it up. It wasn't until we flew home that I started to realise the emotional baggage that we were carrying. We arrived back in Christchurch at about one in the morning. We had flown three times more miles as any other team that season, so every departure and arrival tended to blend into one another, but this was different. The airport was packed full of supporters. The emotion hit me. I let the result of the game go and started to understand the impact of the earthquake on the city, its people and our fans. This was bigger than rugby.

Our run into the final had taken people's minds off what was happening in their lives. It had helped them look away from the geonet apps on their phones, which they would check every time there was an aftershock or rumble beneath the Earth's surface. They wanted to thank us for that. Man, I wished we could have won it for them, but this was about much more than the result. By not playing at home, ironically, we had forged a closer connection to our community.

The city had also received the news that there would be no World Cup games in Christchurch because of the damage to Lancaster Park, another blow to the region.

Having never prepared for a senior World Cup before, I had no context for my expectations, but the leaders of the squad had been looking deeply into the 2003 and 2007 campaigns for clues as to why they hadn't been successful. It sounds basic, but they decided to turn all the negative emotion into a positive.

All the questions we were getting in the lead-up – whether it was Richie McCaw or the newest guy in the team, which was me – implied a fear of not winning in front of our home crowd. We heard it so often: 'You're playing at home – what happens if you don't win at home?' We turned the question around: 'Yeah, but what if we do? How cool would that be!'

A lot of that positive talk had been inspired by the 2009 season, when the All Blacks had been unsuccessful against South Africa. I wasn't with the team then but they'd got together and made a conscious effort to turn their language around. In previous campaigns, they had tried to create a bubble to keep out all the extraneous pressure – to almost ignore that it existed. This time around, they decided to acknowledge the fact that there was going to be a massive amount of noise and pressure. We were playing at home at a tournament we hadn't won for 24 years. We couldn't pretend that pressure didn't exist. Instead, we were embracing the challenge and 'walking towards the pressure'.

I know phrases like that can sound trite, but they really helped me. It meant that when I met friends for a coffee or bumped into a familiar face in a hotel reception area, it felt weightless when they asked about the World Cup.

Before we even got to the World Cup, though, we had a Tri Nations Test at Port Elizabeth to negotiate. The selectors left out most Crusaders who had played big minutes and collected a lot of air miles, but because I'd missed a big chunk of the season, I was chosen to play. It was an interesting side. There was no Richie, Reado, DC or Thorny. We had three halfbacks – Jimmy Cowan, Andy Ellis and Piri Weepu – in the match-day 22. I started with Ali Williams, while Jarrad Hoeata was lock cover off the bench. We kept it pretty close for a while, and in fact scored the game's only try, but the Boks ran away with the match 18–5.

The only reason this Test lingers in my memory is because there is a photo from it that people love to bring up. It happened immediately after a scrum. I don't want to say it was 'the good old days', but let's just say somebody – not me – threw an elbow, opinions were exchanged and Bakkies Botha ran around the corner to grab me and tell me I was too young for Test rugby, to which I came back with some wisdom of my own. It's a classic old-bull, young-bull image, and it still tickles me to see it. One of the benefits of playing Test footy so young was that I had the opportunity to bump heads – sometimes literally – with the likes of Bakkies, Victor Matfield, Nathan Sharpe, Donncha O'Callaghan, Pascal Papé. It was the best kind of rugby education.

*

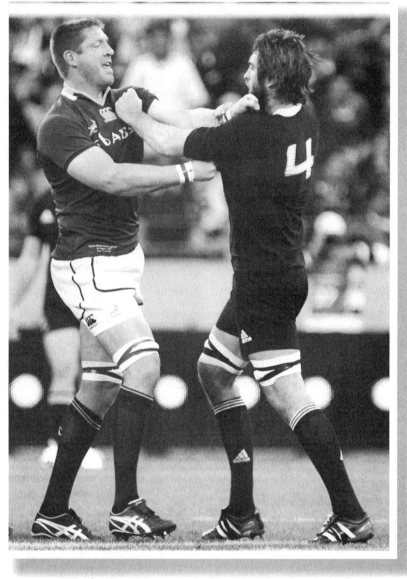

Our Tri Nations loss to South Africa, in Port Elizabeth, August 2011. A classic old-bull, young-bull image. It still tickles me to see it. *(AFP via Getty Images)*

Most people remember the All Blacks' injury chaos at the 2011 World Cup, especially with our first five-eighths, but it actually started before the tournament. After Port Elizabeth, some players flew home and others, including me, went to Brisbane to play Australia in the final Tri Nations match. The guys who had been given the South Africa game off flew to meet us.

I didn't have great vibes about Suncorp Stadium. Just a few minutes into the match, it looked like Reado's year might be ending prematurely when he suffered an ankle injury that would see him leave the ground on crutches and wearing a moon boot. Shortly before half-time, Adam Thomson hyperextended his elbow. Victor Vito, whom the coaches had told recently that he was a blindside flanker only, replaced Reado at No. 8. When Thommo left, Ali Williams came on and told me I was now on the blindside. 'Okay,' I thought, trying to remember what that role entailed. Australia beat us that night and with it took the Tri Nations.

We were disappointed to lose but the result sharpened our focus. We didn't want to enter the World Cup on consecutive losses, but it fed into our narrative about embracing pressure and walking towards it.

Reado and Adam were in a rush to come back in time, but for our opening match – against Tonga at Eden Park – Ali and Brad started at lock. I was cover on the bench for number six and Anthony Boric for lock. As it turned out, I went on to play lock after 55 minutes, and AB came on late to replace Victor, with Jerome Kaino switching to No. 8. I was learning quickly that it paid to be adaptable. We were expected to beat Tonga and did so, but even still it felt important to put a marker down because there had been sniping in the media about our pre-tournament performances. The coaching group hadn't got the previous World Cup campaign right, so they had few credits with the public.

The game was important for another reason: the Tongan supporters showed New Zealanders how to support your team. When 'Ikale Tahi (the Sea Eagles) arrived in New Zealand, there were Tongans lying down on the streets from the airport to slow the convoy down so they could wish the team good luck and shake their hands. You could almost see the switch flicking in New Zealanders' minds: 'This is big. I want to get my flag, support my team and get some tickets.' It had been a low-key build-up, but that Tongan fervour made the tournament. From that moment, Kiwis could show their colours. Our typical reserve was washed away.

I started and finished the next Test, against Japan in Hamilton. The most memorable moment was trying to jump and accidentally kneeing Tony Woodcock in the head. He reckoned that set him up for when he got knocked out against Canada a fortnight later, but it probably did more damage to me. His head was pretty hard and I had a sore knee for the rest of the tournament.

We prepared for our pool game against the French in Christchurch, which was nice. There was still a bit of World Cup fever, though it would have been better if we'd been able to play there. There was a lot of chat during the week about which France team we'd find when we got to Eden Park, but in the event it was a fairly subdued one. Cory Jane put on an absolute show, scoring one try and having the French in fits. DC was in top form too, controlling the game with his passing and his boot. It was hard to say if the French were holding much back because we got on top early and didn't give them a sniff, winning 37–17.

Richie told us later that night that several of the French team had approached him after the game with the same message: 'We'll see you in the final.' They'd put themselves on the tough side of the draw with the loss (they would also lose to Tonga in pool play, but still qualified for the quarters) and Richie was amazed at their strength of conviction. We weren't talking as confidently about making the final and we were in a far better place than them.

By this time Richie's foot had well and truly broken, but we were keeping that news under wraps as best we could ahead of our final pool game against Canada in Wellington. He was given the game off, which meant that DC would be captain. The loose forwards mix was Victor at openside, Reado – back finally from his high-ankle sprain – at No. 8, while the indestructible Jerome patrolled the blind side. I started in the second row with Ali, while Thorny and AB were on the bench to cover lock and loose forward.

The game became a smorgasbord of chaos. Andy Ellis replaced Jimmy Cowan at halfback, and when Mils Muliaina got injured, Piri Weepu came on to replace him, with Colin Slade moving from first-five to fullback. Isaia Toeava was already on shortly after half-time to replace Izzy, who had started on the wing and took a knock on a leg that was already sore. Sladey then got injured and we had no choice but to bring Thorny on for him. AB was already on for Reado, whose minutes were being closely monitored. This was also the Test where Woody was knocked out after a head clash with Adam

Kleeberger. We ended the match with Victor playing right wing and all four locks on the field.

I had started at lock and shifted around all three loose forward positions. I'd never played openside flanker in my life, and when Canada had a scrum five metres from their own line, I had horrible visions of them breaking away off the back and going 95 metres to score. It didn't happen, and I now hold that match as one of my claims to fame: the time I played openside flanker, the most cherished position in New Zealand rugby, for the All Blacks in a Test. It might only have been for 30 seconds, but I'm taking it.

Yet the biggest story of that match happened on the eve of the game, at training.

My first clue that something was wrong was hearing one of the guys yelling, 'Where's Dr Deb?' I turned around to be greeted by the sight of DC rolling on the ground in obvious distress, while somebody ran to fetch Deb Robinson, our head of medical. While you always hope for the best, there really wasn't much suspense. We could tell just by looking at DC that he wasn't going to play another minute at the World Cup.

Ted got us into the sheds soon after and confirmed that DC had ripped his groin, and that others were going to have to step up to fill the void. It was gutting. Players like Dan only come around once in a generation, if that, but the great thing was we had guys on the team who wanted more responsibility. Piri at halfback was stepping up more and more as a leader and wanted to be the focal point of the team. Andy Ellis was another brilliant leader coming off the bench at halfback. Colin Slade was looking for a chance to prove he could drive a team around the park.

I was a bit naughty that week in Wellington, but with the safety of distance I can share the story. Our physio Pete Gallagher, Johnny Afoa, Keven Mealamu and I were all huge basketball fans. Pete and the basketball coach Kenny McFadden were also good mates. We used to sneak off on Wednesdays to go and play basketball, but with so many injuries in the camp we wondered if the time was right to put that little addiction to one side. Kenny had got hold of Pete, however, and said he had this kid down at his gym who'd love to have a game with some All Blacks. We agreed, but I said to Pete that he'd better strap my ankles well just in case something went wrong.

We walked into the gym and there was this young kid who must have been seven feet tall. I'm 2.03 metres and he was towering over me. We had an awesome pick-up game for about two hours, and at one point the kid and I challenged for the same rebound, and he grabbed the ball with two hands and dunked on my head all in the same motion. Pete couldn't watch. Kenny said he was going to be leaving Wellington to try his luck in college ball in the United States, and we thought it sounded like a plan. In another life I might have done the same thing.

It turned out that the kid, Steven Adams, made a good choice. After being drafted to the NBA in the first round of the 2013 draft, he's since played over 700 matches. I hope he's still living down the moment I got a fingertip to one of his attempted hook shots. It counts as a block!

Having qualified for the quarter-final, we set up camp on the North Shore. On the Monday morning before our match, the coaches were walking around in a foul mood. Meetings were being called. I couldn't work out what was going on, but obviously something was up. One of the boys texted me that 'the boys had a big night'.

I grew up playing with Israel Dagg through all the age groups. He was a phenomenal talent and always his own man. But he had a rebellious streak and liked to tweak authority. If I was going to pick a couple of guys who'd push the boundaries around curfews, Izzy and Cory Jane would have been near the top of my list. Plenty of people had seen them on their big night out in Takapuna, so it was obvious there were going to be repercussions. It wasn't just management that was pissed off – a few senior players couldn't believe they would let themselves down in this way before such a big game. Izzy was nursing an injured leg and wasn't going to be considered for quarter-final selection, but that didn't make the situation okay.

CJ knew he was under pressure for his spot. Izzy was in his ear, telling him he had to play well for both of them, and to his credit he went out against Argentina and had an unbelievable game. He took every high ball aimed at him and played like a champion.

The other critical figure in that match was Piri. He'd heard all the talk about us having no chance without DC, and he took it on himself to prove them wrong. DC himself was great, too. He put his own disappointment aside to help Sladey and Cruds prepare. He'd go back to his room each night a broken man, but you wouldn't know it by the time the next day rolled around. It showed that sometimes it's not always the people playing the game who are the most important, but also the ones helping them prepare. That was something I'd be reminded of four years later, when Liam Messam, despite a limited playing role, emerged as one of the key figures in our title defence.

We were in Auckland from the semi-finals on. We were stuck in our rooms because every step outside saw ten people emerge for a signature or a photo. Even the reception area was fraught. We loved and appreciated the support, but you can't prepare for a big game like that. It was so different to anything we had encountered before.

We found a quiet little coffee shop around the corner and they were amazing to us. Being a central-city cafe, it normally shut on the weekends, but they agreed to open on game day for us so Reado, Andy, Richie and I could escape our rooms to play 500. Our order was always the same: Reado – mochaccino; me – hot chocolate; Richie – peppermint tea; Andy – quadruple-shot flat white. We'd have two each. It was a good way to get away from the World Cup pressure and relax, even if I was playing against some horrendous card cheats.

In our semi-final against the Wallabies, we wanted to set the tone by stamping our physicality on the match. We talked about the threat of David Pocock and how we wanted to isolate him and make him tackle, so he couldn't come in as second man and steal the ball. We did that really well and forced him into a couple of early penalties.

You could go through every person in the team that night and shower them in praise. Cory Jane and Richard Kahui were great under the high ball, while Piri carried on his leadership and playing form from the quarter-final. Aaron Cruden was singled out by the Australian media as a potential weak link after the injuries to DC and Colin Slade, but he was brilliant and a gamebreaker. Izzy Dagg, despite his North Shore misadventure, had supplanted 100-Test veteran Mils Muliaina as our first-choice fullback, and he was arguably the best player on the park. We knew what a freakish talent he was and now he was showing the world.

Then there was Jerome Kaino. He basically played the entire tournament and was immense for every minute. He pulled off a tackle against the powerful Digby Ioane that was one of the greatest defensive interventions from an All Black I've seen at a World Cup. Jerome deserves to be remembered in the same way as his loose forward comrades Richie and Reado.

We won 20–6. The scoreline looks comfortable but it never felt that way. The game had an edge that never dulled. It was a special night. The crowd at Eden Park was rocking. As a rule, I hated finishing games on the bench but on this occasion we were far enough ahead that I was reasonably comfortable and could soak up the atmosphere.

Just as their senior players had insisted would happen, France were in the final after they squeaked past a 14-man Wales in the semi-final.

There was such an intensity to the final week of the 2011 World Cup, though on the Tuesday I gave my teammates something to laugh about, even if it was a long time before I saw the funny side.

Johnny Afoa and I had been to the Les Mills gym just around the corner from our hotel. We'd played a bit of one-on-one basketball on the outdoor hoop they have, and got absolutely drenched on the short walk back. On returning, I packed up all my soaking washing and put it in my laundry bag to drop off on the way to a team meeting.

We were on the fourth floor and had permission to use the service elevator, although it was pretty small and tight. A few of us were waiting to use it, but then Isaia Toeava came from nowhere to cut in front of us in the queue. I decided to mete out a bit of rough justice and hurled my laundry bag at him. Being a fleet-footed back, Ice used his *Matrix*-like skills to sway out of the way, and my bag – much heavier than usual because of all my wet gear – smashed straight through a large window.

Time stood still. I could hear the crash of the glass below and the car alarms activating. Just a few hours ago, there had been 500 to 1000 people gathered in that spot to get a glimpse of us as we boarded our bus to go to training. 'I've killed someone,' I thought in blind panic.

My teammates were laughing at me, but I'm not sure if it was nervous laughter. I eventually got to the ground floor and sprinted outside, where, thankfully, I saw that nobody was hurt, although my laundry bag was sitting guiltily in the middle of the road. I gathered the bag and swept the road clean of glass. When I reported the incident to the hotel staff, they told me not to worry and that incidents like these were covered.

That night at the team meeting, I comfortably picked up the 'Dick of the Day' award and had to neck a couple of beers that went straight to my head. Oh, and when I went to check out a week later, there was a $1000 charge on my room for the window. By then I was in such a good mood, I was happy to pay.

*

Everywhere we turned, the country was hyper-focused on a match that we were, to be blunt, expected to win easily, considering our respective paths to the big game. We knew it was going to be a lot harder than the public expected. France had defeated England and Wales, and in doing so shown that they were comfortable playing forward-dominated knockout rugby.

The journey from the hotel to the ground was unforgettable. There were crowds waiting to cheer us onto the bus, and it felt like every New Zealander capable of standing was lining the streets as we wound our way slowly to Eden Park. It was like nothing I had seen before, and it hasn't happened since.

As expected, the French kept it very tight, though we did score a training-ground try through Tony Woodcock. The move, known as 'Teabag', involved setting up two jumping pods. I was the dummy jumper at the front lifted by Reado, but the ball went to Jerome at the back, who immediately shovelled an offload to Woody, who was wheeling around to hit the gap between the two pods. When you watch the replay, you can tell I was pretty happy about it. I was showing a lot more emotion than Woody, but perhaps he knew better than me what was coming.

The rest of the match was a grind. Stephen Donald came off the bench for Cruds, who became the latest in a long line of players to get injured. Stephen then wrote himself into history by scoring the penalty that pushed us out to an 8–0 lead, but then Thierry Dusautoir scored and his try was converted. The bulk of the second half was an agonising experience, as we clung to a one-point lead.

As usual, I was subbed off with about half an hour to go. You're never quite as helpless as when you're sitting on the sideline knowing you cannot do a thing about the result from there on. I hated every minute of it. Time slowed to a crawl, right up until the moment referee Craig Joubert blew his whistle and Andy Ellis kicked the ball out.

It was well past 11 pm by the time all the formalities were over.

Exhausted, Owen Franks and I sat slumped in our seats, dreading the prospect of having to peel our sweat-soaked jerseys from our aching bodies.

I'd just completed my 25th Test, but I was still as green as the grass on Eden Park. Of those 25 Tests, I had been part of the starting line-up in only 12, and only five times had I managed to play the full 80 minutes. I wasn't complaining. Not much, anyway. Of course I wanted to start and play every minute of every match, but a few years later I would look back on those days and come to realise how perfectly my early forays into international rugby had been handled by the coaches. But all that was a million miles from my mind at that moment.

Owen wasn't saying a lot. He never did. Ten months older than me and ten months more experienced in international rugby, he'd just finished his 31st Test. We'd both play a lot more, but again, that wasn't on either of our minds. After the drama of the past two hours, coherent thoughts were difficult to muster. We just took everything in. Don't ask me what the specifics of our conversation were – we could have been just filling the air with white noise. It didn't really matter.

The room wasn't as loud and as jubilant as you might expect for the team that had just scaled its Mount Everest, a success 24 years in the making. The tone was set by our skipper, Richie McCaw. He had left everything of himself out on Eden Park. All he could do was slump in his seat, sucking as much oxygen as he could into his lungs while he removed his broken foot from his Adidas boot for the final time that year. Drinks were being opened and passed around, but I don't know if Rick had the strength to get a bottle to his lips just yet.

Andrew Hore, the hooker with so many rough edges that he was immediately identifiable as both a front-row forward and a farmer, plonked himself down between Owen and me, clutching a beer. I might not be able to tell you what Owie and I had been talking about, but I remember like it was yesterday exactly what Horey said: 'You guys have no f***ing idea what you've just done.'

What had we done? At 23 years old and in just our second and third seasons of Test rugby respectively, Owen Franks and I had just won a World Cup. Over the next 12 years, I came to understand perfectly what Horey meant. He was 100 per cent right. Well, I can't speak for Owen, but he was right about me. I had no idea what I'd just done. How could I? I was so naive.

Wasn't winning a World Cup just what we were meant to do? Wasn't it always going to be like this? It was time to party, and the next four years would only prolong that sense that this was something that was always going to happen.

On this day we'd clung on to record a single-point victory. There'd come a day, years later, when I'd sit on the other side of that equation.

8

BLOOD ON MY HANDS

I'M AN OUTDOORS PERSON.

Hunting has been a big part of my recreational life for a long time. If you step inside my place in Christchurch, you'll quickly see that the mounted heads of a couple of beautiful animals take pride of place on the walls.

When it comes to shooting, I follow all the rules, whether they're designed for safety, the environment or animal management. I know there are people who don't believe there is any such thing as a 'good' hunt, and that is their prerogative, but the aim of a well-run hunt is to respect your environment and kill the animals as quickly and humanely as possible. What type of animal depends to a large extent on where you are.

Which brings me to Bloemfontein, on South Africa's Highveld.

It was an open secret that if you had a few hunters in your midst, Bloemfontein was a great place to visit. This had been going on for a long time in rugby circles, where you'd hook up with a professional hunter who would take your group out for an expedition. You pay for the experience – by no means is it a freebie – but if you're an enthusiast like me, it's worth it.

Early in my career, every time I'd flown out of South Africa I'd look at the magnificent zebra hides in the airport gift shops and think about buying one, but I'd decide, 'No, buying a pelt is not the same as taking one yourself.'

When we went to South Africa in 2014, we played the Lions in Johannesburg before heading south to Bloemfontein for the week to prepare for a match against the Cheetahs. The opportunity to visit a lodge and go for a hunt presented itself, and a few of us decided to avail ourselves of it. That's how my brother George, my cousin Ben Funnell, Tyler Bleyendaal, Tom Taylor and I found ourselves at the lodge, eating a fantastic *braai* – a South African barbecue on coals, not gas – and looking forward to a big next day. On the *braai* there was kudu and impala; if that sounds a bit exotic, consider that the locals there would think nothing more of it than we would at home eating venison.

We were all aware of what we were doing; it was all legal and above board. We had the right people with us. They were licensed professionals and had connections to some of the Lions players. Some had played professional rugby themselves. It was nice to get out and spend some time with locals rather than spending the whole time in our team bubble.

The following day, I shot a zebra and a gemsbok. A couple of the other guys shot other animals. The meat was donated back to local villages, as it has always been done. We then had the opportunity to have the zebra skins sent back and the gemsbok heads mounted. Once it was organised, it could take six to 12 months to get them through quarantine. Again, this wasn't a fly-by-night operation. It was highly organised and professionally run.

We played the Cheetahs at Bloemfontein, enjoyed a 51–32 victory and flew home. That was the last I expected to hear about Bloemfontein until my zebra pelt and gemsbok head were cleared through New Zealand customs.

The Super Rugby campaign finished in devastating fashion for the Crusaders. This was the Bernard Foley last-minute-kick final, when Craig Joubert had pinged Rick late on for a ruck infringement, conceding later that he had got it wrong. A lot of our fans found that tough to take but I remain fairly sanguine about these things. Yes, it was gutting to lose, but we'd had plenty of opportunities to take the final out of the ref's hands but we'd come up short – again.

The All Blacks squad had been named and we were sent in various small groups around the country, to engage with the public in communities that didn't normally get the chance to see us. Wyatt Crockett, Ben Franks and I were sent to the West Coast and Buller. From Hokitika up to Westport, we stopped at all these little towns and places, many of which reminded me of where I had grown up. It was a fantastic day. We were at the airport in Hokitika doing a few interviews before jumping on a plane back to Christchurch when my phone started blowing up. I could feel it constantly buzzing in my pocket, but I was talking to the local media and couldn't stop to see what was going on.

I hopped on the plane, took a quick glance at my phone and saw a bunch of missed calls and about 50 messages from friends and family. A quick scroll indicated that a lot of them were jokingly giving me some grief and asking me what I had gone and done now. I didn't have a clue. I'm not the sort of guy to get myself in strife, so my curiosity was certainly piqued.

It was a bumpy old flight, and as soon as we landed I switched my phone back on. It didn't take me long to work out what I was in 'trouble' for. The guys from the lodge had posted some pics of our hunt on social media, and a woman in Cape Town had seen them and sent them to the world's media. She thought it was disgusting – that we had blood on our hands.

On one level, I was fine with it. I know that hunting rubs some people the wrong way, and that it doesn't matter if there are sound conservation and ecological reasons for culling animals. There will always be those who believe we're just doing it for thrills. If I'm being honest with myself, posing with the recently killed zebra in my Crusaders branded kit – although it was all I had to wear – wasn't the smartest PR move on my part.

But this had happened a couple of months ago. It seemed to me that she'd waited until I was in camp with the All Blacks to try to give her stance maximum impact. There might be a more innocent explanation, but that was my reading of it.

By this time Crocky and Franko were also well aware of the situation, and I received a text to say there was a woman from New Zealand Rugby waiting for us when we got off the plane in Christchurch. That seemed like an unnecessary escalation, but as we were walking through the airport to make our connecting flight to Auckland, there were two or three TV cameras. The NZR employee panicked. Her stress levels were going through the roof – she didn't know what was going on, which wasn't her fault.

One of the camera operators said to me, 'George, can we have a word?'

'I'm not George, sorry, I'm Sam,' I said politely, and just kept walking.

That was the signal for them to chase me, although I use that word lightly. It was more of a fast follow. Crocky thought the whole thing was a huge joke. He took his jacket off and was trying to put it over my head, as if I were a criminal being led out of court. He thought it was the high point of his comedy career but I was getting pissed off with him. I knew that his antics, and the fact I now had an NZR minder with me, were actually making it look like I had something to hide. It was just Crocky being Crocky, but I got the hump and told him to cut it out.

One of the journalists yelled out: 'Hey, Sam, what did you do with the meat?'

I turned to the NZR staffer and said that this was getting silly, and that I'd rather just stop and politely answer some questions. I knew the answers wouldn't please everybody, but it was better than trying to avoid them. She agreed and I did a brief interview. I told the journos what had happened and explained that the meat had been donated to a local village.

As soon as I said that, the questions basically stopped. One of the journos later told me that the story they'd heard was that we'd killed these creatures and just left the carcasses to rot.

To an extent, I understood the outrage. I'd never hidden my love of hunting, but I'd never gone out of my way to promote it either. Hannah hasn't killed anything in her life that didn't involve a can of fly spray, and even then there's a little bit of a squeal involved. There's nothing wrong with that, but I'm from a farm and I have a fair understanding of where our food comes from.

Hannah rang once we landed in Auckland. She'd been reading a few of the comments under the stories and was a bit worried, because threats had been made against us. I suggested she should stop reading them. Eventually the matter would die down, but for a while there it seemed like there was a real town and country divide.

I was happy to do more promotional media – as much as was necessary – but NZR told me not to do any for a couple of weeks. I studied conservation and ecology as my minor at Lincoln, so I was looking forward to using some of that knowledge in the real world and perhaps educating people that just because a zebra could be seen in a zoo in New Zealand, it didn't mean there was a shortage of them in Africa. In 2023, there was a report in Bloomberg that stated that South Africa was looking to promote zebra meat for international menus due to the surplus from the tens of thousands culled each year.

After my experience – the only real brush with personal controversy I've endured – I can give them the tip that the idea of zebra meat in New Zealand restaurants is unlikely to be a hit.

9

BACK TO BACK

ALONG WITH GRAHAM HENRY calling it quits as All Blacks coach after the 2011 World Cup and Steve Hansen coming into the top job, there was a fair bit of player turnover. Brodie Retallick, Dane Coles, Julian Savea, Beauden Barrett and Aaron Smith were introduced. It was great to see Nuggy in national colours. He was the same as he was at Feilding High, an irrepressible personality, just a big kid really, with a bullet pass that he worked on hour after hour after hour until it was as close to perfect as you could get.

Those guys all took to Test rugby in 2012 like ducks to water. It was impressive.

Meanwhile, it was a watershed year for me. Brad Thorn was gone, as was Anthony Boric, who had been in a constant battle with his body to stay on the park. Ali Williams was still around, but in a reduced role, so although I was a long way from being the 'senior' lock, I was expected to take on a more prominent role and help shepherd 'Guzz' Retallick and Luke Romano into the environment.

It was also the year when Steve Hansen upped the ante with me – which, if I'm being honest, led to a couple of seasons of introspection and second-guessing of myself that I didn't really enjoy.

After a 22–0 win over Australia at Eden Park in August 2012, Shag came out in the media and said I was playing averagely and made it clear I was about to be dropped. I thought I was playing decently. I wasn't incredible, by any stretch of the imagination, but I didn't think I was playing poorly. Even more confusingly, in the Tuesday review following the Bledisloe Cup win, I was voted defensive player of the game in a match where we'd held the opposition to nil, so I must have been doing something right.

I was duly dropped to the bench for the next Test, against Argentina in Wellington, with Guzz and Luke picked to start. That was a hard one to take. It felt weird. I was pretty sure Shag was trying to send me a message, but was I arrogant in thinking that? Was I actually in poor form and too ignorant to see it? It took me a while to realise he was trying to make me better, make me grow, and maybe it even worked in the short term, but I'm still convinced there would have been better ways of going about it.

I remember thinking, 'Shit, this is not good – I need to play better.' My preparation was different that week because I had become used to starting, and there was the added wrinkle of me having to practise at No. 8 because Reado flew home for the birth of his second daughter, and there was doubt as to whether he would get back in time.

There was a whole lot going on in my head that week, and when I came on – after a storm-induced power cut kept the teams in the sheds for 20 minutes at half-time – I played really well. The whole experience was a turning point. I had gone from being the baby of the team, where my main job was to look after myself, to having a massive expectation on me to perform with excellence every time I pulled on the jersey.

I played 14 Tests in 2012 and we won 12, drew one and lost one. The draw came in Brisbane in a dead-rubber Bledisloe Test, and stopped us from setting a record for most consecutive wins. We had put together 16 wins on the bounce, all of which I had played a part in, starting in 14 and playing 80 minutes in nine. That was probably the biggest change from the World Cup year to the start of the next cycle: I was now considered robust enough to play full games.

Even after the niggly performance at Suncorp Stadium, my bogey ground, which had halted the win streak, we still had the opportunity to finish the year unbeaten. We'd had comfortable wins against Scotland, Italy and Wales, which left us with one more match to negotiate: a Hillary Shield clash against England at Twickenham.

That didn't go so well. It was, as Shag likes to say, the 'rock under the towel' for the summer. England totally outplayed us in front of a packed Twickenham, and although it was three tries each, they deserved the 38–21 win because they kept the scoreboard moving, kept punishing us for our mistakes – and they had a lot to work with – and rode the crowd emotion.

I can honestly say I don't hate any team I play against. I do hate losing, though. At anything, from games of euchre or 500 to Test matches. And, yes, there are certain teams I hate losing to more than others. I have nothing but 100 per cent respect for every opponent I play, whether they're from a huge rugby country like South Africa or a relative minnow like Uruguay. There are obviously teams I like beating more than others because of their history and long-standing rivalries. England is a team I enjoy beating, not just because of the rivalry, but there's a personal element to it as well because the win against England in 1954 was Grandad's greatest moment as an All Black. Twickenham is such a cauldron and captaining the side to a draw there in 2022, when we'd been comfortably leading late in the match, would be one of the more gutting experiences of my career.

My 2013 season was similar to 2012, in that I remained a favourite target of Steve at team review sessions. This coalesced around a Bledisloe Cup Test in Sydney, where I thought I had gone pretty well in a big 47–29 win. The problem was I was yellow-carded by referee Craig Joubert with about 30 seconds to go. There was a penalty, and as I went to give the ball back, the Wallabies halfback Nic White pushed me. I tripped over the ball and struck it with my heel as he went to pick it up. Joubert pinged me because he thought I was trying to be a smartarse. When he looked at the incident after the game, he made a point of apologising to me because he knew he had misread the situation.

But that hadn't made any impact on Shag, who absolutely lined me up in the team review. It was the full hairdryer treatment. Andrew Hore came up to me after to see how I was going, because, in his words, he'd never seen anybody take that sort of roasting before. I was pissed off and confused, but I was a big boy and could handle it. I usually had a reply at the ready when I was challenged in review situations, but on this occasion it was clear that Steve had made up his mind that I was an idiot who needed to be taken down a peg.

One or two guys got around me that night. Reado told me not to worry – that Shag was firing the big bullets at me because he knew I could handle it, and that it helped keep everybody in line. There might have been some truth in that – and, in fairness, when he did have a crack, I tended to come out and play really well. I guess that's what kids with older brothers tend to do – we're on a lifelong mission to prove our elders wrong.

I wasn't the only one catching Shag's eye for the wrong reasons. He was bloody hard on Ma'a Nonu too. Like me, Ma'a was still growing into his game, even though he was a veteran All Black. Ma'a was arguably the best second five-eighth in the world, close to unstoppable at his best and one of our key drivers, but Steve always wanted him to deliver more – and Ma'a usually did.

For me, though, after an initial 'I'll show him' response, the targeting started to have a negative effect. I called a meeting with mental skills coach Gilbert Enoka and told him that I was way down on confidence, and that while I thought I was still doing my job, I had lost a bit of spark. I needed to start enjoying my rugby again, so I talked with Bert about ways to absorb the criticism and to learn from it without it hanging over me during games. I wanted to get better, and to please the coach, but I needed to play freely and with the natural instincts I'd grown up with.

After meeting with Bert, I had a sit-down meeting with Shag at his place. I told him exactly what was going through my head during Tests – how I'd make a tackle but it might not be a dominant one, and as I ran to the next ruck all I could think about was how that would be mocked in the review, rather than what I should be doing next. I had to bite the bullet and tell him that I knew that he was trying to spur me on to better and bigger things, but that it wasn't helping. We needed to start doing things differently.

Believe me, it's not easy to look a tremendously successful coach in the eye, someone you have an enormous amount of respect for, and tell him that you're not enjoying his methods. Shag reckoned I was overthinking things, but to his credit he said, 'I'll give you some space for a couple of weeks to get your mental game sorted.'

What he also did was subtly let me know that he didn't view me as just an All Black now. He saw me as somebody who had a responsibility to drive the high standards he was demanding from the team. He wanted me to grow into that responsibility, not shrink from it, and that was the balance we had to find.

That was nice to hear and gave me more insight into his thinking, but it took a while to find a happy medium. To use a familiar metaphor, Shag thought the best way to prompt me towards greatness was by constant use of the stick. Every now and then, however, I was hungry for a carrot. Although it troubled me at the time, now, with more distance, I appreciate his thinking better. He was trying to get the best out of me, and my reward was playing more than 100 Tests with him involved as either assistant or head coach.

*

For the All Blacks as a team, the rewards were some of the most dominant years enjoyed by any professional sports team anywhere, ever. We followed the rock-under-the-towel summer with 14 wins from 14 Tests in 2013. I played in 12 of those matches, including a satisfying 26–19 win over France in Paris and a 30–22 win over England at Twickenham.

The Paris win came with a sting in the tail for me, as I lost an improbable seven games of credit-card roulette in a row, including an extremely expensive occasion at a white-tablecloth restaurant at the top of the Eiffel Tower.

To walk you back a little: Luke Romano, Kieran Read, Wyatt Crockett and I were spending a lot of time together on that tour, playing 500 at various cafes around Europe, drinking our coffees and hot chocolates, and watching Crocky cheat horrendously at cards. When it came time to leave and pay, we'd all put our credit cards in the middle and let the proprietor choose one to pay. When you've got four competitive guys together, it just adds that extra shot of adrenaline at the end of the cards session. Somehow, I lost six in a row. Those losses were starting to add up and I was getting a bit twitchy.

One evening we were in Paris and on our way to a team dinner when the restaurant rang Darren Shand to tell him they could no longer take us. We were let out on the streets of the city and told to sort ourselves out for the evening. It was a blessing and (for me at least) a curse.

Paris was one of those places I never realised how lucky I was to visit until my career was almost over. Rugby players can be bloody hopeless like that. We live our touring lives to a schedule and rarely deviate from it. It was Conrad Smith, a great tourist, who alerted me to this. Rather than just live his touring life from meeting to training to game, he identified gaps in his schedule and got out and explored wherever we were, visiting a local market or a museum.

In that spirit, Reado, Luke, Crocky and I decided to use the last-minute opportunity created by the cancellation to have dinner atop Paris's most celebrated landmark. We were dressed fairly shabbily and the security staffer at the bottom seemed reluctant to let us into the elevator. After a bit of bilingual back and forth, he said there had been a late cancellation and there was a table of four – 'but you do know it's fine dining, don't you?'

The view and the atmosphere were amazing, the portions tiny. Even the bread was struggling to fill the farm-fed-sized hole in my stomach. Still, it was a nice evening until we came to pay. I thought we were splitting the bill, but Crocky made a late call for roulette and once again my card was chosen. Seven in a row! And this time the stakes were higher – much higher.

I was sure my card was going to bounce. Luke and Crocky thought it was hilarious, but Reado, being the empathetic bloke he is, sensed my discomfort and slipped me 200 euros, which covered his share. Crocky had no such qualms, comforting me by saying he'd buy me an ice cream on the way home. I refused that kind offer.

Crocky further blotted his copybook in my eyes by revelling in my misfortune with his wife, Jenna, who promptly told Hannah about what was going on. As a potential end-of-season holiday in Fiji was whittled down to a night away at the beach somewhere near home, she was unimpressed enough to ban me from ever playing that game again.

Incidentally, Crocky reckons my misfortune didn't equate to his in 2012, when he lost roulette after a trip to Wagamama's, the noodle-house chain, in the week before the Test we lost to England at Twickenham. Norovirus swept through the team and its symptoms presented themselves later that night. Crocky, whose vomiting was so loud that Dr Deb thought a large animal was dying, was distraught that nobody could keep the food that he had paid for down.

Back on the field, we ended 2013 with a remarkable win against Ireland at Dublin. That was the Test where they had the ball in our half and were leading 22–17 with 30 seconds to go. Then we won a penalty turnover, and 12 clinical phases later Ryan Crotty scored in the corner. Cruds added the conversion on the second go after the Irish had broken early while charging his first, failed, attempt. That kick preserved our perfect season.

There were some quirks during the lead-up to Ryan's try that spoke to the all-round skills of the squad, like the Franks brothers combining in midfield, and our blindside flanker, Liam Messam, doing a really good impression of a right wing. Of the 15 players on the field, only Guzz, a brilliant ball carrier, and Rick, the skipper, didn't touch the ball during those 12 phases, but they did a lot of work off the ball. We hadn't played very well, but those final couple of minutes were a reminder of where we were at as a team – capable of winning from anywhere.

It was the opposite of where we were at the Crusaders. We had great teams but struggled to close out the big moments, including in that year's Super Rugby final. Put a black jersey on, however, and I never felt like we were beaten.

By now, Guzz and I were getting to know each other's games really well. We got most of the starts, and – after Ali moved overseas at the end of 2012 – my Crusaders mate Luke Romano rounded out a great trio. We were three young locks who just loved getting stuck into the work and had an old-school mentality.

Both Guzz and Luke played with a bit of a chip on their shoulder because nothing had come easily to them when they were younger. Although both had attended the talent production line at Christchurch Boys' High, they were far from schoolboy stars. Luke had only made the Third XV, while Brodie had left Canterbury for Hawke's Bay to get his rugby opportunities. It's not all 'the system's' fault that their talents weren't recognised – Guzz would be the first to admit that his habit of stopping at the bakery most days meant he didn't exactly have the diet of champions – but it's also a good lesson. Too often talent identification starts and ends at secondary-school level, and far too many kids leave the sport because they're not on a performance pathway. People develop at different paces and in different environments – Luke and Guzz are perfect examples of this. As a rugby country, we have to guard against them being the last.

Our old-school mentality shone through at different times and in different ways, probably not all of them healthy. When we got injured on the field, we'd challenge each other to get back in the line and make the next tackle. Reado once told Luke to walk off a broken leg. I told him to toughen up when he ripped his groin. We can laugh about it now, but at the time I'm sure Luke wondered what the hell he'd got himself into.

It wasn't until midway through 2014 that our 22-match unbeaten Test streak ended when South Africa beat us 27–25 at Ellis Park, Johannesburg. Neither Luke nor Guzz were beside me that day as we were under the pump through injuries. Jeremy Thrush started at lock and we had no genuine lock cover on the bench. Steve Luatua and Liam Messam were covering the loose forwards and locks between them, and it was the latter who gave away the critical penalty in controversial circumstances. It was the early days of the television match official, or TMO, and referee Wayne Barnes had missed Messam's no-arms tackle on Schalk Burger with time running out. The TV director kept playing a replay of it on the big screen, causing the crowd to go nuts, until finally Barnes referred the incident upstairs. It was the right call, but the way it came about left a bad taste.

Although we would have loved to keep our streak alive, in the long run a few setbacks ahead of the World Cup probably didn't perturb us. If anything, our loss to the Wallabies in Sydney in the truncated Rugby Championship the following year just reinforced the message that nothing was going to be handed to us at the 2015 Rugby World Cup in England.

*

We wouldn't have frightened too many with our performances early at the World Cup, especially after we struggled to a 26–16 win over Argentina in our opener at the iconic Wembley Stadium. Rick got a yellow card early and was pretty filthy on himself, because it was a cynical, easily avoidable foul and it put us under pressure. It also gave those who like to get on the McCaw-is-a-cheat bandwagon an opportunity to get stuck in.

We stayed in London for a win over Namibia, travelled to Cardiff to beat Georgia, and then to Newcastle and their treasured football cathedral, St James' Park, to play Tonga. All three matches were comfortable but relatively subdued victories.

While you never take any Tests lightly, our physical preparation was primed for what came next: a rematch of the 2007 quarter-final against France – in the same Cardiff stadium, no less.

Most of the 'rematch' noise came from outside the group, but we weren't shying away from the fact that this was where it had all come unstuck eight years earlier. We had veterans of that defeat, including our skipper, so we talked about it, but it wasn't a huge deal. Any talk of revenge was coming from outside the camp.

From the moment Guzz charged down Frédéric Michalak to score the first try we were in control. DC was at his brilliant best, Julian Savea was unstoppable and we got contributions all across the park. The 62–13 scoreline did not flatter us. It should have been more, but Ma'a dropped the ball over the line with time up on the clock.

One of the most common things you hear after a thumping win is: 'Why can't you just play like that every time?' There are many reasons, mostly to do with the fact the opposition doesn't just let you play how you want. You have to earn it. One of the things we learned from 2011 was that after each game we had to review it, then draw a line under it and reset for the next match. It doesn't matter what sport you're playing, or whether you're in an individual or team sport – that's the aspect a lot of people struggle with. Being able to back up really good performances is tremendously difficult.

We knew the semi-final against South Africa was going to be different. There was no way we'd be putting 60 points on them. My main memory of the week leading up to the match was a simple message: 'We've got to get off that wave and get on to a new one.'

The semi-final at Twickenham was classic Test rugby. That's not the most eloquent analysis you're going to find, but it doesn't make it any less true. We felt in control of the game, but we'd talked all week about the three-point threat posed by Handré Pollard, an outstanding young kicker who could nail goals from a long way out. Every time we gave away a penalty, it seemed like we were around that 40- to 50-metre mark and he'd take the shot and score. We were not under any massive pressure around the field, but we were under scoreboard pressure.

Jerome Kaino, who was having a monster tournament to back up his efforts in 2011, scored a try down the right-hand edge early in the first half. I remember it clearly because he fended off Lood de Jager. There had been a lot of talk about how Lood hadn't missed a tackle all tournament, but here was our own tackling machine brushing him off. Nice.

The Boks weren't posing any threat to our line but Jérôme Garcès kept penalising us and Pollard kept nudging them over. DC hit the post from a penalty in a handy position that would have given us a 10–9 lead and instead they crossed our half, kicked another penalty and made it 7–12 at half-time. A further wrinkle came when Garcès put Jerome in the bin for a professional foul. Not so nice.

There was no panic, but it was a strange feeling to be a man down and behind on the board when we felt like we were playing the better rugby. If anything, we'd been too keen. We pushed our dominance at the breakdown too far and kept getting pinged. It was frustrating but fixable. We needed to pull back from thinking we needed the miracle turnover at every tackle.

The second half was much the same. I felt like we had a stranglehold in terms of dictating play and being more enterprising, but they would not go away. DC dropped a goal while we were still at 14 men, and then Ma'a put our supersub, Beauden Barrett, over in the left-hand corner to steal back the lead.

It rained hard, so territory became as important as the scoreboard. They brought on Patrick Lambie for Pollard and he continued the theme, drilling the Boks' sixth penalty of the match to bring the score to 20–18 with just over ten minutes to go. There must be a psychological boost you get when you know you've been second-best in most areas but you look up at the scoreboard and you're one kick, one blow of the whistle, from playing in a World Cup final.

If anybody was to make a highlights reel of my career, what happened next would be somewhere near the top. With the Springboks deep into our half and preparing for their favourite attacking platform, the lineout, I got up and in front of the great Victor Matfield and stole the ball. It was an important moment in the match – almost certainly the most important moment of the closing minutes – but it was born out of frustration as much as anything.

It had been a messy period of play. Sam Cane had spilled the ball on attack and they pounced on the loose ball, with Patrick Lambie kicking it deep into our 22-metre zone. All a retreating DC could do was kick the ball off the sodden turf into touch about ten metres out from our line. We didn't compete on that ball and instead concentrated on our maul defence as Duane Vermeulen took it unopposed at the back. We defended that one well, and when they spread it one off the ruck to Damian de Allende, Keven Mealamu and Sam Cane got over the ball and stole it. That was a great chance to kick deep and regain control, but Nuggy sliced his punt and put it out on the opposite touch, just 30 metres from our line.

I knew they would organise their drive better this time but I also saw an opportunity. We'd competed at the lineout all game to try to prevent them getting those easy piggybacks down the field but had enjoyed no luck. There had been times when I could feel my fingers on the ball but it was never quite enough. The plan had backfired because we'd committed so hard to the jump that they had been getting behind us to get a good drive on. At the last lineout we hadn't competed and we'd defended well, and I reckon the Boks believed we had changed our strategy.

I saw Victor chatting to their hooker, Adriaan Strauss, and I was sure they believed they were going to get another free jump. Victor would call the ball to himself. It's what big-time players do in big-time moments. I made the call that I was going to compete.

It was a risk. If they won the ball with me in the air, we would be defending the drive with a man down, and they could be clinical in those situations. Even if they didn't win the penalty, they would be in drop-goal territory. Still, I preferred the proactive option. Every now and then, rugby comes down to these man-on-man moments, and this time

I won, getting my timing right and tapping the ball back on our side. When I watched it back on replay later, I thought I should have caught it cleanly rather than tapped, but Nuggy did a great job reeling it in. From the ruck we then box-kicked back into their half.

The game still wasn't decided, though – we still had more than five minutes to go – but it felt like a big moment. We'd jumped in ten lineouts and lost nine of them, but when it counted we won one, and that proved the difference.

That moment had its roots in 2009, before my time in the All Blacks. In that year, the side had played three Tests against the Boks and lost them all. They had learned they could not afford to be passive and let the South Africans win their lineout ball as their maul was devastating. The best way to stop their maul was to deny them the ball. Sometimes, even if you don't win the ball, the act of competing can throw off their system. Six years later, that lesson paid off in a big way.

We never let them back in it from there. We played tight, smart rugby to close it out. We were happy for the Boks to have the ball as long as it was well in their half. We weren't that scared of being beaten through the hands from a long way out, and the contest finally ended when Ben Franks crunched Victor in a tackle so hard that he spilled the ball. Another World Cup final to look forward to.

I later learned that my lineout steal was the only one by either side in the match, and it was a pretty pivotal one, so it was nice to know I'd played my part. I've tried over the years not to acknowledge the moment too much, because it's my job to be a threat to the opposition ball at the lineout and it's not in my nature to blow my own trumpet, but there are some great photos of that moment, and when I see them there's a bit of quiet pride there, for sure.

At the final whistle, Nuggy and I were attempting an awkward tall-guy, short-guy cuddle. There was a camera right in front of us, so we turned the other way to take in the moment on our own. We'd been in the same group class from the age of 13. He was a day pupil but he liked to hang out where the action was, so he was always around the boarding hostel. He was exactly like he is now, except chunkier. He wasn't ripped and running everywhere, but he had that same pass. He worked on that pass relentlessly, obsessively.

We're polar opposites in many respects but he's like another brother. Dad loves the little bloke too, and will defend him to the hilt because he knows he hasn't had anything handed to him. We were like, 'How good is this? Two kids from a small-town co-ed school winning a semi-final in front of 80,000 people at Twickenham, where we're coming back to next week to play a final.' When we started school, the outer reaches of our dreams were to one day play for Manawatū, but even that felt fanciful. That photo of Nuggy and me having a heart-to-heart in the middle of one of world rugby's great arenas is still on the fridge door at Mum and Dad's. It means a hell of a lot to me.

The other famous image from that semi-final is the 'Gulliver' photo I had with Prime Minister John Key. It's become a meme.

At the conclusion of big games, we often have a parade of people through the sheds. He was the PM, so we couldn't not let him in, but he was sitting in my spot and I was absolutely knackered. I couldn't tell the PM to get a wriggle on but I

Getting up in front of the great Victor Matfield to steal the ball in the closing minutes of the 2015 Rugby World Cup semi-final. It was an important moment in a tight contest. We would go on to win 20–18. *(Matthew Impey/Photosport)*

hovered in the hope he would get the message. When I said, 'G'day,' he took the cue and stood up to shake my hand. The photographer was crouching and had a 16mm wide-angle lens, which created an unnatural perspective. It made my hand look bigger than his entire head and shoulders. He was in the process of standing up and I was hunched over, which added to the effect.

The image went viral and I felt a bit sorry for Mr Key. After the final, I walked back into the sheds and he was there again. He got up straightaway, laughed and said: 'You're not getting another photo out of me.'

That semi-final was a game that might not have been an amazing spectacle of running rugby for the viewer, but I loved every moment of it. Neither team submitted an inch without a fight. It was hard, physical rugby. Tests against the Boks have always been my favourite to play. Even when they look one-sided, they're really not. When we beat them 57–0 at Albany in 2017, we sat in the dressing rooms afterwards wondering how on earth we'd managed that, because to a man we were sore from head to toe.

There's an unspoken understanding between South Africans and New Zealanders that we're both going to go as hard as we can. Two proud nations, the old foe. The Boks were part of my dreams and nightmares way before I ever got to play them. When our neighbour Gary Knight had taken a flour bomb to the head in the third Test in 1981, the All Blacks scraped home to a 2–1 series win that was remembered more for what happened off the field than on. That was well before I was born, but in 1995 I got out of bed to watch the World Cup final and was absolutely heartbroken by the result. That

In the sheds after the semi-final match with South Africa in 2015.
(Phil Walter/Getty Images Sport)

affected me so much I went through a period of practising drop goals, as if I could single-handedly prevent another result like that happening.

My respect for them as a rugby nation only grew when I played with Damian de Allende in Japan. He was a big man, very strong, but with great feet. It was incredible to be able to sit back with him and talk about 2015, when we were successful, and 2019, when they were, and to understand the commonalities in those campaigns. They timed their run beautifully in 2019. We beat them in pool play comfortably enough, but by the time they met England in the final they were at the top of their game, and from very early on it was obvious that there was only going to be one winner of that game.

After any game against the Boks, all the brutality of the previous 80 minutes is immediately put to the side. It doesn't matter if you're playing away or at home, in a World Cup or the Rugby Championship, the relationship doesn't alter.

*

The week before the 2015 final felt so different to 2011. Back then, there'd been a lot of injuries to deal with, and in truth I probably wasn't quite ready to be elevated in the way that I had been, although it all worked out. This time, we talked about how no team had ever gone back to back. We had given ourselves an opportunity to do that. As we had in Auckland, Owie and I roomed together. It felt right – one of those omens that shouldn't mean anything but gives you a little bit of comfort. We didn't say anything, but I could tell we were both thinking, 'History repeating itself here.'

It was nothing comparable to the carnage of 2011, but we had lost front-row linchpins Wyatt Crockett and Tony Woodcock. Joe Moody had been brought into the squad and was starting, with Ben Franks in his familiar role off the bench. Luke Romano had done his groin too, but he could still scrum. He'd push in the scrums in training, but when we did any running he'd shuffle off to stand with Mike Cron. Luke had no chance of playing, which left Jerome as lock cover.

We were playing a silly game at the start of training a couple of days before the final. Brodie slipped on the wet turf and took me out at the same time. I could just feel my knee start to hyperextend. Shag was standing next to us, and I swear I could hear his intake of breath. The physios did the same. For a second it looked like every lock we had had been taken out on the eve of one of the biggest matches of our careers, but we both dusted ourselves off gingerly and said a little thanks to whoever was looking over us.

It might sound strange, but that was such an enjoyable week. We were staying at Pennyhill, a resort in Surrey which England often used before home Tests. It has massive spa pools and the guys were doubling down on recovery, trying to get everything straightened out in our bodies as much as we could, so we could squeeze 80 more minutes of juice out of them. Hannah was staying with friends just down the road, so it was nice to spend some time with her.

We studied our opponents, the Wallabies, who were surprise finalists in some pundits' eyes. Our focus was just on what we needed to do. As arrogant as it might sound, we felt that if we played near to our potential, Australia would not be able to stop us.

I was involved in everything from the word go. The first few minutes have been clipped for coaching demonstrations as an example of how to set the tone in defence. I love that, but I also hate it.

Let me explain. I took the kick-off, Aaron Smith kicked the ball back and, following the chase, Kieran Read cleaned up Israel Folau with a bit of help from Owie, ball and all, perfectly timed. The Aussies just managed to secure the ball. Ma'a Nonu came in with a big tackle with help from Brodie Retallick, which was followed by a huge hit from Conrad Smith on Michael Hooper. Australia swung the ball the other way and it was my turn, but compared to everybody else's it was a passive tackle, which is why I don't like the clip. It was a secure tackle, but it didn't put the carrier on the back foot, as the others had. Australia went to the blind side again, taking it into one more ruck, before Brodie charged down Will Genia as he went to box-kick.

So for the first minute and a half, we didn't have the ball but we still managed to assert our physical dominance on the match. It really did set the tone. Wayne Smith had us doing so much work on defence during training early in the tournament that it had become second nature and the team was just hustling at every opportunity. It was almost like we didn't want the ball – we preferred to attack with our defence.

I certainly wished we didn't have the ball when I stuffed up our first attacking opportunity. I'd won the first lineout, Ma'a made a bust in midfield, Nehe Milner-Skudder and Reado made good yards from quick ruck ball, and before we knew it we were five metres out in front of the sticks. Nuggy and I got our timings a bit wrong, though, and he fired it straight at me when I was trying to get out of the way. An opportunity to really put the Wallabies on their heels in the first few minutes was lost. That wasn't a great feeling, but I pushed it out of my mind and got straight back into it.

We often talked about the mental side of these moments. Errors will happen; it's how you respond that counts. After that mistake I played really well: I was constantly involved and was doing my core roles. I received the kick-offs because they were trying to avoid Reado, I won my lineout ball, I carried well and I made tackles. We were humming, but the only thing that wasn't moving as well as we would have liked was the scoreboard. On the stroke of half-time, Nuggy doubled around Conrad, who fed Rick, who then put Nehe in at the corner. DC added the two and we went in 16–3 ahead at the break.

Reado had done his ankle, so he needed it strapped. He was key for us. Richie might have been our captain and talisman, but so much of our attacking game plan revolved around Reado, who had been World Player of the Year in 2013. He was our lineout caller, and a lot of our strike moves were based around him. Every man and his dog was telling him what he needed to do.

'Get on the bike, Reado!'

'Keep moving!'

He had one too many guys in his ear, because at one point he let rip: 'Bloody hell, boys, you worry about yourselves and I'll look after me.'

The coaches made a change in midfield, with Sonny Bill replacing Conrad, who was gutted for his 94th and final Test to end that way. Sonny was the perfect man for that moment, though, and two offloads later Ma'a made an arcing run to the try line. I flew after him, and while I couldn't keep up, I was at least one of the first to give him a cuddle.

We were pretty comfortable at 21–3. It wasn't like we thought the job was done, but we were dominating every facet of the game and the Wallabies knew it. From out of nowhere, however, Ben Smith got the first yellow card of his career when he tip-tackled Drew Mitchell. Bender knew straightaway he'd made a mistake and gestured to apologise as soon as Mitchell hit the ground. To compound matters, Australia scored a try from the penalty and, after we couldn't get the ball out of play when Bender's time in the bin was up, Tevita Kuridrani scored too. After being in complete control at 21–3, now it was 21–17 and we had to try to claw the ascendancy back.

We did that. DC was brilliant and snapped a dropkick and nailed a long penalty to put us up by ten with less than ten minutes to play. We were running on fumes. With Bender off the field, we'd been scrambling a lot into the backfield. The Wallabies needed a try. Kurtley Beale and Mitchell spotted me out wide, tried to gas me and then made the cut. I over-chased and dived. As I was in the air, I saw the cut, and as I twisted to follow the ball, my legs flicked up and clipped Mitchell, who dropped the ball.

Everybody was watching Bender and Beaudy, who created a magical runaway try, but I was lying on the Twickenham turf thinking they were going to pull it back and ping me for a leg kick. DC was down the other end, nice and relaxed as he prepared to kick the conversion with his right foot, and all I was thinking was, 'Hurry up and kick the damn ball before they ask for a replay! KICK THE BLOODY BALL!'

I've since looked back at that moment a few times, and my infringement was a figment of my own mind, but at the time I couldn't enjoy the try like the rest of the team and the country watching at home. Even so, the clock expired and we were victorious. The difference between being on a winning team and being on the field at the end was massive for me, even if I had spent too long worrying unnecessarily about blowing Beaudy's try.

Winning in 2015 was more satisfying than 2011 in many ways. It's hard to explain why without sounding conceited, but in 2011 I was as naive as could be, and there was a definite sense from within the group that year that New Zealand *needed* to win a World Cup after 24 years of failure. This time, it felt like we truly *deserved* it. That's not to say we expected it to be given to us. Almost the opposite. But deep down we knew we were the best team in the world.

Without being a doomsayer, I guess there was only one place to go.

SECOND HALF

10

WATERSHED YEAR

IF YOU LOOK AT most players who have enjoyed long, successful careers, their game evolves. They accrue different strengths and leave other parts of their game behind. Sometimes it's to try to stay ahead of the opposition; at other times it's to play as their body allows.

Richie McCaw was a devastatingly good fetcher in his young days, but became a more heads-up player towards the end. Reado was one of the best edge forwards there has ever been, with an offloading game similar to Sonny Bill, but as he got older and more beaten up, he played tighter and more towards the middle of the park.

Because I'm a tight forward, my evolution has been a bit subtler, but I've definitely become less of a ball-carrying option as I have got older. The peak of my athleticism, if you want to call it that, came during the 2015 season, when I scored the best try of my career, amateur or professional.

People still bring up that five-pointer, which is nice, because when I'm old and withered, my grandkids are not going to want to sit on my knee and listen to me tell stories about a great ruck cleanout, or the time I changed the angle of a lineout drive to our advantage.

In the lead-up to the try, scored against the Reds at AMI Stadium, I'd been doing a bit of work with Aaron Mauger, 'Azza', around using my footwork. It had been a real strength of mine when I first started, the result of my basketball background, when pivoting off both feet was a critical element of a big man's offensive game, but then I'd started listening to everyone who was telling me I needed to get bigger and stronger and be the typical Kiwi lock.

In the All Blacks, I was just chasing rucks. I was allowed to carry one off the ruck and that was about it. If the backs wanted the ball, or if Brodie wanted it, or Luke in the middle, they'd get it and I'd run past them. Romano would be standing there going, 'Come on, hurry up,' while I'm running past thinking, 'Okay, Luke, I'm just off to do what you could be doing.'

I had largely forgotten about my ball-carrying until I got a bit of feedback that said I needed to work on it, because it wasn't where I needed it to be. And so I went to work with Azza.

Against the Reds I called for an inside move and my cousin Ben Funnell received the pass. I called 'no' because there was a brick wall in front of us, but he just threw me the ball thinking, 'Shut up and get on with it, Sam.' Everything happened super-quick, then super-slowly. There was no middle ground. I stepped inside the first tackle, broke it, then took off. The next two defenders were split with a bit of acceleration and a fend. I beat a bit of cover, then turned the final defender, Nick Frisby, with a left-foot step before pushing off his attempt at recovery. He dived and tried an ankle tap, though, and that was where everything went from hyperspeed to no speed. I was running out of gas and thought I was going to fall just a little too short to be able to place the ball for a try. I just got there, though, in the clutches of two defenders. I know all this because Mum's still got the video on her phone.

The TV broadcast then cut to the sideline, where McCaw was grinning like a Cheshire cat and Tom Taylor looked like he'd just seen an alien spaceship land in the middle of the Addington Showgrounds.

Scotty 'Sumo' Stevenson was commentating the game and had a fairly colourful interpretation of events: 'Sam Whitelock, please tell me this isn't happening! What the . . . My goodness! Even the skip's into that. Well, his mum and dad train Standardbreds, put a sulky behind that.'

It was just as I'd been practising with Azza: make the most of those first couple of steps and then fly into it, get some momentum and trust my skills and footwork from there. I was absolutely gassed, and had to deal with all these boys jumping all over me. Jordan Taufua – a funny man – kissed me in the middle of the huddle and I had no energy left to resist. I got a bit of a kick seeing how happy it made everybody. I went back to the halfway line absolutely spent. My quads and my Achilles were screaming at me, because this wasn't what I did. It might have been run-of-the-mill for your Will Jordans and Sevu Reeces of the world, but my legs didn't get used that way.

Todd Blackadder took me off, to be replaced by Dom Bird. He scored about five minutes later, and the cameras panned to the bench again and I was still heaving. I couldn't quite reciprocate the joy the boys felt when I had dotted down.

I have only one other try to compare with that: a 50-metre effort against Manawatū in 2009. I cut Owie off for the ball, hit the hole and ended up dummying the fullback to score. Nuggy knew that I liked to throw an extravagant dummy, so he'd warned his teammates never to fall for it, but Tomasi Cama, the sevens genius, was playing fullback and I sucked him in.

No one has fallen for it since.

*

After the 2015 World Cup, my game tightened up again. An easy description for me in the All Blacks was that I was one of the 'glue' guys who held our structures together and enabled our ball players, including emerging leaders like Ardie Savea, to shine.

The year after the World Cup was, sadly, standard for that period of the Crusaders' history. We made the playoffs but lost heavily to the Lions in Johannesburg, 42–25. It was Todd Blackadder's final year in charge. It was very similar to previous years. We had all this potential but never fulfilled it. We played some awesome rugby and some really average rugby. Guys were starting to get frustrated because we felt like we had the players to win, but since our last title in 2008, we'd watched on as the Chiefs, Highlanders and Hurricanes had lifted the trophy.

In the All Blacks, so many senior guys left after the World Cup that we knew it was going to be a completely different campaign. There was no Rick, but Reado was more than ready to move into full-time captaincy. We knew he was going to create a different feel and style, and he did.

I don't want to say 2016 was an uneventful year, because it wasn't. We won 13 out of 14 Tests but lost our unbeaten record against Ireland, losing to them in Chicago, a match I wasn't involved in. The national side already had an eye on the visit of the Lions next year.

Before we knew it, the calendar turned over to 2017. Nothing has been the same, for the Crusaders or the All Blacks, since.

Scott Robertson came in at the Crusaders, along with a few other new coaches. It was a big change. Some of the sports science staff stayed on but a lot of Todd's team left. I was made captain. It was a challenge I was ready for. I'd been in the team for a while and had been getting frustrated with a number of things. I'm not saying we'd been going poorly, but we were getting too comfortable about being okay. Just making the playoffs should never be a satisfactory result for a team with such playing riches.

My frustrations centred on what I considered to be our underachievement relative to our talent. If you look at that 2015 side, for example, nearly everyone played for an international side, and those who didn't were bloody unlucky. Some of us had played more than 100 games for the Crusaders, living and breathing the red and black, yet had no titles. We just hadn't played consistent, winning rugby. Worse, we really struggled in derbies, and those are the games on which you really mark yourself.

Razor came in with a different energy and a different way of doing things. There was a freshness to everything we were doing. We had a beautiful balance between older guys who had won big games with the All Blacks and other Super Rugby teams, and young guys with talent like Richie Mo'unga and David Havili. Bryn Hall had come down from the Blues, and he was mixing with guys steeped in Crusaders lore like Ryan Crotty and Matt Todd. We could tell straightaway that we had a good thing happening.

We got off to a couple of good, tight wins, against the Brumbies and Highlanders. We probably shouldn't have beaten the Highlanders but we got over the line. It was the sort of game we might well have lost in previous years. Suddenly, winning tight games became infectious.

We played the British & Irish Lions during their tour. We lost to them quite easily, but I learned so much as a captain that day because they didn't do anything special. They just played high-pressure rugby. Just before half-time we had an opportunity to score, but I got too stubborn in attempting the seven points. They wouldn't have done that – they would have just taken the points on offer. We lost that game 12–3, and for the next few days the only thoughts in my head revolved around the same thing: an all-out attacking New Zealand style isn't the only way to win rugby games. As captain, I had to be adaptable and understand that you could build a different kind of pressure by moving the scoreboard along in threes. It was something my brother George had understood intuitively as captain, but it took me a bit longer to get comfortable with that approach.

The lesson came in handy when we reached the 2017 Super Rugby final against the Lions – the Johannesburg-based ones –

at Ellis Park. We were attempting something that year that hadn't been done before, and this was the theme of Razor's campaign. We had to cross the Indian Ocean and beat the South Africans on their home territory, at altitude, where they had everything going for them.

Just before half-time, we received a penalty and I opted for a shot at goal, which we missed, and another one early in the second half, which we got. Previously, my instinct in both cases would have been to kick for the corner and try to maul, especially as we were a man to the good after Kwagga Smith had been sent off for taking David Havili out in the air, but that penalty stretched our lead beyond three tries. In the end, that got us over the line because the Lions finished fast. We were out on our feet, but we had that buffer and held on 25–17.

The Lions were a seriously good side. They'd lost to the Hurricanes in Wellington in the 2016 final, so to beat them in front of a packed house in Johannesburg was hugely satisfying. It had a Test match feel to it. Physically, we were wrecked by half-time. Jason Ryan was ready to give his address to the forwards, but Reado asked him to give us a moment because we weren't ready to process any new information.

There's one clip from that game I love watching. It is the last minute and a half, and it's shot from behind the posts. You can see the amount of energy and work we're putting in, even though the game is pretty much done. In the ref's mic you can hear everyone demanding so much from each other. We're yelling at each other to get up off the floor and make another tackle. We were out on our feet but still pushing.

There's no better feeling than doing the job with your mates and then getting to spend the next day together as a team. That virtually never happens, but it did in Jo'burg. It was a beautiful day and the sun was out. It was perfect. As a player, whenever someone asks what your favourite title is, you're conditioned to say the next one – but for me 2017 takes some beating.

As a captain, I was a long way from perfect, but I had some great leaders in the team to lean on, not least Reado. Izzy was still around and Richie Mo'unga was developing into a player who could drive the machinery around the field.

I was definitely a lead-from-the-front skipper in those early days. If there was a decision to be made, I made it quickly and committed to it, whether it was right or wrong. The intent and action from the decision would outweigh the validity of the decision, I believed. I was the rooster, as Razor would say, but sometimes he needed a sheepdog.

I knew I had to work out a different way of leading, because while my body was not failing me, it was starting to show the effects of the massive minutes I had compiled for Crusaders and country.

I read a book around this time called *The Captain Class: The Hidden Force that Creates the World's Greatest Teams*. The 2017 book by American *Wall Street Journal* journalist Sam Walker identified the on-field captain as the most important precursor to extraordinary success. Walker listed what he believed were the 16 greatest teams of all time; pleasingly, the All Blacks were the only team to feature in his 'Tier One' twice, while a third side from the 1960s just missed out. He wrote:

> On a whim, I decided to make a list of the primary
> player-leaders of these 16 teams to see if any of their
> careers also served as bookends for their teams' Tier One

performances. The results of this exercise stopped me cold. [Every team's dominant] performance corresponded in some way to the arrival and departure of one particular player. In fact, they all did. And with eerie regularity that person was, or would eventually become, the captain.

In the case of the two All Blacks teams, the captains were Wayne 'Buck' Shelford, who became captain after the 1987 World Cup victory until his controversial axing in 1990, and Richie McCaw, who had captained us to consecutive World Cup victories.

Walker found seven common traits among the most successful captains: extreme doggedness and focus in competition; aggressive play that tests the limit of the rules; a willingness to do thankless jobs in the shadows; a low-key, practical and democratic communication style; motivation of others with passionate non-verbal displays; strong convictions and the courage to stand apart; and ironclad emotional control.

The biggest thing I took out of reading this book was that while the underlying character traits might have been the same, all successful captains had their own leadership style. It made me realise that I didn't have to be the guy who was talking all the time if it didn't come naturally to me. I didn't have to jump up and down and be demonstrative when things weren't going well.

I became comfortable saying to Richie Mo'unga and Jordan Taufua, 'You lead the team chant – I don't need to be doing that.' 'Crots, you know what's going on with the backline defence a lot more than I do – you lead that and I'll get my head down and focus on pushing in this scrum.' What I realised was that it's the group that drives your processes.

That was one of the things we implemented at the Crusaders. We had a formal leaders' meeting on the Sunday if we were travelling back from a game, or on the Monday morning if we were at home, and we'd sit down as players and work out what we needed from the week, what we were doing well and what needed more attention. We'd report back to Razor at the end of that meeting. We gave direct feedback to him and he let us know what he thought we needed to focus on.

It gave us an edge, because we were always on the front foot in terms of work-ons.

One saying we had was: 'Whinge up.' That meant you should go to somebody above you in the pecking order with your complaints, rather than whingeing to those at the same level as you. Talk to somebody who can actually do something about it – as long as it was a genuine gripe or complaint, of course. That might be the back-seat guys, the senior leaders, the coaches or even, if needed, the Crusaders management. The accountability within our organisation grew instantly. We self-policed it at first – 'Hey, don't whinge to me, whinge up' – but it didn't take long before we didn't need to, because it became part of what we did as a team. When you get good at nipping potential issues in the bud, it's amazing how few of them you have.

We also became a lot more inclusive. The players' and coaches' partners had always been friendly but we made a point of doing more things together as a team. Razor's wife, Jane, was outstanding. She'd been 'mentored' when Razor was a player by Penny Deans, and we quickly understood why

Robbie had been so successful for so long. Penny was one of the major factors in his success. She instinctively understood that if partners, wives and kids were in a good space and felt valued, the players' on-field performances would be all the better for it.

We went from those dark years, those inconsistent years, to real consistency. One of Razor's great skills was to make the players feel that they were driving that.

*

That British Lions loss was pivotal to the Crusaders' season because we really thought we had the team to beat them. Our All Blacks were available, and even though they played their best side, I thought we still should have had their measure. That was a great lesson in game management. Sometimes skill is not enough.

That Lions tour still grates on me to this day. You only get one shot at it, and I didn't feel that the Crusaders or the All Blacks did themselves justice in 2017. It had been built up so much in my mind and in the media, and – from my perspective at least – it all fell a bit flat.

I had been at the Palmerston North Showgrounds 12 years earlier when the Lions came to town with the aim of putting 100 points on Manawatū, and they'd done just that. They had just lost to New Zealand at Christchurch – the scene of the Brian O'Driscoll incident – and they were determined to put on a real performance before the second Test at Wellington, which became known as the DC show. Even if I was dreaming big back then, the idea of one day getting a shot at the Lions would have seemed far-fetched, but by the time 2013 rolled around I was already starting to think, 'Hey, the Lions are only four years away.' That was how long they'd been in my head.

After the 2015 World Cup, I was thinking, 'Two more years – two more years is nothing. I can do that.' It had massive appeal, because in the space of 12 years you have amazing players who come and go and who never get a shot at the Lions. I was lucky that the middle of my career was falling in a Lions year, and I didn't want to blow it. Reado had just missed them in 2005, so he was sticking around in part because he really wanted a crack at them. We both knew that this was it – 2029 was not going to wait for us.

We'd played Samoa in a lead-up Test with Ben Smith captaining. Samoa didn't have all their best players available and we won comfortably, 78–0, but didn't learn a lot about ourselves. Then the Lions arrived and the circus started.

From day one Shag tried to play the media, in particular to needle Lions coach Warren Gatland. That was where a lot of the noise came from. The two were sniping away at each other. They were the head coaches and could do what they wanted, to a certain degree, but I tried to tune out the noise. I knew it wasn't going to help me, so I didn't read anything or listen to anything. If I got texts from friends or family about the matches, I didn't engage. I just let people say what they felt they had to say and got on with my job of preparing for four hard games of rugby.

We won the first Test at Eden Park 30–15. The weather was good. There was intent and fire. It was good, open, dry-weather rugby. It happened pretty much how we thought it would: we dealt with whatever they threw at us and everything went to plan. That was about the last time we could say that.

During the match, Bender took a head knock and had to leave the field. This wasn't new. He'd also been concussed against Samoa, the game when he was captain, so there was understandable caution. He was replaced by Aaron Cruden, which necessitated Beaudy moving from first five-eighth to fullback. The only reason I mention this relatively insignificant detail is that with less than five minutes to go, Reado was replaced by Scott Barrett, and as Ben wasn't on the field either, somebody – I can't even remember who – yelled out, 'Sam, you're captain.'

It was only the last five minutes or so and I didn't have to make any decisions, but when I thought about it later, it struck me that it was a pretty big moment for me. There might not have been any flashpoints, but hey, I had captained the All Blacks in one of the biggest Tests I would ever play. It was nice to think that I was the one put in control, even if I didn't have to do anything much.

The Lions had scored in the final minute to make the score seem a lot tighter than the match had been, but they'd figured something out in the final quarter of the Test and had something approximating momentum. They would take it with them to Wellington.

In between, the Lions drew with the Hurricanes, but really they were running two separate squads – a midweek and a Test squad – but we couldn't read too much into that. In fact, their record against the Super Rugby franchises was two wins (Crusaders and Chiefs), two losses (Blues and Highlanders) and this draw. But their weekend squad had lost just the once all tour – to the All Blacks in the first Test.

In the lead-up to the second Test, the noise got even louder. Gats and Shag were going at each other constantly. It seemed relentless and there was a real edge developing. You compound that with some pretty miserable weather and the Test became what I'd describe as a Northern Hemisphere–type encounter. I don't mean that in a negative way because it's exactly what we try to do in reverse when we travel up there. We always tried to get the northern teams into an up-tempo game, because we felt we'd have an advantage, so it made perfect sense for them to try to slow the game down, moving it from set piece to set piece and dragging the play out. We didn't deal with it as well as we should have.

Sonny Bill got red-carded early and that cost us. We were in control. We had some points on the board, but losing a man has consequences. We weren't scoring tries but Beaudy was knocking over penalties. We were playing in the areas we wanted to, and everything we had planned was coming off. Then Sonny made his league-style shoulder charge in the 24th minute and it was an easy decision for the ref. He took the blame for the 21–24 loss in front of the boys at the end of the game, which he didn't need to do. It wasn't playing with 14 men that killed us, it was feeling that we had to play differently.

We watched the game back the following week, and I could see us making strategic decisions that proved costly. Really, we stopped playing our style. We became passive, and the Lions saw an opportunity and took it. It was the first time we had not scored a try in a Test since 2014, when we drew 12–12 with Australia in terrible conditions in Sydney (we had also played some of that Test with 14 men). Twice we had handy leads but sat back and watched the Lions score tries.

We were frustrated afterwards because we were still level when Charlie Faumuina was penalised for taking out Kyle

Sinckler in the air. It was hard on Charlie because Kyle had jumped into him. What was Charlie meant to do – let him go? There wasn't much Jérôme Garcès was going to do about it, no matter how hard Reado pleaded Charlie's case, and the Lions nailed an easy penalty to seal the win. A series that we felt we'd done enough to wrap up was now level with one Test to play.

This was another Test in which I learned so much. But I didn't want to be taking lessons from losses in a series that comes around once every 12 years.

During the next week, we had a playing group leaders' meeting. We discussed how, when the Lions had beaten the Crusaders, they'd done it by building a scoreboard lead, three points at a time, and then squeezed us into mistakes as we tried to chase it. It wasn't the rugby we liked watching, but it was winning rugby, and people sometimes forget that playing attractive rugby comes second. We are paid to win games, and if we have to do it in ways that aren't as pleasing on the eye, so be it. It was a tough meeting. We recognised many things we should have done better in Wellington – although, to be fair, we had moved the scoreboard along in threes. Our problem was the fact that we'd stopped playing.

We headed back to Auckland for the decider. I love playing at Eden Park. It is our ground. The history of the place – and the All Blacks' winning percentage there over the past 30 years – only added to the occasion. But there was something strange about playing there against the same team twice in three weeks. The Lions' half of the crowd were up for it – they're always amazing supporters – but our half seemed to be a bit jaded.

Steve Hansen said the 15–15 draw was like kissing your sister, which probably summed it up. Joe Locke, our comms guy, came up to me following the game and told me I had a really good resting bitch face. I was like, 'What are you talking about, Joe?' I'd come off with about two minutes to go, just as the Lions scored to make it 15–15. Then a kerfuffle happened with a penalty that somehow turned into a scrum. I don't want to rake over that, other than to note that there's never been a plausible explanation for what went on between the ref, the assistant and the TMO. Anyway, there's a photo of me standing there, arms folded and with blood coming from my nose. Talk about negative body language – you could tell I was having a very bad day.

I felt like the Lions were happier with the draw than we were. I couldn't have been any unhappier. People wanted to find out who the better team was, and I was in favour of getting a result, whether that meant extra time, golden point or some other method. It might sound like crazy talk – and maybe I wouldn't feel this way if it had actually happened – but I reckon I'd rather have lost the series. That way, you'd be able to sit back and say, 'Hey, we weren't good enough.' Instead, we were left in this kind of purgatory that still hurts to this day.

So I haven't won a Lions series. I haven't lost one either. That's something on the CV that's never going to be rectified. At least I played in one, I guess, but for me the itch remains unscratched.

If you took the five franchises and the Tests, the whole tour was a draw for the Lions, though they came out on the right side of the ledger by beating the Māori All Blacks and the New Zealand Provincial Barbarians. We were joking that the TAB must have fixed it.

I had a lot of respect for the job Warren Gatland did. The Lions side gelled as the series went on. It comprised men from four different nations that don't normally like each other, and they were playing in a country where they'd never enjoyed success.

I can't help but feel something changed for the All Blacks then. We went on to have a successful 2017, putting 50 points on the Wallabies in Sydney and thrashing the Boks at Albany, but we also lost to Australia in Brisbane and just squeaked past Scotland. A certain patchiness was starting to become evident in our work.

The year had a nice postscript for the Whitelocks. In November I officially captained the All Blacks for the first time in a 33–18 win over Wales at Cardiff, in a match in which Luke started at No. 8. The year had been one of wild contrasts, and that Test was too, but that was the right note on which to end it.

A question I always got in the principality concerned the fact that the last time Wales had beaten the All Blacks, my grandfather was playing. The fact that it was 70 years ago should probably be of more concern to the Welsh than who the All Blacks were that day, but there's always a Welshman with a smile on his face asking me if there's any chance there's a family curse. On this day I hoped not, because there were plenty of us in town. Luke and I, obviously, but Adam and his wife, Tiffany, were also in the crowd with Mum and Dad.

It was one of my favourite Tests. Wales were playing really well. We were tight. It was a strange game where we had control on the scoreboard but not in the match. With about 12 minutes to go, I was put in the sin-bin for hands in the ruck. As I was running off, I looked up to the big screen to see how long was left, worried that it wouldn't be a great look if I finished my first Test as captain on the sidelines – and even worse if Wales were to come back and win. As I made my way to the naughty chair, someone snapped a shot of me, and somehow that was the image that ended up on the next year's Weet-Bix cards.

When kids came up to me, all excited, to have them signed, I had to give myself a little pep talk because I'd have mixed emotions: it had been my first Test as captain, we'd almost lost (Rieko Ioane got us out of trouble with a late try), I'd played a Test with my brother and I'd got a yellow card.

That was probably the perfect way to conclude such a mixed-up year.

11

TERROR

TO GET THE FULL armband for the first time with the All Blacks confirmed to me that captaincy was something I enjoyed doing. I believed it was also improving me as a player.

The Crusaders won the Super Rugby title again in 2018, beating the Lions at home in the final. We'd lost only two games all year, and had won our quarter, semi and final by 30, 18 and 19 points respectively, so we'd definitely recaptured that winning feeling.

Razor brought Ireland legend Ronan O'Gara – 'Rog' – into the coaching team to replace Leon MacDonald, who took the head coach role at Tasman before ending up at the Blues. Rog's influence on me was profound.

Both Razor and Rog have talked about how it was a tough first few months in a new rugby environment, but I never really saw that. I thought Rog was fantastic. I enjoyed checking in with him after each game. To be able to have open, direct conversations with a guy who had played 127 Test matches and some 240 games for Munster was invaluable. He might have been new to coaching, and could sometimes get lost in his thoughts in front of the boys, but we loved him.

Rog definitely grew my game, and he grew our game as a team. He changed the way I looked at things. He tried to take me out of the mindset of having to have the Crusaders 'play like a Kiwi team' all the time. He emphasised playing between the two 10-metre lines, of trusting our defence and squeezing the opposition. He wanted us to start defending the ball, not just concentrating on our opposite man. We ended up playing a hybrid of 'man' and 'ball' defence, and even in that first year, when we were trying to bed in some of his ideas, we conceded 48 points fewer than the next-best side. The following year we were a massive 95 points stingier than the second-best defensive team. It's no surprise to anybody who was coached by Rog at the Crusaders that he has been so successful at La Rochelle in France.

I retained the All Blacks captain's armband for our three-Test series against France, as Reado was recovering from back surgery. Luke started in all three Tests, and performed superbly. His rugby had reached a really high level. I'd always loved playing on the same team as him, right from our school days, and might have expected to do it more often, but he'd left the Crusaders in 2016. On the one hand that was gutting, but moving south to the Highlanders was the right move for Luke. He'd made just two starts for the Crusaders in 2015, and he emerged as a real leader at the Highlanders almost

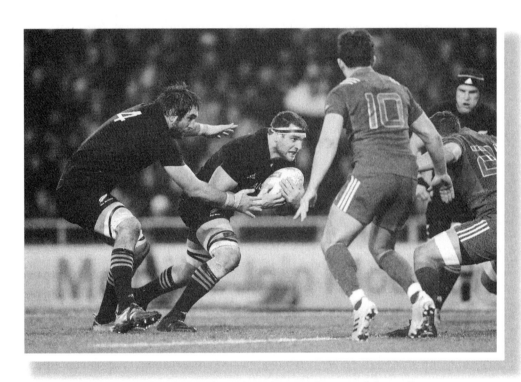

Supporting my brother Luke as he takes on the French line of defence, Dunedin, June 2018. *(Anthony Au-Yeung/Getty Images)*

immediately. I think that, being the youngest of four rugby-playing brothers, Luke always had a desire to make it on his own. I'm biased, obviously, but I thought Luke was playing awesome rugby during those Highlanders years and was unlucky not to play more than eight times for his country.

I had a bit of trouble leading into the French series, as I'd knocked myself out on Beauden Barrett's hip about three weeks before the first Test. I wasn't quite right. I was sleeping more than usual, and just when I was feeling better the headaches would return. I had to concentrate more on getting myself ready to play rugby again than on my leadership, which was perhaps a blessing in disguise. You can become obsessed with the big picture when you're captain, but some of the great leaders I've played alongside and against have told me that the first and most important thing you have to worry about is your own performance – if you're playing well, then leadership becomes easy.

I also had to make a point of trusting the wider group, not just the Crusaders guys I was used to playing with. It was a chat with Robbie Deans that emphasised that message. We had Ben Smith at the back, playing exceptionally high-level rugby. It was important that I asked him what he was seeing on the field, to bring him into the fold early and not make him feel like he had to wait for permission to talk. There was Beaudy, too, who was a big communicator for us, as was Nuggy. Rieko and Ardie were emerging as big voices, so I didn't have to worry about a lack of leadership in the group.

I thought back to all those years ago, when Thorny had told Owie and me that we could both play 100 Tests. As ridiculous as that idea had sounded at the time, that milestone was now hovering on the horizon. The two of us were neck and neck to get there first, but he missed the French series with an Achilles problem. He was stuck on 98 Tests at the start of the Rugby Championship, whereas I had 99, meaning the opener against the Wallabies in Sydney was where I got to raise my bat.

A big crew went over to support me, including friends who made a big weekend of it. I admit I felt a little jealous – all these mates were going out on the town, eating well, drinking beers and catching up, while I was stuck in my hotel room preparing for the game. Having Luke in the squad took some pressure off, so I would grab him for a walk just to get away from the hotel. On my day off, Hannah, Fred and I snuck down to one of the beaches near Bondi and just lay on the sand for an hour or two. The week was overwhelming at times. Rob Jones, a teacher at Feilding High, had made a great video of a whole bunch of people from my life congratulating me. I'd been trying to suppress all this emotion because I wanted to treat the match the same as every other Test, but it was getting harder.

Reado had been the last guy to hit the century, and he'd warned me to prepare for my phone going crazy. He was 100 per cent right. It's what I have told other guys now. You get these messages from everyone who has played a role in your career, whether it's your under-7s team manager or the friend of a friend who watched you play in the under-12s. I had more than 150 text messages on my phone, and it took me three or four days to get back to all of them. Even then, a lot of my replies would have been nothing more than a thumbs-up. Sorry. It was so humbling, but I needed to put all the good wishes to the side and concentrate on winning a game of rugby.

I got to run out of the tunnel first, but was so anxious that I think I jumped the gun. Nobody was ready for my entrance, especially the Australians. I loved the fact that I shared my 100th Test with Tim Perry, who was playing his first. I'd played with him at New Zealand Schools, and I was so impressed that he'd stuck at it when he could have easily walked away and done something different.

It was awesome to get the win, 38–13, and I thought I played well. Guzz, playing his first Test in nearly a year, stole my thunder when he sold an outrageous dummy and flashed the devil's horns when scoring in the second half. I had an opportunity myself later in the game when I found myself in a bit of space, but I could hear somebody screaming for the ball. I looked up but he was too far away, then I lost momentum and the opportunity was gone. If they'd said nothing, I would have had a red-hot crack at the line. I'm pretty sure Nuggy was the guilty party. It would be in keeping with his behaviour at Feilding High. There were a number of times when somebody would make a break and Nuggy would be yelling for the ball even though he was ten metres behind the play. It was always him because he was on a $5-per-try bonus with his mum. (If it wasn't Nuggy in Sydney, then I'm sorry, mate, but I've thrown you under the bus anyway!)

My family was allowed on the field following the game as Reado presented me with my silver cap. I'd played so much rugby with him at Test and Super Rugby level. We're still good mates now. The photo of us together that day is pretty instructive of how many Tests there were between us. Friends have commented that it looks like we're both being held together by strapping tape. I'd actually tweaked my elbow two days before the game, and in other circumstances might have sat the match out, but I knew I had all these people coming over so I just instructed the physio to strap it up and let me out there.

A small bonus was becoming the youngest player to hit 100 Tests, a couple of months shy of my 30th birthday, but Michael Hooper and Wales' George North have since beaten that.

It was Owen's turn in the return Test at Eden Park. Nobody deserved it more than him. When I first started, Owen had written 'Play 100 Tests' as a goal on his wall. This blew me away. It still does when I think about it, because when we started playing for the All Blacks nobody had played 100, and only Richie McCaw was anywhere near it.

My school coach Rick Francis always told us that numbers were the easiest way to set goals. They were tangible. Want to lose weight? Pick a number to get to. Want to get faster? Set a time as a target. But going from zero to 100 Tests – that just seems so far away. Thorny always said that it was pretty simple: play ten Tests a year for ten years. I banked my 100th Test one week, and seven days later Owie did the same. Thorny would have been stoked for both of us.

That year, 2018, was another curious one for the All Blacks. We were successful, but something indefinable was missing. The best way to sum it up was to say that while we were still capable of playing quality rugby, teams did not fear us like they once had. When we were at our very best, leading up to and immediately after 2015, we felt we had teams beaten before they took the field. In 2018, South Africa defeated us by two points in Wellington, and although we only played two Tests in Europe at the end of the year, we could have lost both had Courtney Lawes not been a few centimetres offside when he charged down TJ Perenara. We got out of jail at Twickenham, but not so in Dublin, where Ireland beat us 16–9, holding us tryless. That was their second win against us under coach Joe Schmidt, and they played without any fear.

The year before a World Cup is always a bit cagey, and while there was nothing to panic about – we were still winning a lot more than we were losing – there were ominous signs. The Crusaders, on the other hand, were primed for a hat-trick of titles in 2019. While we would achieve that, it wouldn't be what the season was remembered for.

*

The Crusaders' Super Rugby season had been tracking nicely. We'd racked up four victories from four matches, including a narrow win over the Blues at Eden Park and a thumping home win against our bogey team, the Chiefs. We were gathered at Christchurch airport, ready to fly south to play the Highlanders in Round 5, when we started to hear news of a possible shooting in town.

In those early moments, we wanted to convince ourselves it was the rumour mill getting ahead of itself. Either that or somebody was playing a terrible, sick joke. Soon it was confirmed, however, that there had been a mass shooting.

Everybody had their head down, their attention fixed on their phone. And I don't just mean the team. At Christchurch airport, anybody who was old enough to read was either talking to somebody on their phone or reading the news. It was eerie. Messages from loved ones started rolling in, warning us to be careful because there was a potential terrorist attack ongoing.

'Wait, what? A terrorist attack? In Christchurch? You have to be kidding, right?'

One confirmed fatality turned into two and possibly three, and then we were on the plane with our phones switched off, flying off to play a game of rugby.

One thing I remember with crystal clarity was that when we landed in Dunedin and the 'fasten seatbelt' sign was switched off, nobody moved. It was like we were bolted to our seats, reading our phones and trying to comprehend what the hell was going on back home. Some videos had started circulating on social media; a couple of guys were sent clips that they watched in disbelief, convinced it was a video-game simulation.

The most worrying aspect was that there was a gunman, or potentially gunmen, on the loose. The guys in the team with kids realised that school was due to finish, then Matt Todd received information that kids were being held in lockdown at school. So it was a rattled Crusaders team that eventually made its way to its hotel. All the guys spoke to their families to make sure everybody was okay. Still, I had a bloody terrible sleep, and I know I wasn't the only one.

One look across the breakfast tables the next morning confirmed that nobody was thinking about rugby. We had a game to prepare for but none of us were in the mood. By now it was clear that it had been a terrorist attack aimed at the Muslim community, but for us religion and ethnicity were secondary: we all called Christchurch home, and this was an attack on our city and our people.

As the day evolved, Luke and Ben Smith, both senior players at the Highlanders, were messaging me and a couple of other senior Crusaders players. Postponing the game was raised as a possibility. We called a team meeting. Everybody was equally affected and in a world of disbelief. Guys like Jordan Taufua, who had huge mana (respect and standing) within the squad, wanted to play to send a signal that this terrorist could not win. While I understood, respected and to a degree agreed with that point of view, the more compelling argument to me was that for us to play a game so soon after such a shocking and senseless tragedy could be seen as disrespecting the victims' lives.

The meeting was emotional and the conversations started to flow. I remember looking around the room and realising that it didn't matter where team members were from – whether they'd been born in Christchurch and spent their whole life there, or if they'd only recently arrived to play rugby – there was nothing that was going to make us play that game. Even those who were inclined to play as their own way of giving the middle finger to the gunman started to understand that while we would never regret it if we didn't play, we might if we did.

The team was looking to me to make the final call. I decided that we wouldn't play, and made it clear that we all had to commit to the decision, even those who, in their heart of hearts, disagreed.

A big crowd had been expected at Forsyth Barr – the students were in town and a sell-out crowd was expected – so there were external factors to consider too. But we all knew we had to put that to one side and do the right thing. Once I made the decision, I called Luke and Bender, and they gave us their full backing. They offered to organise a dinner or a get-together so we had people around us, but we decided to charter a bus home, because that was where we were needed.

During the five-hour bus ride, the players and coaches were largely silent as we read the news and gained a fuller picture of the terrible events. After Pike River and the earthquake, this was another level of surreal. While grim, mining disasters are always a possibility; so too natural disasters. But a terrorist attack in New Zealand, in Christchurch? No, that just didn't happen.

Chat restarted as we got north of Timaru and into our 'territory'. What could we do as a team to help? We talked about 2011, and how we'd galvanised around playing good rugby and giving folks affected by the quakes something to feel cheerful about. This was trickier, because our team name and emblem were rightly coming under scrutiny.

I don't think any of us had really considered the historical connotations of the term 'Crusaders', but it was impossible to ignore them now. As rugby players, we talk about things like playing for the badge – but what if that badge was now upsetting, even offensive, to a number of people? I knew there was an argument that if you looked at the names of any number of teams you could find reasons to be offended, but this wasn't the time for whataboutism.

I admit I didn't really have my head in the right space for a couple of days. I took my role as captain seriously, and my focus was on my team and what I needed to do for them. It wasn't until I got home and had made another round of calls to check in on teammates that Hannah said to me: 'Look, you need to stop for a second. Go and watch the news and just take in what has happened – not to your team but to your city.'

I turned on the TV and sat there with Hannah for an hour, taking everything in properly for the first time. It was devastating. All the emotion that I'd suppressed by going into protection mode for my team now hit me. I began to understand the gravity of what had happened to this beautiful city that I had been calling home ever since leaving school. It felt personal.

I was incredibly moved by the national and international outpouring of sorrow, support and mourning for the city and the 51 victims. I wanted to do something to let the Muslim community know they were a valued part of our city's fabric. I know my teammates felt the same. I talked to Sonny Bill Williams and Ofa Tu'ungafasi, two Muslim players at the Blues. Their advice at that time was to stay away, which went against our natural inclinations, but we did not want to be a complication or a distraction, so we gave the Muslim community space to grieve.

Later, Richie Mo'unga, Ofa, Sonny and I would have the opportunity to meet some of the survivors, people who will always carry mental scars from that day. We shared a couple of hours, and Sonny put smiles on a lot of faces as he played indoor football with the kids. I found it hard to keep my emotions in check as I watched them play and realised that many would have little understanding yet of the horror they and their community had been through.

Hannah, Fred and I picked a bunch of flowers from our garden at home and went down to lay them at a makeshift memorial at the Botanic Gardens. It was both numbing and gratifying to read all the words people had put onto cards. It brought the community and city closer. The sad thing was that it had taken such a horrific act of violence to do that.

We travelled to Sydney to play the Waratahs the following week and promptly lost. Effort and energy were not a problem.

We were so motivated to play for our people, but we probably wanted it too much, and our game suffered because of it. The Waratahs, led by coach Daryl Gibson and captain Michael Hooper, were amazing, offering their support in whatever way they could. They did themselves proud on and off the field that night.

After that setback, we did enough to qualify for a home advantage throughout the playoffs. We turned over the Highlanders comfortably enough, but the Hurricanes gave us a huge fright in the semi-final. It was a classic match, in which we felt in control for three-quarters of the game, but every time we had a handy lead they would come back. With 18 minutes to go we were leading 27–26, but they had all the momentum. They weren't able to score, however, whereas we pushed another penalty over to win by four.

By contrast, the final – against the Jaguares from Argentina – was a bit of a grind, but that suited us. People had been quite dismissive of the Argentines leading into the final but they had been playing fantastically all year and had carved a number of teams up. They'd put 39 points on the Brumbies in the semi-final, so we knew they could play. We were the only side to have conceded fewer and scored more points than them during the regular season, so it was a worthy final. Pablo Matera was playing great rugby, they had a big, gnarly forward pack, a scrum that put teams under pressure and a backline full of size, strength and skill.

They got over our line three times, but got held up twice and dropped it once. Rog had been drilling it into me all week that we didn't always need to look to score seven, so I took every opportunity we had for three, played for field position and squeezed them 19–3. There was just one try and it wasn't the prettiest game to watch, but it was three titles in a row. After eight long years of winning nothing, that was all that mattered to us.

12

TROUBLE IN YOKOHAMA

WINNING THREE SUPER RUGBY titles on the bounce was nice, but you know what would have been even nicer? Three Rugby World Cups.

I have talked before about how there were certain things, some bigger than others, that gave the impression we weren't the omnipotent force we had been leading into 2015. The tea leaves were becoming clearer as we started the season with a disappointing, disjointed draw against the Boks in Wellington, and then a record loss to the Wallabies in Perth.

Our performance against the Boks was ugly, but I thought we redressed that with a good week of preparation in Perth. We were playing pretty well too, until Scooter put his shoulder into the back of Michael Hooper's head towards the end of the first half and saw red, and then we were put to the sword 47–26. They scored tries from all over the park and Nic White ran the show like a conductor. We were a little bit slow and a few guys missed a few tackles, myself included. It wasn't the best game to look at from a New Zealand perspective and we got absolutely slayed in the media. There was talk of us losing the Bledisloe Cup the next weekend for the first time in 17 years.

Despite arriving home late on the Monday night, we were straight into our work first thing on Tuesday morning. Some weeks you just know when the boys are on. No matter what room you walked into that week, there was an edge to it. At Eden Park that weekend, we beat Australia 36–0.

When we got to Japan for the World Cup in September 2019, we could feel it was different from any other campaign. The heat was stifling, especially that first week. We would weigh ourselves before training, and even after a light 'clarity' run the bigger guys were losing three to four kilograms in sweat. We tried to adapt quickly without being silly about it, with liberal use of slushies before and during training to try to drop the players' core body temperature. It was important that we adapt quickly, because we had a massive game straight up – against South Africa.

The opener was not a game I remember in a lot of detail, which is unusual for me. My memories largely revolve around how good we felt. Nic Gill had done a lot of hard work with us before we got to Japan, and it felt like we hit the ground running. We built a good lead early, and it was only a late Pieter-Steph du Toit try that made the 23–13 game seem closer than it was. We were playing at the vast Yokohama Stadium, which would be hosting the final, and I did briefly wonder if it might be the same two teams meeting back here if everything went to plan.

We had a break before playing Canada at Oita, and I came off the bench in a 63–0 win. With a short turnaround before the Namibia game, Reado was rested and I was handed the armband. The backline had a slightly experimental feel: we started with Jordie Barrett at first five-eighth, with TJ Perenara covering that position from the bench. I got off my World Cup scoring duck, too, scuttling over from about a metre out in a 71–9 victory. They all count.

With our place in the quarter-finals all but guaranteed, we looked forward to sharpening our game against Italy in our final match. Instead, we spent a lot of time putting this question into Google: 'What is a typhoon?' How did it stack up compared to a hurricane or a cyclone? Or was it more like a tornado? The game, scheduled for Toyota City Stadium, was called off due to safety concerns.

When Typhoon Hagibis hit Japan, we soon learned what they were all about and realised very quickly that it was the right call not to play – although I would have been filthy if I were in Italy's shoes, as they had to pull off an upset win to qualify for the quarters. We were staying in Tokyo and the wind was amazing, funnelling through all the high-rises. A few of us stuck our heads out the door, but not for long. Rubbish was constantly flying down the road, which is very rare for Japan, a country noted for its cleanliness.

Nature thus gave us extra time to prepare for our quarter-final against Ireland, a team that had waited 111 years to beat us, and had then done it twice in three Tests. I think it was a match we wanted more at that stage of the tournament than they did. We prepared well, started well, accumulated points early through a couple of snipes by Nuggy close to the line and didn't give them a sniff. We were 22–0 up at the half, and had 34 points before they scored their first. They scored a couple of consolation tries, but it was close to a complete performance on our part.

It also came with a bit of pain. As I was attempting to tackle hooker Niall Scannell – on for Rory Best, who played his last Test that night – we went knee to knee, bone to bone. My knee immediately swelled up and became painful. I didn't feel like my place in the rest of the tournament was in doubt, but I knew I'd have to manage the pain during the week.

We were drawn against England in the semi-final, which pitted Shag against his old mate Eddie Jones. The week had a different feel to it than others. I was up at 6 am every morning to get on the bike and get my knee moving so I could get through training. I would classify its condition as 'not great but good enough'. It was nowhere near 100 per cent, but by that point in my career I couldn't remember a time when I was playing without pain. I managed to get myself through training each day, but spent a lot of time with an ice pack strapped to it. Reado, too, was struggling with a pulled calf, so he didn't train much.

It wasn't a smooth week. We allowed ourselves to enjoy the good win we'd had over Ireland, but we probably sat on it for too long. We didn't get off the wave quick enough to catch the next one.

Despite all that, we were confident in our game plan. We certainly did not underestimate England, but we hadn't played them a lot in the four-year cycle, unlike Ireland, and while our plan was sound, it turned out it wasn't good enough.

They came out absolutely hissing and flying and put us under a heap of pressure, scoring early. That was their plan – they wanted to shock us at the start, score points and then frustrate us into errors when we tried to respond. It wasn't overly complicated but it was definitely effective.

We, on the other hand, wanted to get to the middle of the field and play with a two-sided attack. The English were smart and used some clever defensive options that they had learned from Gats and the Lions. We didn't get the results we were after from that mode of attack and were too slow to adjust. England were just very good at everything they did that night. They were always in front, and had an answer to everything when we attempted to fight back.

My night ended in forlorn circumstances. We were working our way back into the game and had won a penalty, before I fell for the oldest trick in the book, shoving Owen Farrell to get the ball and having the penalty reversed. One of the easiest ways to slow the game down is to pretend you think the penalty has gone your way, grab the ball, quick tap it and run five metres before you stop. When Owen tried to grab the ball after we had been awarded the penalty, I assumed that was what he was about to do. I grabbed him at the same time and gave him a shove. Farrell, love him or hate him, is a competitor and he went down holding his throat. The replay screen showed it a bunch of times and I got a telling-off from Nigel Owens, while I tried in vain to plead my case that he had fallen for England's gamesmanship.

It was a bad mistake. It was one of a hundred errors made in the game, but this particular one is etched in my memory.

Just when I thought my mood couldn't get any darker, I was pulled from the field immediately – humiliation heaped upon embarrassment. I felt pretty shitty, as you can imagine.

That was my World Cup over right there, as I missed the squad for our win in the bronze-medal match against Wales. That really stung. I really wanted the opportunity to right a few wrongs, but instead I had nothing but my thoughts to stew upon.

Yeah, 2019 … I've had better years.

13

'WHY HAVEN'T YOU RETIRED?'

IT WAS A QUESTION I hadn't been expecting, but it hit home.

Dr Ceri Evans, sitting opposite me, came straight to the point: 'So why haven't you retired?'

I'd started using Ceri to work on my mental game towards the end of my career because I needed a new message. All Blacks mental skills coach Bert Enoka had been great throughout my career, but when you've been around as long as me, you sometimes need a change. I still relied on Bert, especially in social situations, but I needed Ceri's directness and his knowledge of my personality traits.

His question was one of those moments when you open your mouth and expect the answer to emerge naturally, but to my surprise the words didn't come. I really had to think about it.

Why hadn't I retired?

In many ways, retiring would have made sense. I had played 100 Tests, had enjoyed a successful career, including winning titles with the Crusaders, which I'd been desperate to do. My body was also starting to give me hints that less rugby at my age – by then I was 32 – might be advantageous.

I also had opportunities to take up lucrative offers overseas. There was unfinished business in Japan.

At the conclusion of the World Cup, I moved to Japan having signed a 'sabbatical' year contract with Robbie Deans at Panasonic Wild Knights. I wanted to improve as a player and at that stage of my career, playing in a different environment under a highly successful coach was going to be the best way to do that. It was a new challenge and every time I had been challenged in my career I had improved as a result. The intention was to play the full 2020 Japan Top League season before returning home, but this had been cut short by the global pandemic. I loved the short time I had there and could easily have seen myself returning for another campaign.

Ceri was really direct in posing this question to me. That's the kind of communication that's important to me. Succinct and direct. I like that. Don't bullshit me, because I'll pick up on it and hold it against you for a while. Importantly, he'd put to me the question I needed to answer for myself. Because if I didn't have the answer, then I was wasting everybody's time.

The blunt question really made me look at my game. It made me really realise just how much our loss to England in the 2019 semi-final had hurt. I wanted to do something nobody had done before and win three World Cup gold medals.

Ceri also helped me realise that if I was going to go around again, I had to do it properly. I needed to make sure I was playing so well that the selectors – whether for the Crusaders or the All Blacks – weren't going to say, 'Yeah, he's going alright, but this kid has got potential and Sam's not so much better that we can justify holding the younger player back.'

Ronan O'Gara was another guy I had a really good conversation about all this with. He told me the story of how he got to 100 Tests. He understood that while he might have been rating 8/10, a younger guy who was rating 7/10 would get another mark because of his potential, so suddenly a clear-cut decision wasn't so clear-cut. I remember this conversation like it was yesterday. 'Just play so well that there's no debate,' Ronan said. 'Play so well they have to pick you.'

That hit home. I wasn't the young guy coming in and asking every question I could to guys like Brad Thorn, Isaac Ross and Ross Filipo. I was now the guy being asked those questions by hungry young players, who themselves had dreams of playing 100 Tests for the All Blacks.

In terms of the physical side of it, the pandemic provided an unanticipated boost.

The only time I've felt 100 per cent was back in 2010, after I'd trained with Brad Thorn for six weeks, but after I spent the Covid-19 lockdown on the Hawke's Bay farm Hannah and I bought in 2017, I must have been at 95 per cent. I know the lockdowns were tough on a lot of people and I'm not minimising that, but it was a godsend for me. I had the rare opportunity for uninterrupted family time while also recharging my batteries.

We'd just say to the kids, 'So, what do you want to do today? Let's go and get pinecones and light a bonfire!' Our daughter Iris turned one during that lockdown. I think we managed to get her a tiny bottle of bubble mixture from the supermarket, and we sat down under the feijoa tree and had a party. She won't remember her first birthday but I will. It was the best time.

It was just a nice time for us to reset, to enjoy each other's company and embrace the simplicity of menial tasks like cleaning out a shed. There was no television in the house, so it was the longest I'd been without watching or even thinking about rugby. It was the longest period I'd spent on the farm, too. We had planned on spending whole summers there while I was still playing, but the reality of the rugby season always seemed to get in the way.

When the lockdown restrictions changed I had a fortnight to get fit because we were going back to work in a pandemic-era Super Rugby competition.

The first thing I noticed was how fresh I felt. My body felt amazing, like I'd done a Benjamin Button. There was no gym on the farm, so I was running down the road to get some kilometres in my legs. I had to be pretty creative in how I trained. I actually fell out of a tree while trying to do some chin-ups. Our son, Fred, had been playing under the tree, so I took the opportunity to do some lifts. The branch broke and before I knew it I was lying flat on my back, sucking in some big, deep breaths and checking I was still in one piece.

'Are you alright, Dad?' Freddie said. I can't have looked too bad because when I said, 'I think so,' he just went back to his game.

When I finally got back to Rugby Park a couple of weeks later, we did a lot of testing and found I had shaped up pretty much exactly as I had left off the season before. I was amazed at how quickly I could get myself in shape. That's what ten years in professional sport does for you – fitness becomes almost subconscious.

It wasn't always like that, of course, and there was a time when I used to think any bump or niggle was a harbinger of bigger things to come. One of my first lessons came from Dr Deb Robinson, the All Blacks' team doctor. She told me that if I had an injury that wasn't going to get worse by playing, I had two choices: I either learned how to handle the pain or I didn't – in which case I should probably find a different occupation. This was particularly true of upper-body injuries. If you can run, you can play. You can manipulate your body position and catching technique to mitigate most shoulder, chest and hand injuries.

There were times, however, when I shouldn't have ignored what my body was telling me. I played through a torn groin and thoracic injuries, and both affected my form. I also played a Test against Argentina in 2018 with hyperextended fingers. I felt compelled to play because Kieran Read was out with a wrist injury, but I struggled to lift, catch and missed a couple of tackles I would normally have made. To the average punter it looked like I had a shocker – and it's hard to argue with that assessment, although there were reasons for it.

My thoracic spinal injury still gives me grief. The doctors reckon it might be the result of where my GPS unit sat in my jersey, constantly putting a tiny bit more pressure on two vertebrae. It's a real mess in there, and my back still screams at me. It's also one of those injuries where you don't see day-to-day improvements during rehab, so it can mess with you mentally as well.

Even on a good day, my left-side Achilles tendon takes a long time to warm up, so I spend the first part of the morning hobbling along until it catches up with my right.

I've had a couple of concussions where I've taken knocks early in games, but no symptoms have presented themselves so I have stayed on the field and felt fine. In the changing sheds afterwards or later that night, though, I have suddenly felt sick. I'm not sure why it happens this way, because I have no interest in putting myself in danger by playing while concussed, but very rarely have I taken a blow to the head and immediately thought I was in trouble.

I've always looked after my body. I enjoy a beer from time to time and there might have been occasions where I've had one or two too many, but I'm not a big drinker. I watch my diet. I try to get a power nap around midday. I take cold-water swims or have an ice bath in the morning. I use saunas and recovery pumps. Stretching. Pilates. Yoga. I do everything to get the marginal gains. I brush my teeth standing on one foot every day. I sleep well.

Early in my career, when I was a student, I lived in a typical flat with others. After a year or two of this I realised I was spending six months of the year with cold symptoms. Nowadays I'm a zealot when it comes to maintaining a warm, dry home.

I'm not blind to the fact that the higher up the ladder you go, the better you get paid and the better you can look after yourself. Things I take for granted now might not be accessible to every aspiring young player. Hannah and I are lucky in that we don't have to scrimp on food or the quality of ingredients. Not every player or family has that luxury. You can play Test rugby these days while being a poor trainer with a poor diet and drinking too much, but you aren't going to last long. Rugby has changed too much for that. It's far more physical, for one thing, and the players are bigger. If I rocked up these days to play lock for the All Blacks at 106 kilograms I'd be laughed at, yet 14 years ago I got away with it.

The body is only one part of the equation, however. Giving your mind the necessary motivation is just as important and in that respect some of my desire to continue came down to personal goals. I had begun to understand that Richie McCaw's record for Test caps – he'd won 148 – was within my reach. I also wanted to be the first player to win three Rugby World Cup finals. I also really wanted to play a pivotal leadership role, which brings me to a bit of a sore point.

Following the 2019 tournament, Ian Foster had been appointed to take the reins from Steve Hansen as All Blacks coach. I would have loved him to appoint me as the permanent All Blacks captain. I'm not going to lie – I thought I could have been a great captain and was looking forward to the challenges it would have brought.

I was confident I would have made a good job of it because I had genuine connections with every player, from the newest to the most experienced. I had learned how to get better results from individuals in terms of how I communicated with people: who needs a kick up the butt and a direct message versus those who need a cuddle and a caring message. I had an understanding that some players needed detail, and others needed to be left alone.

I had become good at reading body language. I was a people watcher, I got that off Mum, and got to know the little 'tells' that indicated how they were feeling at any given moment.

Speaking bluntly, I was pissed off when I was passed over for the role.

I thought I had the credentials, having led the Crusaders to three titles in my first three years of captaincy. There was also the fact that I'd captained the All Blacks in six Tests under Steve, five against Tier One nations, and we had won them all.

Since becoming captain of the Crusaders, I realised I found it easier playing with the (c) next to my name. I'm convinced it made me a better player. I still felt I was playing well and had room for growth in my game. I didn't think I had plateaued.

Let me emphasise that in saying this, I am not saying anything against Sam Cane, who is a great player and leader. This is not a dig at him. It's not even a dig at Fozzie, who was well within his rights to appoint the guy he wants.

When I was at Panasonic Wild Knights following the World Cup, Fozzie was in regular contact with me, pumping me for information. There was at least a part of me that thought this fact-finding was a precursor to naming me as captain, which made his decision, when it came, just that bit harder to take. Hannah often has better insight into how I'm really feeling than I do, and she was gutted for me because she knew how much I wanted the role. But we had to suck it up. I'm sure Fozzie's reasons would have been valid, even if I didn't agree with them.

Perhaps he doubted whether I had enough left in the tank to get through to another World Cup, or thought my body might let me down. More brutally, perhaps he was of the mind that other locks were ready to usurp my place in the starting side. Perhaps he didn't rate my communication skills,. something I had worked on pretty hard in my early years of leading the Crusaders.

Anyway, it didn't really matter what his reasons were. I just had to get over it and understand that my role was to work out what sort of support Sam needed and offer it to him. You've got to manipulate your style to support the captain. That can be challenging, and sometimes you get it right, sometimes you don't. You don't need to be captain to be a leader. I'd like to think that when I'm not captain, I still demand the same sort of accountability from myself and others as I would if I had the armband.

As I had been with Reado, I became a placeholder captain for Sam, who spent a bit of time in and out of the side due to injuries. Eventually, Ardie Savea became the first-choice deputy. When I thought more about it, I came to see that it didn't matter so much who had the armband for the 80 minutes: captaincy, like coaching, isn't really a one-person job. I'd like to think Reado was a better captain for the Crusaders and the All Blacks when I was alongside him helping, and I'd like to think it was the same for Sam and the All Blacks.

Reado was still at the Crusaders when Razor made me captain. He still wanted to be captain and probably deserved to be, but he sucked it up and we worked really well together. I was a better captain for him being there. At times we didn't even need to speak; I'd just give him the nod and he'd know exactly what I needed from him and would do it without question. Those roles were reversed in the All Blacks.

Reado had a tough task in taking on the job after Richie, a godlike figure in New Zealand rugby, who had grown his captaincy over a staggering 110 Tests. There was a time that playing 110 Tests would have seemed far-fetched; now it seems impossible to comprehend that anybody could go beyond his captaincy total. He and Reado were very different leaders, just as Sam would be in his time. I'm pleased about that, because if Reado had tried to be Rick, it wouldn't have worked. Their personalities are so different.

Most of us are finely tuned to detect inauthenticity. It's that feeling you get when you walk into a room and know that something is a bit off, that someone isn't being themselves. You can't have that in a captain. Captains can have faults – and, let's be honest, they all do – but as long as they own them, that's far better than having a skipper who is trying to be all things to all people.

As a leader, Rick was, if not first off the bus, then second. He'd get out onto the training field first and be running laps at a really good clip just to set the tone. He was telling everybody we were there to work, so we wouldn't be mucking around. He was an incredible lead-from-the-front guy. That was dictated somewhat by the position he played. As a number seven, he had to show that he was prepared to get beaten up every weekend and still be first in line for more punishment at training. There were many times I knew he had a sore knee or that his shoulder was killing him. The physio would come around the team for check-ups and he'd say, 'Yeah, I'm all good,' and walk away. I'd be sitting there thinking, 'How is this guy getting through this work unscathed?'

Once I'd played with and observed Richie for long enough,

I noticed that this was done for the benefit of the rest of the men in the team. An hour or two later, when nobody was watching, he'd sidle up to the physio and book in some time to get his knee or shoulder sorted. Publicly, he refused to show weakness, and that set the tone for his leadership.

If you watch Rick's film, read his book or see any of the media reports on him, you quickly see what drives him. He'd play 80 minutes on the weekend, make ten more tackles than anybody else and have five more ball carries. When you have someone like that leading the team, it puts your own game in perspective. You tell yourself to get on with it and be more like the skipper.

Reado was a lot more empathetic as a leader. I don't mean that Rick was an unfeeling guy, because he wasn't. It just wasn't his style to show it, whereas Reado had a really good way of communicating with everyone in the squad. He was happy to sit down at anybody's table and could hold meaningful conversations across the board. Being a tall, skinny, white, curly-haired cricket boy from South Auckland, he was used to growing up in a diverse place with a range of kids from different backgrounds. He was as comfortable talking to a farm boy like me as he was with hanging out with a Pasifika kid who'd grown up with his extended family in the city.

Kieran, like Rick, was a phenomenal player. It might sound strange to say this about somebody who was World Rugby Player of the Year, but he was underrated in New Zealand. He was a wonderful No. 8 who could play in multiple modes. He could play tight, he had ball-handling skills on the edge, he could dominate the lineout and he was a physical beast. I loved playing with that guy.

In very general terms, Richie showed what it meant to be a great All Black by his actions, whereas Reado could talk about it in a way that was relatable to everybody. You need both types on a team. Richie benefited from having someone like Keven Mealamu alongside him for most of his career, because he could fill some of the communication gaps. He also had leaders like Andrew Hore and Tony Woodcock, who never said a lot, but when they did everybody stopped to listen.

Sam is different again. He sits somewhere between his two predecessors, although he's probably closer to Reado than Richie.

The numbers tell a story here too. Richie was captain in more than 100 Test matches. Reado led in more than 50, and Sam ended the 2023 World Cup having skippered in 27. Everyone is going to evolve and grow as a leader, and their style will change with that. That makes it nearly impossible to compare the effectiveness of these captains' styles because they have vastly different volumes of experience to back it up.

Rick lost a World Cup quarter-final as captain but got two more campaigns to rectify that and put those lessons into play. Most other captains only get one shot at a World Cup. That's not to diminish Rick's achievements, which are monumental; it's more to say that failing to win a title doesn't necessarily make Reado and Sam lesser leaders.

I get on really well with all of them. With Sam it's different because I was there before him, so I've seen the entirety of his evolution as a player and leader. Rick was fully formed by the time I was an All Black, and Reado, too, was a world-class performer when I arrived on the scene.

Geography means I see a lot more of Richie and Reado. Hannah gets along really well with Gemma McCaw and Bridget Read, Richie's girls swim with ours, while Reuben Read plays in the same Rippa Rugby team as Fred. They play for Christchurch, not Lincoln, as much as that pains me!

It was a pretty cool team in 2023. There was Owen Franks' son Beau, Matt Todd's son Lochie, Jimmy Marshall's boy Toby, Izzy Dagg's son Arlo, Ben Funnell's boy Easton, and Luca and Ayla-May, Codie Taylor's son and daughter. In fact, there's only one player in the team whose dad didn't play professional rugby. We counted 450-odd Test caps and more than 1000 first-class ones. It can get a bit awkward sometimes, because we turn up and all the opposition kids and their fathers want to get photos with us before the game. We all ended up at the same club because the partners know the dads are going to be away a lot, so they decided it was an easy way they could help each other out with pick-ups and drop-offs.

When we watch our kids play, we're just like any other fathers cheering them on. But we know everybody is watching us, so we have to be squeaky clean and make sure we're encouraging every kid.

I want to add in here that I became a better player when I had kids. It was my sister-in-law Kayla who alerted me to this, and I think she's right. She was a brilliant hockey player: she went to four Olympic Games and is recognised as one of the best to have ever worn the Black Sticks' singlet. She told me that having kids makes you understand the limitations of a 24-hour day, so you prioritise only what's important: you organise and plan your day to the minute, and cut out a lot of the rest. She and my brother George became quite ruthless in the way they ran themselves and their home, and they got much better at saying no to things that weren't going to help her achieve her goals.

Gelling a team together can sometimes be complex and require work. At other times it happens easily and organically. Israel Dagg, when he came into the All Blacks team in his first year, connected better with Dan Carter than he did with Andrew Hore or Keven Mealamu. As a country kid, I initially found I had more in common with Horey. The younger Pasifika boys gravitated towards Kevvie.

Kevvie is one of the world's great human beings. In fact, there is something seriously wrong with you if you can't get on with him! In Super Rugby, though – and I found this out the hard way – he was ruthless. He cut me once, early in my career: he saw that I was too high at a breakdown and just blew me out of there. I'd played with him the year before in the All Blacks, and I was like, 'What are you up to, Kevvie?' After the game he was sorry about splitting me open, but he was just so competitive and so driven to win that he could only play one way.

The All Blacks team I walked into in 2010 had a massive edge to it. They'd crashed out of the Rugby World Cup in 2007, and had been poor in the Tri Nations in 2009. They were well aware that we hadn't even made a World Cup final since 1995, and they didn't want to go through that feeling again. The side was so driven to be World Cup winners in 2011. The senior guys didn't care if you'd been there one minute, one year or 80 Tests: they expected the same standards from everybody. Training, playing, representing the team away from the field – you had to be on your game all the time. You had to get on board or you were not going to be there for long.

Horey and Kevvie had a reputation as being Richie's henchmen – the guys you had to answer to if you stuffed up. Some of that was more myth than reality, but it's true that those guys were integral in driving standards. They were key figures on and off the field.

I had a great conversation with Robbie Deans back in 2017, when I took over the Crusaders captaincy.

'The most successful week you'll have as captain will be the week you don't have to say anything,' he told me.

That sounded weird – wasn't it my job to speak to and for the team? I told him I wasn't sure where he was coming from and pressed him for more information.

'The best week will be the week you say nothing,' he repeated, 'but that doesn't mean you won't influence the team.'

Robbie was very clever like this. He would offer information only in droplets. He wanted to make sure you were curious enough to ask questions, and weren't just looking for instructions. I must have passed the test, because he explained his thinking.

'Look, if you've identified an issue with the defence, go to your defensive leader – let's say it's Jordan Taufua – and say to him, "Hey, at the end of training I need you to address the huddle and tell them that we need to be squarer on defence." You load the gun for him, but get him to pull the trigger.

'You can do the same for attack, the set piece, whatever. The idea is to get others invested in leadership, in delivering consistent messages. You need to frame what that message is going to be, but you don't need to be the one always delivering it, because then it becomes very monotone.

'You develop these intra-squad leaders, work with them on the messaging and give them the confidence to deliver it. The messages will keep evolving and you'll keep giving them the nod to speak. When the leadership group is fully matured, you won't even have to give the nod – Jordan will instinctively know when it's the right time to hammer home a point about the defence.

'That will be your best week.'

Occasionally, Robbie explained, I would still need to 'top up' the message, but he believed that a common pitfall of captaincy was to think you needed to be the one in constant control of the message. But even if one of my leaders didn't nail his message 100 per cent, he said, I shouldn't feel the need to jump in, because they'd get frustrated when they realised they'd missed something. They'd want to circle back and it would get messy – a bit clunky and ineffective. The other guys would start to roll their eyes and think, 'Here we go again.'

That was the best piece of advice I received on captaincy, because I was that guy he said not to be. As captain, I'd always felt I had to be the top performer: I had to be the guy who always fronted the media, always fronted the meetings, always delivered the messaging. That might have worked at the start. It might even have been momentarily inspiring for the younger guys to see someone who wanted to win so badly that he was trying to do it all on his own, but that approach would have a very short shelf-life.

What Robbie taught me was that the messenger was as important as the message. Take the example of Richie Mo'unga and Sevu Reece, who are great mates. Sevu wasn't the greatest timekeeper and had a habit of getting to meetings as they were due to start, which pushed everything back a bit. I could have gone to him and said, 'Hey, Sevu, I need you to be early for this meeting,' and explained why. He'd have done it, but he would have been thinking it was just the captain asserting his authority because he could. But if Richie said to Sevu, 'Come on, mate, you need to give yourself five more minutes to get to meetings so you're ready to start contributing as soon as we begin,' it would be so much more powerful. Sevu would realise there was a good reason for the message, and that it wasn't some petty power trip.

This line of thinking made me recall discipline in my childhood home. Dad was the chief disciplinarian and the one who tried to keep us four boys in line. When Mum was trying to square us up with 'Charlie' the strap, we knew we had crossed a line.

Working out how to deliver effective messages is a hugely important part of captaining teams. It's all about knowing when to use the carrot and when to use the stick.

Another thing we did well at the Crusaders was to develop future leaders. We had a group of five or six of us who would meet every week, but we also had another group of guys we had identified who would replace us in the next few years. It might have been a young George Bridge, Mitch Drummond or Bryn Hall. Before we knew it, these guys were taking over and captaining their provincial sides.

It was gratifying to know the part I'd played in their development, but even more so because I knew the Crusaders had given them space to develop in their own way.

14

THE GRITTY STUFF

IF THERE IS ONE question I get asked more than any other as an All Black, it is this: 'What is [insert name] really like?'

Often the question is directly about my coaches. That's a hard one to answer honestly. Every rugby coach at the professional level knows the game inside out. They might have more specialist coaching expertise in specific areas, but as a person they have been immersed in the game for most of their lives.

They want to win, too. I have yet to play under a head coach who hasn't wanted the best for their team. There are times when I might not have agreed with certain selections, tactics or strategies, but I have (almost always) known they are making those calls for the right reasons.

When people ask that question, then, they're not really interested in what I think of the coach technically, but in how we get on personally.

I like to keep the details of my coach–player relationships fairly private. If I didn't agree with a coach, or was struggling to get on the same page as them, I would have those conversations in private.

The trickiest period I've had to negotiate in this respect was, not surprisingly, during the Ian Foster/Scott Robertson debate which in reality covered nearly the entirety of the 2020 to 2023 World Cup cycle. Fozzie was always going to be a favourite to get the top job when Shag retired at the end of 2019, but Razor's success at every level he had worked at, from age-group through to Super Rugby, made him a genuinely compelling candidate.

When the All Blacks started losing in ways they never had and against teams they never had, Foster's position became precarious and in 2022 it was widely reported that Razor had been prepped to take over, only for Fozzie to 'save' his job with a win against South Africa at Johannesburg.

I know both men well, and had worked closely with both. So I had a tremendous amount of respect and affection for both. I took zero pleasure in Fozzie's struggles and never publicly advocated for one over the other. Being a Crusaders lifer, every man and his dog wanted to know if I thought Razor should be brought in to take over from Fozzie. It was never my decision, and nor should it have been, so I tried not to waste any energy thinking about it.

I played under three All Blacks head coaches, and they were all, to some extent, products of their upbringing and vocations. Graham Henry was a former school principal who watched over everything with a helicopter view and a discerning eye. Steve Hansen was a former cop, always needing to know everything that was happening in the background. And Fozzie, a clergyman's son, was a very caring, empathetic guy who believed in fairness.

What was Ted really like? Honestly, I didn't have a lot to do with him. In some ways I treated him like a Year 9 would treat the principal. I'd keep my head down and hope that I didn't attract his attention. The only time we really talked was on the Grand Slam tour in 2010, when we had a chat about my grandfather, Nelson Dalzell, who had played every Test on the tour of Great Britain and France in 1953–54.

Ted was the head coach I needed at the start of my All Blacks career. I didn't need somebody constantly in my ear and filling me up with detail. He wanted me to work things out for myself. Like a good headmaster, he let me know when I'd done something wrong, but he wasn't micromanaging every aspect of my rugby education.

Shag was definitely a cop, keeping a close eye on everything like a detective. He could also be brutally gruff, in keeping with his persona. He had no trouble looking a player in the eye and giving him a blunt and brutal gee-up. What Shag did brilliantly was come into the top job from being an assistant and immediately set new goals, making them extremely tough and aspirational. He intuitively knew that, as a continuity appointment, under his watch things could easily get stale if he didn't push the team in new directions.

We got great evidence of that when the press revealed a message on a whiteboard in our team room that said we wanted to be known as the 'most dominant team' in history. Steve was obsessed by going back-to-back as world champions and being the first All Blacks team to win a World Cup away from home. His leadership was really fresh for some of the older guys, who had been around for a while, whereas I was still new, so I was going to be excited no matter what direction we were headed in.

My own relationship with Steve was the most complicated of any of the coaches I have had. I have to frame everything I write here by acknowledging that I believe everything he did had the intention of getting the best out of me. Do I think he went about it the right way? No, I don't, and there were times when his prodding of me probably had the opposite effect. If I had my time again, I would have brought the matter to a head earlier, because I let him chip away at my confidence more than I should have.

Shag was the coach who dropped me in 2013, saying my play had become one-paced. He was the head coach so I had to listen to what he said. I could argue until the cows came home, but ultimately there were just three people I needed to impress. You can stop anybody in the street and ask them for their best XV and their favoured players in each position, and they'll have their own opinion, but it means nothing unless they happen to be one of the three All Blacks selectors. And at that stage I wasn't impressing those men.

Steve was a great rugby coach. His first four or five years in charge of the All Blacks were close to flawless. We were dominating rugby, and it was invigorating to be part of that. The World Cup win in 2015 cemented his legacy.

We couldn't repeat that in 2019, though, and it's fair to say Shag and I didn't finish on the same page, as I was dropped for his final match in charge, the bronze-medal playoff win against Wales. I'd gone from playing every game I was available for to not making the 23. Shag and his assistants, including Fozzie, knew I was pissed off about that. I didn't bother hiding my emotion. They wanted to give others opportunities, and that's what they did.

After that campaign ended and Steve stepped down, New Zealand Rugby was left with a choice between continuity or a new direction. In picking Ian Foster ahead of Razor, Jamie Joseph and Dave Rennie, they chose continuity. For the next four years, I reckon every second question I answered – whether it was from friends, family or random people in the supermarket – was about the coaching of the All Blacks.

It feels like a lifetime ago when the debate first started, and never really died away over the four-year World Cup cycle. I cannot remember how the selection process worked, but as a senior player I would have been asked for my thoughts on the applicants.

My view on this has always been consistent: my job is to play, not to be the high-performance manager and appoint people to those roles. I've always been amazed by how much information gets leaked to the media around coaching appointments – much of it obviously leaked on purpose – and by how much of it is wrong. I decided pretty early on that getting involved in any of that would likely leave me with egg on my face, so I've never done it.

My job is to go out there and play good rugby. Whether Coach A or Coach B is selecting the side, you've got to work hard and impress them, and the best way to do that is to worry about rugby, not politics. That's the sad thing about our sport – and I mean this in general, whether it's the under-7s at the local club or international rugby. Too often there is politics involved and it does affect the team. The back-room machinations never really seemed to disappear over the four years of Foster's reign.

As I said, I liked the guy – still do. Fozzie had a lot of good qualities. He was dedicated to the job and the sport, and he was a more empathetic frontman than either Ted or Shag. He was dealt a bad hand with Covid-19, which caused chaos in the world of professional sport just as it did in all other areas of life, but there were times when I felt we preloaded that excuse a little too readily.

The Covid period was a fascinating time – but let's be honest, the way it affected rugby was far less critical than the effect it had on the physical and economic health of the world more broadly. The administrators jury-rigged up some Super Rugby, and we also got a chance to play a North vs South game, which was a lot of fun. South was dominated by Crusaders, but we also had the likes of Brad Weber, who had made his NPC debut for Otago, and Jordie Barrett, who did the same at Canterbury.

Brad headed up the social side of the week, and we were being true South Islanders. Team North was throwing out some chat about where some of us were from, which was just what was needed to give the game a bit of needle. The match itself went down to the wire, and we won when Will Jordan hauled in a cross-field kick over his best mate, Mitch Hunt, and scored in the corner. After the game it was like we were back in club footy: we had boat races (drinking games), and the referees had one too, run by Ma'a Nonu. Even though we were playing at an empty stadium, it's one of my favourite rugby memories.

Because of the result, everybody was talking about how cool it would be to have a three-game series – home and away, with the third alternating year by year. There is merit in developing the concept, but a lot of thought needs to go into where you'd fit it in, who would be available, who would select and coach the teams, and what the criteria would be for playing for North or South – especially when there are a lot of guys who, like me, have claims to both.

I can't say that the Super Rugby Aotearoa titles the Crusaders won in 2020 and 2021 and the Super Rugby Pacific titles we took out in 2022 and 2023 gave me as much satisfaction as the others. In 2017, 2018 and 2019, we were thrown a whole bunch of different challenges, having to travel to Argentina, South Africa and Japan. It was just different. Having said that, it was still fantastic to win those trophies.

It grates on me to this day when people say we won seven Super Rugby tournaments in a row. We didn't. While we did win titles every year, we didn't win every title available. We had an opportunity to win the hastily assembled trans-Tasman competition in 2021, but we didn't. We won all our games against Australian opposition but failed to pick up a bonus point against the Rebels. They scored a couple of late tries and so we missed out on the final by a differential of six points. Along with the Blues and Highlanders, we won all our games but missed the final. The Highlanders went up to Auckland and were beaten by the Blues. It was our own fault. We couldn't feel sorry for ourselves, because we'd known what we had to do and we hadn't done it.

So I get a bit annoyed when I hear people talk about our 'unbroken' run of Super Rugby titles, because it was broken. Talk like that belittles the Blues, who won that competition fair and square. We all had the chance to win it and they did. End of story.

*

The Covid-19 pandemic did affect international rugby in a pretty big way. The All Blacks were scheduled to play 15 Tests in 2020 but would only play six.

Of those, I played in five. The first, a 16–16 draw against Australia in Wellington, which was becoming a bit of a bogey ground for us, was accompanied by a hit to the head that gave me a delayed concussion. It felt like a minor bellringer during the game, but shortly afterwards I crashed and burned, so I missed the next Test, in Auckland.

We then travelled to Australia for a set of Tests that came with a few red flags. We split two Tests with the Wallabies but also, shockingly, lost to Argentina for the first time on a tough night in Sydney.

We'd had tight games against Los Pumas in the past, but we'd always found a way to finish stronger than them down the stretch. On this night we got frustrated. We wanted to use the ball with width and score tries, but our penalty count was through the roof. Their flanker Marcos Kremer was immense, while Emiliano Boffelli was kicking everything within 55 metres of our try line. We had an opportunity to snatch the win at the death, but our discipline cost us.

That was one of those games I'd love to go back and play

again. It was like losing to Ireland for the first time – once the aura of invincibility is gone, it's gone forever. Now your opponents know that you bleed just like other teams. I liken it to a household power struggle: big brother dominates for years, but when the little brother wins a fight for the first time, everything changes and everyone knows it. The big brother might long for the days when his mere presence was enough to win battles, but he knows that time is over. That match was Argentina's awakening, as they demonstrated when they beat us in Christchurch the following year.

We ended the season by winning the Rugby Championship (without South Africa), after thrashing Argentina 38–0 in Newcastle in some of the hottest conditions in which I've ever played rugby, but the title felt hollow.

Being placed in quarantine for two weeks on our return home was another hurdle I had never expected to have to jump during my rugby career, and something Fozzie and his team had to plan for that no other All Blacks coaching group have faced.

I'd been talking to Nic Gill about how I was going to cope, because I needed to train and couldn't afford to sit on my backside for 14 days watching movies and eating room service. Gilly had a stationary bike delivered to my room. Others had rowing machines or treadmills. I'd mentioned to Gilly that my brother Adam was trying to run the equivalent of the length of New Zealand in a year. There was no way I could catch him because he was too far ahead, so Gilly said, 'Why don't we bike it?'

I'd get up, flick the telly on, jump on the bike and chip away 50 kilometres or so at a time. Eventually we did it, all in a straight line. A teammate who had a rowing machine paddled the Cook Strait for me.

That was pretty much how I filled in my quarantine, although my in-laws also dropped off a couple of Wasgij puzzles – these are jigsaws where you have to imagine the scene based on the picture on the box. I'm not a gamer. Most of the other boys were on PlayStations or Xboxes day and night, probably loving the fact that they had an excuse to do nothing else. I was just going silently crazy. It took me a week to complete one Wasgij. I was getting myself ready to put the final piece in but it was nowhere to be found. I could have cried. I turned over the entire room trying to find it but it was officially missing in action.

The next year, when we had a ten-day isolation followed by a two-day home isolation, a few of us did a 24-hour Wattbike challenge. We did it to raise money for the Chalky Carr Trust. Chalky was the All Blacks' logistics manager and a Christchurch earthquake hero who had died from pancreatic cancer in 2018. I had a saddle-sore arse for a very long time afterwards, but it was worth it. Brad Mooar, who was a trustee, did it with us and put in an awesome effort before he blew out. I had numb fingers and hands for about two weeks and a numb foot for three. It was insane. I thought I did pretty well with 611 kilometres, but Gilly ended up breaking a record by covering 781 kilometres.

The pandemic exposed us to a narrower range of opposition, as it did with everybody. It was around this time that the All Blacks had a noticeable drop-off in form, and didn't improve in areas we needed to be better at. Whether it was through not playing enough, and not playing enough different teams, or simply through us not performing on the field or the training track, I'm not sure, but it was a pretty bumpy road from 2019 through to the end of 2022 at least.

In 2021 I was named All Blacks captain, as Sam Cane was on the sidelines for some time with a neck injury, but it wasn't all smooth sailing. The team assembled but there were two of us – Richie Mo'unga and I – who were joining a couple of days later, as our partners were expecting what our teammates dubbed 'lockdown babies'.

Penelope was due in two weeks, just before the All Blacks were flying out to play Australia in the Rugby Championship. Our crystal-ball plan was to have Penny on time, smoothly, calmly, with everyone happy and healthy. In August, at the captain's run just before we played Australia at Auckland, though, Hannah rang to say something was up. She'd just had a scan, the baby hadn't grown and had actually regressed in weight, so the doctors were starting to get a little worried. Although I felt quite stressed, I kept it to myself.

Hannah and I agreed that we'd go home to Christchurch in two days and would see our midwife, who was a family friend, and make a decision. Our midwife took a scan and said, 'Yes, we need to induce – the baby isn't growing.'

Because of Covid restrictions, we couldn't go back and forth from the hospital. Hannah went in first and was induced, then I went in a couple of hours later. Penelope was safely born, and while I wouldn't have used the word 'scrawny', that was what the midwife called her. It was probably fair. She also developed a boil on her hip, which needed to be carefully monitored.

Penelope was slowly getting stronger and I had my bags packed about four times, waiting to go to the airport. I was told I had a room at a quarantine hotel and was booked on a flight, but every time team management would get in touch with me at the last minute and say my room was no longer guaranteed, which meant I faced the prospect of flying to Australia, having no spot, flying home and having to do two weeks in quarantine here before having the opportunity to fly out again. There was no point going until that bed was confirmed, and it kept getting pushed further and further out.

Richie and I were in the same boat. He'd just had his son Marley, and finally we got the call but there was only one spot. They gave it to Richie because they thought it would be easier for a back to come straight from hotel quarantine and be ready to play.

So I sat at home and watched the guys play Test matches in September and October that I would have been skippering, had everything gone to plan. The side beat Australia in Perth, comfortably beat Argentina twice and split two games with South Africa, the margin being two points in each. Watching on like this was a new experience for me, and I hated it. This was the first time in more than a decade that I had watched a string of All Blacks games from home. I watched them alone, because Hannah soon understood that I didn't want a running commentary – I just needed to be able to mutter at the TV screen.

One positive spinoff of this international lay-off was that I enjoyed a rare outing for Canterbury. We played Wellington and lost 30–35 after extra time. Dane Coles was playing for Wellington and we were chirping away at each other. It was a lot of fun to get back out there with guys I'd played a lot of rugby with – Luke Romano was playing for Canterbury, and

Dom Bird was in the Wellington team. It had a bit of an old-school feel to it. There were a couple of youngsters with big raps playing too – Tamaiti Williams and Dallas McLeod – so it was good to get a sense of them.

I finally made it onto a plane and met the team in Washington DC, where I retook the captaincy armband when we played the United States later in October. It was a great occasion to be part of, although the score was a lopsided 104–14. We had a small ceremony for former Crusaders and Chiefs player Sean Wainui, who had died suddenly just prior to the tour. That was nice because the boys who had played a lot of rugby with him were definitely hurting.

The whole time we were away, we were under Covid restrictions. We were allowed out late at night and early in the morning, but we had to stay away from people. We had routine testing to make sure we didn't get Covid rampaging through the team. People could join the group, but they had to be tested too. After the Australian leg, Scooter Barrett and Patrick Tuipulotu had left the team to get back to New Zealand for the birth of their children, but their coming and going had to be managed carefully because there were limited spots in MIQ – the hotel-based system of managed isolation and quarantine – and we were acutely aware of criticism that we were getting favoured treatment because we were rugby players.

The team became pretty tight during these times. Traditional socialising – getting out and about in cities, and eating out or having a couple of beers at a pub – were off the table. We had to make our own fun, and we did pretty well. It was such a weird time, though. It didn't matter if you were an athlete, whether you worked abroad or whether you were just trying to live a normal life in Auckland. Nobody had heard of a 'rapid antigen test' in 2019, and yet in 2021 and 2022 it seemed they dominated every conversation.

It was a bit different in the United Kingdom, because they'd already been through their Covid peak. In Wales, we played at Millennium Stadium in front of a packed house of fans who had been starved of live sport, and we were being told that, apart from during the game, we weren't allowed within 20 metres of the sideline. We had friends and family in the crowd so we were trying to have conversations with them, with everybody else listening in. It was so awkward.

We beat Wales comfortably, but I felt a bit sorry for them. The Test was played outside the international window, so they had a whole lot of guys unavailable and their youngsters were a bit outmatched. That was Beauden's 100th test, and he scored a couple of tries to mark the occasion. We ended up with the most points scored in a calendar year, but we'd all remember 2021 for the bizarre time it was.

We handled Italy in Rome pretty well, but the tour took a downward turn after that. We went to Dublin and lost to Ireland for the third time in succession. It was bloody frustrating, and I felt we'd been dragged into playing their style of rugby. There had been a recurring theme of them forcing us into mistakes. It was my first loss as captain, too, so it had an added layer of hurt.

Our final match was in Paris, and some of the frustrations I sensed among the group were coming to a head. I hadn't been on tour for the entire time, but you could tell the boys had one foot on the plane home. They were constantly talking about it.

Winning the lineout against Tom Palmer and England, at Twickenham, 6 November 2010, on the end-of-year tour. We won our matches against England, Wales, Scotland and Ireland, and in doing so completed the Grand Slam. We would win 12 out of 13 games that year. *(Matthew Impey/Photosport)*

The 2011 Rugby World Cup Pool A match against France, at Eden Park, 24 September 2011. We won the game 37–17. When we met again in the final, it would be a very different scoreline. *(FRANCK FIFE/AFP via Getty Images)*

Tony Woodcock scored our only try in the 2011 Rugby World Cup final against France. A game we won by the slimmest of margins: 8–7. *(Dave Lintott/Photosport)*

Left to right: Dad, Hannah, my wife, my granddad John Whitelock, me, my nana Lyndall and Mum, after winning the Rugby World Cup in 2011.

Left to right: Luke, me, Adam and George during the Super 15 rugby preseason match Hurricanes vs Crusaders, at Manggatainoka, Wairarapa, February 2012. (Dave Lintott)

Charging over for a try in our first Rugby Championship as world champions, 6 October 2012, at FNB Stadium, in Johannesburg, South Africa. We won the game 32–16. (David Rogers/ Getty Images)

Going up for the ball during the Rugby Championship against the Springboks, at Eden Park, 2013. The Boks were part of my dreams and nightmares way before I ever got to play them. We had the better of them in 2013. In fact, we were unstoppable that year, winning 14 Tests out of 14. (Dave Lintott)

In the dressing room with Aaron Smith after defeating Australia 51–20 to retain the Bledisloe Cup, 23 August 2014. We'd played a lot of footy since our days at Feilding High. By the end of our careers we'd racked up 280 Tests between us. (Andrew Cornaga/Photosport)

he Rugby World Cup final against Australia, 31 October 2015. Winning in 2015 was more atisfying than 2011 in many vays. It's hard to explain without ounding conceited, but in 2011 was as naive as could be and here was a definite sense within he group that New Zealand eeded to wIn u World Cup after 24 years of failure. By 2015, it felt ike we truly deserved it. (Andrew Cornaga/Photosport)

Enjoying a quiet moment with Aaron Smith after the 2015 World Cup.

Sharing a moment with 'William' and Hannah after the final in 2015.

The lads from Lincoln University. The Webb Ellis trophy doesn't hold as many beers as the Bledisloe, but it still tastes pretty good. *(Richard Heathcote-Handout/World Rugby via Getty Images)*

Shaking hands with Luke after our Super Rugby match on 6 June 2017. Crusaders vs Highlanders, at AMI Stadium, Christchurch, New Zealand. *(Martin Hunter/Photosport)*

Tackling Johnny Sexton in the third Test against the Lions, at Eden Park, 8 July 2017. This was a game (and series) that we would end up drawing. That tour still grates on me to this day. You only get one shot in your career at the Lions. I didn't feel that the Crusaders or the All Blacks did themselves justice. *(©INPHO/James Crombie/Photosport)*

Celebrating back-to-back titles for the Crusaders against the Golden Lions of South Africa, in Christchurch, 2018. The previous year we'd done something special by beating them at altitude at Ellis Park, Johannesburg. Given the challenges we faced, those two titles, and the one after in 2019, gave me the most satisfaction of the seven between 2017 and 2023. (MARTY MELVILLE/ AFP via Getty Images)

Watching my brother Luke captain the All Blacks against a French XV, in Lyon, 2017. All four of us have been captains in our careers. You can trace the leadership traits back to all those nights re-watching games on TV together, pausing and quizzing each other on what we would have done if we were captain. Left to right: Adam, Tiffany, me, Mum, Dad, Claire and Luke.

In the sheds with the Dave Gallaher Trophy after our third game against France in 2018. We won the match 49–14 and the series 3–0. It was my fourth game as All Blacks captain. I'm not going to lie, I would have loved to have been appointed as the permanent All Blacks captain after Reado retired, but I am still forever grateful for the 18 opportunities I received. (Phil Walter/Getty Images)

We got the job done against Argentina to wrap up the Rugby Championship in 2018. That year was another curious one for the All Blacks. We were successful, but something indefinable was missing. The best way to sum it up is to say that while we were still capable of playing quality rugby, teams did not fear us like they once had. *(JUAN MABROMATA/AFP via Getty Images)*

My boots commemorating 100 matches for the All Blacks. My school coach Rick Francis always told us that numbers were the easiest way to set goals. When I first started, Owen Franks had written 'Play 100 Tests' as a goal on his wall. This blew me away. It still does when I think about it, because when we started playing for the All Blacks nobody had played 100, and only Richie

Four boys, all born within 1770 days of each other, all playing rugby for New Zealand in either sevens or 15s. George is All Black number 1093, I'm 1104 and Luke is 1129. Adam is All Blacks Sevens number 252, the only back among us.

Beating the old foe, the Springboks, in the 2019 World Cup, in Japan. Tests against the Boks have always been my favourites to play. (© ZOPH/ Photosport)

Playing with Panasonic Wild Knights, David Pocock in support. At the conclusion of the 2019 World Cup, I moved to Japan, having signed a sabbatical-year contract with Robbie Deans at Panasonic Wild Knights. I wanted to improve as a player and, at that stage of my career, playing in a different environment under a highly successful coach was going to be the best way to do that. It was a new challenge and every time I had been challenged in my career I had improved as a result. (Courtesy of Saitama Panasonic Wild Knights)

Leading the haka as captain against Australia, at Eden Park, on 24 September 2022. I've been fortunate enough to have never played on a team that lost the Bledisloe Cup. *(Hannah Peters/ Getty Images)*

Four generations of Whitelocks. My first-born son, Fred, is the baby of the Whitelock family.

Richie Mo'unga and me during the Super Rugby final, 2023. Our respective last games for the Crusaders. Final score: 25–20. What a way to go out. *(Andrew Curnaga/Photosport)*

My last game on home soil. The match itself was a dramatic comeback win over the Wallabies after being down 17–3. I'm pictured here with the kids, Fred, Penelope and Iris. *(Joe Allison/Getty Images)*

One of my primary goals in 2023 was to reach 150 caps.

The quarter-final against Ireland in the 2023 World Cup. With Ireland deep inside our 22, Brodie made a low tackle and I went high, so I could release straightaway and seize my opportunity. I got my hands on the ball – then the whistle sounded. Even though I knew I'd got it right, I still felt anxious that Wayne Barnes hadn't seen it the same way. I needn't have worried. We won 28–24. (Lionel Hahn/Getty Images)

The last Test I played for the All Blacks still haunts me. The 12–11 defeat crushed me in ways other losses haven't. As much as losing grates, you learn to take the rough with the smooth. (Adam Pretty/World Rugby via Getty Images)

Luke and I with the kids after our Top 14 match against Bayonne, at Stade du Hameau, in Pau, France, 9 March 2024. *(Icon Sport/Getty Images)*

I'm appreciative of the upbringing I had. I love the farming life because it enforces self-reliance. Sometimes that self-reliance can bite you on the bum if you don't make sure you stay connected with the outside world. That's where my work with Farmstrong comes in. I'm proud to be an ambassador for this rural wellbeing initiative, because while I love the farming life, it does come with unique pressures. *(Emmily Harmer for Farmstrong)*

Left to right: Nana Lyndall, Hannah (pregnant with Iris), me holding Fred, Grandad John and Mum and Dad, gathered around Jum's jersey. We bought the jersey at auction in the UK. Jum wore it in the third match played against Australia, in Dunedin, on 2 September 1905. It's believed to be the oldest All Blacks jersey in New Zealand. There are things in my life I believe strongly in, and one of those is that it doesn't matter when or how many games someone played for the All Blacks, we are all temporary guardians of this magnificent garment we call 'the Jersey'.

The quarantine rules had been relaxed a little and people were thinking about that, too.

As I saw it, we were coming up with excuses for a loss before we'd even played the game. We were talking in the media about how tired we were, and it was like a punch in the face to hear us talking that way. I wasn't insensitive to the fact that many guys had been away from home for longer than me, but we had a Test to play before we got on that plane. That should have been our only focus.

Teams in the past would have never allowed that sort of attitude to creep in. There would have been too many leaders putting a lid on it before it started. This was exactly the sort of thing we'd talked about in 2011: that there would be times when things were not going our way, but we just had to find a way to win. Those victories might not be the prettiest, but they're the ones you look back on with real pride.

The Test was in the balance, but not for long enough. France scored a couple of maul tries, which hurt. We allowed them to stack some easy points and they ran away 40–25.

As captain, I had to hand over the Dave Gallaher Cup for Tests between New Zealand and France. That trophy meant a lot to me, and I know it means a lot to the servicemen and women of New Zealand. Gallaher was our 1905 Originals captain, a guy who fought in the Boer War and signed up for World War I, even though he should have been too old to serve. He ended up making the ultimate sacrifice for his country on the fields of Passchendaele. Playing for a trophy with his name engraved on it is something we should never take lightly.

During my time in the All Blacks, we always tried as a team to embrace that sort of history. A lot of things we aspire to as All Blacks started with that touring team, who left New Zealand on 30 July 1905 and didn't arrive home until March the following year. Any game against France is a huge occasion and a big Test in every sense. I hope the trophy means as much to the French as it does to us, because I hated handing it over.

*

Things started to get crunchy around this period. Serious questions were being asked as to whether we had the pieces in place to reclaim the Webb Ellis Cup. The end-of-year reviews were pretty cutting, but I also questioned why we were waiting for the end of the season before we tried to sort things out. It meant we had not done enough to fix the issues in season.

Still, it was brutal for the right reasons. We knew we needed to be better, we wanted to get better and we expected to get better.

The one thing we hadn't done consistently over the past four years was more important: winning. We had set a number of unwanted records, which was always going to put the spotlight on the coach.

At times it was uncomfortable. I had been captain of a successful Crusaders side who had won multiple titles under Robertson, and it was no secret that if Fozzie lost his job then Razor would be taking over. I wouldn't say it put me in an awkward position, because I knew my lane and stuck to it, but I also knew that people wanted to know what I *really* thought. Well, what I really thought was that it was somebody else's decision to make, and that I would give 100 per cent to whoever coached me.

Things came to a head after we lost the July 2022 home series to Ireland. That saw the departures of assistant coaches John Plumtree and Brad Mooar, with Joe Schmidt taking on more responsibility and Jason 'Mutt' Ryan coming in as forwards coach.

I have good relationships with my coaches, professionally and personally, so it was a tough situation. I was wondering, 'Do I message Plums or Brad? Do I ring them, leave them alone or go and see them?' It was a really tough spot to be in. These were good people, and smart. They knew I was a part of a group that had reviewed their work and found it to be below the standard that was required.

We were not being coached well enough. We needed to change. I recognised that after the northern tour at the end of 2021, when we were well beaten by France and Ireland and, in my opinion, had prepared too many excuses for our underperformance. The balance of the coaching group wasn't right. They all had strengths, but we didn't have enough strengths across the board. There were holes in the group.

Just as I believe the All Blacks is no place to select development players, it should also be reserved for the best of the best coaches, but the appointment process doesn't really allow for that because you're forced to assemble a team beforehand. In fact, the best coaching team might be a mix of candidates from the various groups put forward. Fozzie didn't have enough international experience and skills in his team, and Plums and Brad paid the price for that.

That's not me as a player saying this was the reason we were playing poorly. As a senior player, you can't sit and wait for things to happen. We had to be more vocal and proactive about making sure we were getting what we needed, and sometimes we needed to have hard conversations before issues blew up into full-scale problems. It could have been as simple as me or Guzz having a meeting with Fozzie and saying, 'Hey, our standards in maul defence are slipping – we need to spend more time on it.' Human nature, however, means those conversations can be difficult to have and are easier to avoid, but that's not how the best teams operate.

Putting all the politics and all the bullshit to the side, the thing that hurts the most is that we didn't play as well as we ourselves expected. The standards that we tried to uphold as players were higher than what the public expected of us, but during 2021–22 we weren't playing as well as we needed to. And the results certainly weren't as we would have liked them. It was such a challenging time. People were losing their jobs or being threatened with losing their jobs. All those things that were publicised, rightly or wrongly, were at the forefront of our minds.

It's no great secret that our win over South Africa at Johannesburg in August 2022 saved Foster's job. We were coming off five losses in six Tests, including that unprecedented home-series loss to Ireland. Long story short, there was a group of players that went to New Zealand Rugby chief executive Mark Robinson's room following the Test to lobby strongly for Fozzie to remain in the role. As part of the leadership group I was among them, but I can honestly say I was blindsided by the idea. Others in the group were really keen on going, while some members of the squad didn't even have a clue it was happening.

Was it the right thing to do? Good question.

It's a sticking point for me because, as I've said, it is not our job as players to back or sack the coach. If you flip that scenario on its head and we had a group of players approaching the CEO to have a popular coach sacked, how do you think that would be received by the public? What we had was a group of emotional people, in an emotional situation, influencing decisions that should not be based on emotion.

To me, what happened that night is not what good leadership looks like.

As a player, the first thing you have to be loyal to is the team, the jersey, the fern, whatever word you want to use. That has to come first. Sometimes that means great people, outstanding human beings, miss out. There have been great players who have missed out on being All Blacks, or on going to a World Cup, because someone is better.

The world's worst-kept secret was that Razor was basically given the word by NZR leadership to start assembling his coaching team around that time. It's been widely reported, so I'm not talking out of school.

It's true that I felt stuck in the middle. I have relationships with Razor and Fozzie that are built on trust, and while they're different relationships, I value them both.

I know people find it frustrating that I am hazy on this subject but it is not indifference – it is more that I have always needed to look at it dispassionately. I knew that there was a good chance that if I planted my flag on one or the other's mast and the other person got the job, then I would be compromised. I didn't allow myself to have a strong opinion one way or the other as to whether Team Robertson should be brought in or Team Foster should be retained and I can't suddenly retroactively form one for the sake of a headline. I couldn't afford to get bogged down in that external noise.

I was focused on being a better rugby player and doing my part to improve the fortunes of the team in the only way I could control.

At the risk of repeating myself, my job as a player was not to select the coach, so I stayed out of it, hence my feeling of being blindsided when the leadership group decided to approach the CEO in South Africa and make an impassioned pitch for Foster's retention.

I never looked at it as Foster versus Robertson either, so I might have differed from others in that respect. I've never had a head coach that was perfect. I looked at what the coaching group as a whole could offer. It's the way coaches complement each other's strengths and cover each other's weaknesses that is the key.

We weren't the only team going through this type of drama, either. You look at England replacing Eddie Jones with Steve Borthwick, and in turn, Australia pulling the trigger and ditching Dave Rennie for Jones. In the latter case it created massive upheaval and had no positive effect. There was always a danger we could have faced a similar proposition had we pivoted away from Foster and brought in a whole new group.

In the end, did New Zealand Rugby get the decision right? I'd ask a different question: did we win the World Cup?

Because of the politics, the indecision and the drama of the past year, the only way we, the larger New Zealand rugby community, could get a pass mark was to win it all.

As blunt as that is, there are different things we could have done to win the World Cup, but they didn't happen. Is it because we didn't change the coaching group? That's hypothetical. We could have won with a new coaching group. We could have lost in the quarter-final. It's pointless speculating.

The sad thing about it was that if we as players were being asked who should be the coach, that showed we didn't have the right systems in place. Yes, we were dealing with the coach day to day, but it shouldn't be up to us as players to say he was the right or wrong person for the job, or that he needed to develop more in this area or that, or that he needed assistants who were stronger in one area or another.

All of those things should have been sorted by the time he became All Blacks coach; from that point it should be all about the finer details. Too often during that period we heard that coaches were working on developing in certain areas. I know everyone has to be on a constant search for improvement, but that was a sure sign we didn't have the right building blocks in place to start with.

It was interesting to see how differently coaching and playing were being treated. As a player, you're under selection pressure every single week. I'm not saying that coaches and players should be treated the same – you can't chop and change coaches every week – but I did have conversations with a few people who said, 'This is what we face every day as a player – if we put in a terrible performance, it could be our last one. It doesn't matter who you are or what you're doing.' Meanwhile, you could stack up weak coaching performances and yet a change would be treated as the last resort. If you're being really unemotional about the situation, an expectation of winning is a natural part of a professional, high-performance sports environment. It's what we face every week. That's not to say

Fozzie should have lost his job; it's more an observation about how overblown the entire issue became, though obviously if you were viewing it through his eyes, you'd get a different perspective. This was his livelihood, and in some respects his reputation, on the line.

In the weeks following that win in Johannesburg, Fozzie received the official backing of New Zealand Rugby to continue as coach through to the end of the 2023 Rugby World Cup. But I had stopped reading anything on the subject. I wasn't even going onto websites to check on general news in case I saw a headline that might hook me in. I know I'm like a broken record on this, but I knew that if I got caught up, three hours later I'd find myself scrolling through some comments section at the bottom of a story, which wouldn't be helpful to me at all.

When Mutt Ryan came in as the new forwards coach, I already knew him well. He'd been a Crusaders coach for six years and I'd worked very closely with him around lineout, scrum and breakdown. We worked together well and had a good relationship. Jase's wife, Cath, and Hannah are good friends, so we'd been to the same weddings and parties and I knew him socially as well. While there's nothing unhealthy about maintaining friendships with coaches away from the training ground, perception-wise it can be a fine line to tread because whenever there is speculation about a coach's role or their future, you will be described as being in their 'camp'.

I found it a tight spot to be in. Niggly. I knew and respected people on both sides. I was excited for Mutt and Joe Schmidt, and was looking forward to getting stuck in and working with them, but I was disappointed for Brad and Plums, the guys they were replacing.

Within the All Blacks set-up, the coaching dynamics changed straightaway. We had conceded a lot of maul tries and it was not a strength of ours. We were leaking points through the heart of the tight five. We'd been trying to fix it but had struggled to do so. When Mutt was first appointed, he talked to me about what I thought was happening, but he also had his own views and immediately began work to tighten things up. Joe Schmidt took more of a big-picture view and spent a lot of time studying our defensive structures, which were different from what most European teams were using.

We improved in a lot of areas, although ultimately it wasn't quite enough to win the 2023 Rugby World Cup – which I'll get to soon. These days the ship is being helmed by Razor, but before I get to him, I want to take a short detour to Japan – and to Robbie Deans.

*

It was the coach of the Panasonic Wild Knights who was a big drawcard in convincing me to take my sabbatical in Japan. The club, owned by the Panasonic corporation, was based in Ota-Gunma, north-west of Tokyo, but has since been rebranded as the Saitama Wild Knights and relocated.

I had heard great stories about Robbie from ex-players of his – in particular about how he would challenge you in different ways – and I was stoked to get the opportunity to experience his mentorship. Because we were in a part of the world where we didn't have many friends and could not speak the local language, Robbie often flicked me a text: 'What are you doing? Let's go and get a cup of tea.'

Sometimes that cuppa would last an hour, sometimes it was five hours and Hannah would be wondering where we'd got to. We'd talk rugby, we'd talk leadership, we'd talk coaching. His wealth of knowledge and experience was incredible. Because I'd been in leadership roles at the Crusaders and had a few more miles under the bonnet, I felt like I could contribute, not just listen, and we bounced a lot of ideas off each other in those discussions. This wasn't like I was with Brad Thorn, when I was just a sponge looking to soak up everything I could. This was more like a conversation, but those conversations sharpened my rugby edge, which had started to get a little blunt.

Robbie was a different coach with a different perspective and a different way of looking at rugby and how it intersected with life. I loved chewing the fat with him. At the same time, his wife, Penny, was incredible with Hannah and the kids, and made their transition to living in a foreign country so much easier.

This was a guy who had played for the All Blacks, had coached the All Blacks as an assistant, had coached the Wallabies and the Crusaders, and had had great success in Japan, too. For me it was an amazing opportunity to bounce ideas around, and I didn't waste it. When I came back to New Zealand, our relationship continued. He felt comfortable messaging me about things he was seeing in games, and they were invariably sharp and useful pieces of analysis. To have a person of his experience helping me grow when I was a 100-Test All Black was priceless.

*

Scott Robertson, although very much his own man, benefited from Robbie's tuition when he was a Canterbury and Crusaders player. His appointment to the All Blacks role, which came more than six months before the 2023 World Cup, became a huge story because of the unprecedented timing of the decision, although that was a red herring as far as I was concerned. I can't speak for everybody in the team, but for me it had zero bearing on how I prepared for the World Cup campaign. I would be surprised if it had an adverse effect on anybody. If it did, they weren't concentrating on the right things.

Mutt Ryan had stayed on as an assistant to Razor, but otherwise a whole new coaching team had come with him. I can't predict the future, but I know Razor has always been hyper-focused on being successful, and has so far managed to put together a spectacular CV at club, NPC, age-group and Super Rugby level.

I first met him back in 2008, when I was training with Canterbury. I was on a steep learning curve – just a watching brief, really – and Razor was the same with his coaching. We didn't say anything to each other but we were just learning and growing, me as a player and him as a coach. It wasn't until 2017 that I had him as a coach, because I'd been away with the All Blacks when he was in charge of Canterbury. He had a really good relationship with all my brothers, though. It was actually quite strange when he got the Crusaders job because he got on so well with George, Adam and Luke – I was the odd one out.

Razor is 100 per cent different from the other head coaches I've had. For one thing, he's a total surf bum. Wherever we go, he's always checking the wind and the swell and working out whether he's going to get an opportunity to surf. He lives that saltwater-in-his-veins cliché.

Can he be annoying? Has he got too many ideas? Can it be hard to keep him focused on what he primarily needs to do? Yes to all of those questions, but that's not what defines him as a rugby coach. Razor drives an incredible campaign and never gets less than 100 per cent buy-in from his players.

We complemented each other so well because we challenged each other. You can't have a team full of people like me, or a leadership group full of people like him. But we balanced each other really well. He innately knew what people he needed around him to balance out his coaching group.

Take Scott Hansen, for example. He was a lot like his namesake Steve in that he could have direct, hard-out conversations with his players.

Scott was also very detail oriented. He was a huge influence on my last three or four years as a player in New Zealand. Even in the All Blacks I used him as an external sounding board and the experience he had accumulated coaching around the world and under coaches like Wayne Smith and Jamie Joseph was invaluable.

In his first year as head coach at Super Rugby level, 2017, Razor was definitely green. That's no different to every new coach or captain I've had. As a first-year captain, I was green as well, and I think that helped make the year an enjoyable one for the team. We didn't pretend we had all the answers.

Every day I walked into Rugby Park, there was an energy that's hard to describe. We put a heavy emphasis on skills. We were always playing games that focused on improving our fine skills. It was a high-energy campaign that I will always look back on fondly.

Without doubt Razor sees things differently. Here's a story from our first year working together that sums him up perfectly.

I had played massive minutes for the Crusaders and the All Blacks over the past few years, and my body was screaming at me. A niggly Achilles would plague me for the rest of my career. Razor got me into his office and showed me a photo. He's dyslexic and has had to find different ways to learn, so in that respect he's similar to me, in that we were both written off as dumb early but in reality we just needed different modes of learning.

He showed me a photo of a rooster leading a group of hens across a bridge. He pointed at the rooster and said, 'This is you.'

'Okay,' I said. 'Where are you going with this one, Ray?'

'If there's something that needs doing, you're the first one to do it. If there's a drill that needs demonstrating, you're first up and doing it. But I need this …' Then he showed me another photo, and I saw a dog with three sheep in a little mob.

Now I got really confused. Razor grew up in Mount Maunganui and knew the sea, but he knew absolutely nothing about farms and the way they work. What was he trying to do here, double-bluff me? Ray pointed to this dog in the photo and kept calling it a collie. Well, that was his first mistake. It was actually a heading dog. They are descended from Border collies but technically they're their own breed. By now, though, I was sure the ins and outs of working-dog breeds wasn't the point of this conversation.

What Razor was showing me, in his inimitable style, was that he needed me to bark from behind. To get the flock moving in the right direction without leading the way every time. It was one of the most valuable leadership lessons I ever received, and it was all done with a photo of a dog Ray couldn't even identify properly.

Actually, it was a nice way of framing my leadership faults. That was what might have annoyed Shag a bit, I reflected. I might sometimes have looked like I wasn't listening, but Razor was the first person – from a leadership perspective at least – who demonstrated to me that there were different ways of doing things, and that a bit of back-seat driving wasn't a sign of weakness.

He has a unique way of being able to get through to the most stubborn of subjects. If nothing else, the All Blacks environment will be a bloody interesting place to be over the next few years.

Our head coach Scott 'Razor' Robertson celebrates with some break-dance moves after winning the Super Rugby Pacific final, **2023.** *(MICHAEL BRADLEY/AFP via Getty Images)*

15

DARKENING THE JERSEY

PARIS, 28 OCTOBER 2023. Some guys like to rush through the post-match steps. Off the field, into the showers, soap, water, smellies and into their number ones. They have places to be and people to see.

I've never been that guy. I like to take my time, soak up the scene and fold myself into conversations about the previous 80 minutes. As I've got older and more banged up, it takes me longer to remove all the strapping. It's a job best done with a cold drink and a chat.

On this night I'm particularly slow. There's something nagging away at me. I've never been one for extroverted displays of emotion. It's not how I'm built. It's not that I'm a closed book, you'll know if I'm happy or not – and there are times over the past few weeks when I haven't been thrilled about things – but I'm never overly demonstrative about it.

The sheds at Stade de France were very quiet after the 2023 Rugby World Cup final. I wanted to spend some time in protection mode, making sure everybody was feeling as good as they possibly could after what was a shattering result. There were guys I wanted to touch base with before I started the long process of getting back into my formal wear, my number ones.

There was Nepo Laulala, with whom I'd played a lot of rugby; I felt a special connection with him because my brother George was his first captain in professional rugby. There was Richie Mo'unga, a guy I loved playing with, and one of the biggest reasons why the good times came back to the Crusaders. There was a time when my own kids said that he, not their dad, was their favourite player. Dane Coles – Colesy – who didn't get to play in the final and was leaving New Zealand rugby, was one of my favourite blokes in the sport. An absolute pest to play against but a dream to play with. And Brodie Retallick, Guzz. My connection with that bloke needs no further explanation, other than to say we'd reached that stage where we didn't need to talk to know what each other was thinking.

There was no real anger in the room, just a sense of disappointment. It wasn't about unfulfilled destiny, because it was ingrained in us not to think that we were entitled to anything. We knew we had to earn it. My view on professional rugby tends to be very black and white. There are no style points or moral victories; you either get the job done (win) or you don't get the job done (draw or lose). On this night, we didn't get the job done. South Africa did.

When you view the game through that simple lens, you strip away a lot of the negative emotion and baggage that can come with it, but right then, in that moment, those feelings were welling up in me. By this time I was the very last person to get changed. I found it really hard to take off the jersey, and not just because I was sore. It was something deeper than that.

If you went through my words with forensic detail in 2023, ever since it was announced that I would be taking up a contract to play alongside my brother Luke at Section Paloise, better known as Pau, in the foothills of the French Pyrenees, you might notice that I'd never used the 'R' word – retirement.

Even when those of us who were not returning to Super Rugby in 2024 were given a big send-off after our final home Test – a dramatic comeback win over the Wallabies at Dunedin – I chose my words very carefully. Why commit to something so final when there is so much uncertainty in life?

Still, in that moment, just after a crushing one-point loss in a World Cup final, as I went to remove my All Blacks jumper, with its embroidered details of the match on the front and a number on the back that was 14 or 15 too high for my liking, if I'm being absolutely honest, it hit home. This was *almost* certainly the last time I would get to do this. Once I took this jersey off, the chances were that I wouldn't be putting another one on. This jersey, black as the night, had played such a big part of my and my family's lives.

If my narrative that night had been held in the hands of a more romantic scriptwriter, the story might have ended differently. We might have found another couple of points from somewhere in those desperate final few minutes, but it was not to be.

If we cast our minds back a few months, though, perhaps the writing was already on the wall.

*

Once the truncated 2023 Rugby Championship and Bledisloe Cup season finished, we travelled to Napier for the World Cup squad naming and a training camp. While you never want to take it for granted that you'll make the squad – Owen Franks, my fellow novice in 2011, was a high-profile casualty just prior to the 2019 World Cup – my form and my Achilles were holding up pretty well, and uncertainty over Guzz's knee injury placed a premium on experience.

Before heading to Europe, we travelled to Hawke's Bay. When Cyclone Gabrielle had hit in February, flooding had devastated the eastern region. Hannah and I had bought a farm in Rissington, in the hills above Napier, in 2017, and it was out of those hills that rivers like the Esk, Mangaone, Tūtaekurī and Ngaruroro flooded into the cities and settlements below.

Visiting Hawke's Bay was a humbling experience. The community's attitude to the disaster reminded me so much of post-earthquake Christchurch. People have an amazing capacity to deal with the worst nature can throw at them. Even if all we could offer them was some of our time, it felt important for us to be there.

I'd never been to London in summer, so arriving there to face the Boks in August in our final hit-out before the World Cup and finding it stinking hot was disorienting. Normally we'd be wearing thermals and it'd be dark, but this time London had a much sunnier disposition.

Scott Barrett and I were down to start, and because Guzz's knee was still recovering, Tupou Vaa'i and Josh Lord, who wasn't in the World Cup squad, were on the bench and scheduled to come in at the 50th minute.

We spent most of the first half defending short-handed. Scooter's two yellows had turned into red and Sam Cane also spent ten minutes in the bin. We hadn't fired a shot offensively, and yet we were just 0–14 down at half-time. Instead of working our way methodically back into the game, though, we conceded straight after the break. The coaches stuck with the plan and I came off after 50 minutes, which was the right long-term decision, given my grumbling Achilles, but I didn't like leaving. We lost our way in the remainder of the match, eventually crashing to our heaviest-ever defeat in Tests, 7–35. That was a bitter pill to swallow, as we'd enjoyed a good year to that point.

There was external speculation that South Africa had taken the Test a lot more seriously than us, because we had beaten them convincingly at Mount Smart Stadium earlier in the year, but that didn't wash with me. It was a Test match. We went into it desperate to win and gain momentum ahead of a tricky World Cup draw. We just got beaten up.

There was no post-match panic within the squad, but there was concern. Our discipline was something we had talked at length about, but it was consistently letting us down. Against a team like South Africa, being disciplined was a non-negotiable. They thrived on opportunities to kick the ball to the corners, and their drive was hard enough to stop with a full complement of forwards. When you're a man down, it becomes almost insurmountable. We were dragged too easily into a physical slugfest. That was my area, so I didn't take the loss well at all.

The Boks looked primed for a big tournament, but we always knew they'd be strong. In particular, flanker Kwagga Smith loomed as a focus. Whenever he came on he invariably brought pressure, and he was good over the ball. He had a sevens background and was fast enough to be a back, so we knew the 7/1 forwards/backs 'Bomb Squad' split of their reserves bench wasn't quite as radical as it was made out to be, as he had the rare ability to cover a lot of positions. He might nominally have been a forward, but in reality he was an agent of chaos and a player we hadn't figured out how to combat.

The Bomb Squad was a big focus of the media, but mostly we kept our gaze inwardly focused. How could we ensure that our discipline problems didn't resurface? All through the four-year World Cup cycle they had reared their head. We'd be good for a few weeks, then it would come back to bite us. The phrase we liked to use was 'intent with accuracy'. As forwards, we couldn't lose our physical edge, but we needed to apply it in a way that wouldn't attract the wrong sort of attention.

Famous last words.

Off to Adidas headquarters in Germany we went, licking our wounds. Those included a badly sliced knee to Tyrel Lomax, while I had whiplash and concussion symptoms after a Duane Vermeulen tackle from behind. There was no malice in the tackle, but the field in August was harder than usual. Headaches meant I had a low-key training week in Germany, but – on a positive note – my Achilles was responding to treatment and rehab, and was feeling better than it had in a long time.

The Adidas compound is really impressive, based in a semi-rural setting just outside Nuremberg. We stayed where the German football team prepared for their World Cup. We connected as a group, did some discount shopping and trained hard. I also sat down with a boot designer to discuss what I needed to do to take some pressure off my Achilles. I had used the Kakari model for as long as I could remember, but after consultation I switched to the RS15 with some heel raisers to try to take some pressure off.

There was a real sense that the World Cup was upon us. Typically, time flies during the two years after a World Cup, and then the remaining two years pass painfully slowly. Now, after a turbulent period in All Blacks history, we had finally arrived. The nervous excitement kicked in and I knew I had to start preparing for the unpredictable.

We started our French expedition in the north, in Arras, and took a trip to Caterpillar Valley, a World War I Commonwealth War Graves cemetery. The valley was captured in July 1916 by Allied forces, but was lost to the German advance of March 1918, before being retaken by the Welsh Division in August that year. A small cemetery was created there to house the dead, but this increased massively following the November armistice, when more than 5500 soldiers were brought in from the battlefields and makeshift graves of the Somme. Close to 3800 of the soldiers buried at the cemetery are unidentified. On the eastern side of the cemetery is the New Zealand Memorial, commemorating the men of the New Zealand Division who died in the Battles of the Somme in 1916, and whose graves are not known.

There is an All Black buried there, Bobby Black, who hailed from Dunedin's Pirates club. According to his profile on allblacks.com, 'his speed and quick acceleration made him an asset as a first five-eighth'. He won a place on the All Blacks' tour of Australia in 1914 and might have expected to make some more if war had not intervened.

The visit was a humbling experience, and I donated a signed jersey to the Commonwealth War Graves Commission. It was highly emotional seeing the graves, reading the names and, most poignantly, the ages of the dead. It might be a cliché, but it is no less true to say that Bobby Black's story, like that of the thousands of young men alongside him, helped put everything we were about to go through into proper perspective. It is impossible to visit these places and not come away moved. You try to put yourself in the shoes of those men who every day knew that the difference between life and death often owed more to dumb luck than anything else.

The Pioneer contingent of the Māori Battalion had been based in Arras. There was a network of tunnels and caves they used, both to house soldiers in and launch attacks from. Through the tunnels there was a lot of 'artwork' – silver ferns and 'kia kahas' scrawled on the walls, which had been there since the Great War. There was the Blenheim tunnel, the Nelson tunnel and a bunch of Kiwi street names for the makeshift thoroughfares.

It was amazing watching guys going through these caves and reading headstones to find connections to family back home. I found a Whitelock and put flowers on his grave. There were five Whitelock brothers who enlisted from the United Kingdom, and some served with the New Zealand forces. My understanding is that at least two of them died, but this is something I'd like to research more. Colesy and Tamaiti Williams worked out that they had family in those caves and tunnels. Jum Turtill, Hannah's great-great-grandfather, was buried about an hour away from Arras.

As a team, we continued to train hard, but were doing so with a view to having a mini-performance spike for our opener against France, our key pool match. In this way it differed from our successful campaign in 2015, when a 'softer' pool draw meant that we aimed to peak in the knockout stage. Having said that, Argentina really put us under the pump at Wembley in 2015, and on another day our yellow cards might have cost us, which just shows how different World Cups can be. This time around, with one of the tournament favourites France and another Six Nations team, Italy, also in Pool A, we did not have the luxury of looking ahead.

We moved to our team base in Lyon, which was in the grip of a heatwave. We'd been preparing in saunas in New Zealand, but still the heat was a shock. Lyon has a reputation as being the gastronomy capital of France, but we were limited in how much we could enjoy that side of life while preparing for a huge game. I'd been to the city once before, in 2017, when we played a French XV there in a non-Test fixture. Luke had captained the All Blacks that day but I hadn't played. My abiding memory of Lyon then was that it pissed down all week, so it was nice to get a different view of the place before we moved to Paris by train ahead of the tournament's opening match.

*

Paris is a massive, cosmopolitan city far removed from France's traditional rugby heartland in the south, but it had taken the

Rugby World Cup to heart. We saw so many people in Les Bleus' colours. The heat remained unrelenting and the hotel we were assigned to was questionable, but not as bad as some made out. There was nothing drastically wrong with it, but air conditioning would have been nice. Behind the scenes, management were trying to get answers as to how we were assigned substandard accommodation, but as players we just got on with it, drank a bit more water than normal and kept the curtains closed in the morning to keep the heat out for as long as possible. We were fine.

We spent time at training working on silent lineout calls, because we suspected the noise at Stade de France would be deafening. We felt like we had a great game plan, but just before the game Sam Cane's back started to spasm. He'd been troubled by that in the past, but not to this extent. It meant that, at the eleventh hour, Dalton Papalii was named at openside flanker and Tupou Vaa'i – 'Toops' – a natural lock, went to blindside flanker because Shannon Frizell was still unavailable. With Toops in the starting line-up, it meant Brodie had to cover lock from the bench; his injured knee was, at best, just okay.

We started positively in front of a crowd that remained at fever pitch throughout, scoring early after Mark Telea reeled in a Beauden Barrett cross kick, and played well throughout the first half. Our accuracy wasn't quite where it needed to be, which prevented us from adding to the scoreboard, but we were in a good spot down 8–9 at half-time. We'd seen a lot of what the French had to throw at us and it didn't feel like we couldn't handle it, as long as we maintained our discipline and were clinical with our possession. We were ready to make a real mark on the tournament.

We again scored early through Telea in the second half. But it was the hosts who came home much stronger. A familiar failing showed itself when Will Jordan was put in the sin-bin for taking out a player in the air. We had opportunities but never nailed them. Telea's try after half-time should have been a platform for us to build on, but it proved to be the opposite, being pretty much our last positive contribution to the match.

We kept giving away penalties and they kept kicking us into more and more trouble. We ended up needing to score twice late in the game, and we gave away a late try while trying to run it out from deep, so the 27–13 scoreline wasn't quite as bad as it looked. Even so, it was two big losses in a row. All of a sudden we were one upset in pool play away from being the first All Blacks team not to make the knockout stage of a Rugby World Cup. That was a sobering thought.

I was a grumpy lock forward. The last two Tests had seen us post a record loss against the team we mark ourselves against the most, and then a first-ever loss in World Cup pool play. I was sick of adding to a bunch of records I never wanted, and I wasn't ready to listen to the talk about South Africa losing their first match in 2019 (against us) and going on to win the tournament. As an All Black, you have to win every game. Simple. That was always my mindset. If you indulge the thought that you can afford to lose one and still progress, you're already giving yourself an excuse. I hate that sort of talk.

We licked our wounds and went to rugby heartland in Toulouse to beat Namibia 71–3. I gave away the penalty for their three points, but it wasn't a game we were ever challenged in because our scrum was too good and our defensive lineout was sound. In that type of game, it's about managing your standards – which was why I was gutted to give away that penalty – and picking out a couple of aspects to work on. We decided we wanted to be really smart at scrum time and work with referee Luke Pearce, after – in Fozzie's words – we had 'painted the wrong picture' for Jaco Peyper in the loss to France.

The scrum is such a complex area and warrants special attention. One of the reasons we were able to turn around the Bledisloe Cup match in Dunedin just prior to the World Cup was because Colesy had come on in the second half and worked really well with referee Karl Dickson, talking him into allowing us to increase the speed of our hit.

Following the Namibia Test, we had a fortnight between games, so we staged a camp in Bordeaux, on the Bay of Biscay. Included in the camp was a day out at Arcachon, a coastal town famous for its oysters. I'm not a big fan of the mollusc, but on this occasion at an all-you-can-eat buffet I downed so many I reckon I got gout.

It was a bit of a novelty having such a big break early in a campaign, but we knew we had to switch on for Italy at Lyon, a must-win match. We'd been meant to play them in Japan in 2019, but Typhoon Hagibis had rolled in and the game was called off on safety grounds, which ended their hopes of qualifying for the quarter-finals. This was a chance for them to exact some revenge on Mother Nature and us.

The last time we had played Italy, in November 2021, we had detected some genuine improvements in their play. Their inclusion in the Six Nations tournament and a burgeoning age-group program were starting to produce more consistent performances. In short, despite our record against them, we were not taking this match lightly. We couldn't afford to let another nation score a first win against us.

This was the match in which I took the All Blacks' caps record off Richie. I was named on the bench, which – all diplomacy aside – I was absolutely filthy about. It was a must-win match and a milestone game for me, and I felt like I was playing really good rugby and had earned the start. The coaches knew I was pissed off, but selection was their prerogative. I couldn't bitch and moan about it – the needs of the team always trumps the individual. I was told that my leadership and control were needed at the back end of games. I had to find a way not just to accept that role, but to embrace it.

I had a long talk to my mental skills coach, Dr Ceri Evans, because I didn't want my disappointment to affect me or the team. I knew, too, that managing the end of a game, particularly when it's close, is vital, so I wanted to leave no stone unturned in nailing my role. 'Intent with accuracy' off the bench was just as important as it was in the first few minutes.

Before the game, Rick came into camp and presented me with my 149th jersey. Down the bottom of an All Blacks jersey, along the seam, is the player's name and cap number. It's always embroidered black on black because we want it to be understated. This time it was embroidered in gold, which was a nice touch.

I like to keep the jerseys that mean a lot to me – to be honest, they all do. After the Namibia Test, when I'd equalled Rick's caps record, I was fairly agitated when my jersey went missing in the wash. I contacted the hotel and the laundry, but nothing. I put it on the team WhatsApp in case it had got mixed up, but after a few days of hearing nothing I assumed some local opportunist had picked it up for a five-finger discount. Out of the blue a few days later Jordie Barrett texted me, blasé as you like, telling me it had come back in his washing and he'd had it all along. That boy is going to knock over a few major milestones himself, so I'll be interested to know if he's quite as relaxed about his own property when that time comes!

In Lyon we absolutely thumped Italy. They started brilliantly and threw everything at us, and after we repelled that initial onslaught and scored straight after, they had nothing left. You could see the fight leak out of them. Our defensive accuracy was mostly great, although the Italians did score a couple of tries that gave our coach some ammunition to use in training.

By the time I got on to Parc Olympique Lyonnais, the game was well and truly over as a contest. Even so, I was pretty content with how the reserves kept the momentum up. In the end, 96–17 probably saved a few blushes, as racking up three figures against a Six Nations team would not have been a great look for the sport, but I was gutted. We had a couple of chances late but didn't nail them. Scoring 100 points against a Tier One team at a World Cup was a record I wanted.

Hannah and the kids had arrived in France, and I got a buzz to see them all there. After the game, the new All Blacks record-holder went up to his wife for a cuddle and a chat, but all I got was a frazzled: 'Never again am I taking kids to a game that kicks off at nine pm.' Lovely to see you too, Hannah!

By that point, it felt like I had become a one-man media machine. I'd done several weeks of extra press and speeches to the boys after Test matches 148 and 149, and now I was set to play my 150th in our final pool match, against Uruguay.

My teammates had wanted me to run out of the tunnel early for my 149th Test, but I had resisted. In my mind, there is no difference between a 'game' and a 'Test' in the All Blacks jersey. If you're picked to play for the All Blacks, you're an All Black, whether that match is against South Africa in a Test or the Barbarians in a non-Test match. I knew that Richie had played one match that hadn't qualified as a Test, whereas I hadn't, so for me 150 appearances was the true record (although I might be the only person who thinks like that).

Against Uruguay I was picked to start and we won 73–0, with the zero being the most important number in that score. Sam Cane and Jordie Barrett had recovered from their injuries, so things were starting to take shape as we approached the knockouts. That was probably not a Test that would live long in most fans' memories, but I had a lot of fun. I went back to calling the lineout and playing the role I had traditionally done.

Uruguay presented me with a jersey with 150 on the back. We had a beer with them and spent a bit of time enjoying that win, rather than getting straight into the recovery shakes. There are a few traditions in rugby that we need to protect. Even in this age of nutritional awareness, the beer with the opposition should not be discarded. This is when you get to know your opposition as real people, not just players. That's why I remained jealous of all those who had played for the Barbarians – they always seemed to have a mate on the other team.

I was asked in the mixed zone whether it was nice to have an 'easy-beat' before the quarter-finals, which was so unfair. Uruguay were good. They pushed France big time, and had never relented against us. Those sort of throwaway comments annoy me, because the Uruguayans had well and truly earned our respect. Those guys don't go through the Tier One development paths that we enjoy. They have to work bloody hard to be a Test rugby player without all the advantages we are afforded.

After my 150th, I spoke to the players in our rooms. I focused in particular on the locks, and talked about Guzz and how much rugby we had played together, and the successes and challenges we faced. It was the same with Scooter and our long partnership at both Test and Super Rugby level. I reminded Toops that he was not only the present but the future as well. Richie had earlier spoken about how much he treasured the caps record, and how gutted he was to lose it, but how proud he was of me at the same time. I told the boys that I'd feel the same way. It's the individual record I'm most proud of, but I desperately want it to be broken. Why? Because, like Richie before me, we have broken down barriers once thought impossible; more importantly, losing that record to a younger man means we've inspired the next generation to be even better.

I also talked about how I thought the best players I'd played with weren't only the most spectacular, but those who made those around them better. Conrad Smith sprang immediately to mind. What a player he was. He played 94 Tests and might not have had a highlights reel to match that of some others, but if you asked Ma'a Nonu, Sonny Bill Williams or Julian Savea how important he was, they'd tell you he was a master at doing the small stuff that created space for them to work their magic. I expressed the hope that my teammates would view me in a similar way – as someone who had done a lot of the unglamorous work that helped them shine.

During my various speeches around this time, I also thanked people from the wider All Blacks community who had been there for me – people like Nic Gill, Pete Gallagher, George Duncan, Bianca Thiel, Darren Shand, Gilbert Enoka and Katrina Darry. They'd all seen me grow up as a player and a person. I talked about leaving the All Blacks jersey in a better place. I received a nice text from former New Zealand Rugby chief executive Steve Tew, who said I'd 'darkened the jersey'. In a different context that might sound like an insult, but to us, with black as our colour, it is the ultimate compliment.

*

Second place in our pool meant we travelled back to Paris to face a quarter-final with the winners of Pool B, Ireland. They had achieved that status by beating South Africa 13–8 in a titanic encounter. Ireland were the number one team in the world, and while sometimes the rankings could prompt a bit of sarcastic humour from the boys, this was no false position. The men in green had earned it. Their record against us in recent years was exceptional.

I was named on the bench again. The decision was not as deflating as it had been for the Italy game, as by now I was slightly more accepting of my role, but I was still disappointed. But I knew the match would likely go down to the wire, so that final half-hour was going to be critical and I would have to be switched on. Again I had a good catch-up with Ceri, working through various scenarios and discussing how I could use the mental space to power up.

Ceri could square me up pretty quickly with a direct question or challenge; at other times he knew I only needed a gentle push. In France, when I felt a little grumpy, or perhaps even a bit vulnerable due to my reduced role, he did some of his best work.

Working in that mental space is one of the biggest growth areas in my time in professional sport. I'd always seen my mentality as a strength – growing up with three brothers toughens you up to a degree – but Ceri opened my eyes to the gains I could still make. If you can use professional help to get stronger in the mind, why wouldn't you?

Ireland presented a unique challenge. There was a genuine rivalry between them and us now, and there was some talk in the media about us hating each other after some of the Irish comments following their 2–1 series win in New Zealand. I can genuinely say Ireland don't rub me up the wrong way – not in the way some other teams do. Ireland has earned the right to see themselves as big dogs, and pressure brings out the best and worst in people. We're all competitive, alpha-type males, and we might all say and do things we regret, but it's fans who drive the hate, not players. We take out any frustrations we might have through sheer competition.

As for the game – it's funny comparing the fans' and pundits' views to my own. I've heard a thousand times that this was one of the greatest games ever played, and while that might be true, from my perspective it was a Test we gained control of early and then relinquished too easily.

We got to 13–0 after 20 minutes and were dominating, making all the play and asking Ireland to do all the defending.

An All Blacks side at its peak would have probably put that game away, like we did when we got on top of France early in the 2015 quarter-final, and Ireland four years later. Perhaps that sounds a bit unfair. Ireland are, of course, allowed to play well, but I couldn't help but think we missed an opportunity to go up a gear and apply more scoreboard pressure. Instead, we watched them fight their way back into the game, with soft tries to a couple of guys we knew well, Bundee Aki and Jamison Gibson-Park.

At half-time we were up 18–17. It had been a fans' dream: close, two tries each, the ball in play for long stretches. Just after half-time Will Jordan scored a fantastic long-range try after Richie Mo'unga broke from our half to establish the all-important eight-point gap. That became one point when we conceded a penalty try off a lineout drive. Not only that, but Codie Taylor received a yellow card – our second, after an earlier one to Aaron Smith. More yellow cards in big games was so frustrating, and our lineout drive was leaking points like in the bad old days.

A penalty moved us to four points up, and that was the end of the scoring, but there was a lot more rugby to come. Ireland should have scored again off a lineout drive, but Jordie spotted Rónan Kelleher detaching himself from the drive, so he came in from his position in the line and made a phenomenal defensive play – as valuable as any try he'll ever score – to hold him up. It was a match-winning intervention. If they'd scored, we would have had time to come back, but it would have been bloody difficult.

Much has been made of us defending 37 phases at the end of the match but, as Fozzie noted, they didn't challenge us too much, so it was a case of getting our tackle height right, between knee and hip, getting away from the breakdown quickly and back into line. We had a couple of opportunities to get over the ball. I thought I had a chance on about the 14th phase but decided against it, and Ardie had a chance about ten phases later and was perhaps a bit unlucky not to win the penalty.

Finally, with Ireland deep inside our 22, Brodie made a low tackle and I went high, so I could release straightaway and seize my opportunity. I got my hands on the ball while holding my own weight. The whistle sounded. Even though I knew I'd got it right, I still felt anxious that Wayne Barnes hadn't seen it the same way. I needn't have worried. His arm was pointing in the right direction and, with time well and truly up, the game was over. We'd won 28–24. It was gratifying to play a key role at the end, especially because some specific things I had talked about with Ceri had come to pass. We had talked about the game boiling down to a key moment and that I would have to commit to it fully.

There were a few words spoken after the game, which have been widely reported. I wasn't involved, didn't hear it and didn't think a lot about it. It's just part of the game. I imagine it's just like sledging in cricket. Every team has their talkers and stirrers, but for me it's better when that verbal stuff is left on the pitch and at 80 minutes you shake hands, say 'well done' and have a beer.

I was never much of an instigator of that sort of chat, but if you came at me I'd bite back. Whenever the Crusaders and Hurricanes met, Colesy and I would enjoy a fair bit of dialogue, though you'd be doing well to keep up with his constant dribble.

Freed from the pressure of having to make our way home as early as any All Blacks side before us, we relaxed and had the privilege of watching the France–South Africa quarter-final the following evening. I don't watch a whole lot of rugby because I can't just enjoy it – I'm always analysing. It's the way my mind works. France were arguably the best team in the world at that time, but sometimes the best team in the world loses to the best team on the day. South Africa just found a way, as they so often seem to.

We were not taking Argentina lightly ahead of our semi-final, even if others were. Like Ireland, they had shown the ability to beat us recently if we were a touch off our game. We'd played them in Mendoza earlier in the year and beaten them easily, but this time we were expecting a much more cohesive team.

I was named to start, so I was pretty excited, even if I suspected that it was partly about managing Brodie's minutes ahead of a possible Rugby World Cup final. The maul had been a weapon for Argentina – they loved to drive from a long way out – so that became the big focus in my preparation.

In the nicest possible way, this game didn't feel like a semi-final. Argentina challenged us at the start, but only came away with three points – and then we built a big lead. Just before half-time we scored a brilliant training-ground try, and that felt like a big blow. Nuggy scored just after half-time and we were humming along nicely, accumulating points and fully in control. Everything pretty much went to plan, apart from Scooter's yellow card, which was inexcusable, and which he felt terrible about. For some reason we didn't put him on again when his ten minutes was up, which was not a decision I agreed with. It might have been made with the best of intentions, but it looked arrogant.

After the drama of the quarter-final weekend, our 44–6 semi-final victory was generally seen as a bit of a letdown. But we hadn't given Argentina any chance to get back into the match. Unlike against Ireland, once we got in front we shut them out. We'd been really good, whereas South Africa had not been convincing in their semi-final. England had played to their own strengths and put the Boks under massive stress – but the South Africans, as ever, had found a way to win.

16

THE END OF THE WORLD

GOING INTO THE FINAL, we had everyone to choose from. The grim reaper, Ian Foster, showed himself on Monday night to tell each of us whether we'd made the starting XV or the 23. I'd gone from the XV to the 23. Internally, I took it about as well as you'd expect, but I was pretty sure it was coming and so outwardly I put on a brave face. I didn't agree with the decision – but then I wouldn't, would I? The simple fact was that in a squad of 33, you'd have 18 players gutted they hadn't made the starting line-up, and ten absolutely gutted they hadn't made the match-day side at all.

There was plenty of analysis and learning during the week, but also a lot of laughter and fun. The prize was so close. We were playing the old foe, the team we'd split matches with during the year. They'd had a series of close games, and even though they'd lost Malcolm Marx to injury, we knew they'd still try to beat us up front. Without putting too fine a point on it, their game plan tended to revolve around denial: they'd try to stop us getting the ball to our backs in the right parts of the field. If they could do that, they knew, they'd be more than halfway to victory.

Wayne Barnes was appointed as the referee of the final. Back in 2007 he'd become public enemy number one in New Zealand after his handling of the quarter-final loss to France, but he never bothered us at all. It's a hard job and all refs have their quirks. I didn't care how people reffed, as long as they were consistent. If you go by the letter of the law, then go by the letter of the law; if you're going to let things go, let everything go.

All players had different journeys to the final and different motivations, but mine were obvious: I wanted to be the first man to win three titles, and I wanted to do it in front of my family. I had 14 tickets for the final and used them all. In the stands at Stade de France were Hannah, her sister and the kids (who were obviously over their jet-lag nightmare), Mum and Dad, George and Kayla, Adam and some good family friends.

From our perspective, the first half was a mess. South Africa might see things differently but it was not a great spectacle. It was stop-start, full of whistle and errors. We also conceded two yellow cards, one of which, Sam Cane's, was upgraded to red. The instant I saw the replay of Sam's incident, I thought, 'Oh no, this is not looking good,' but we had solid contingency plans, with Jordie Barrett joining the scrum, and four-man and five-man lineouts assisted by quick calls and throws.

Somehow we went into half-time only down 6–12. The difference between Stade de France and Twickenham a couple of months earlier was that we were more composed and showed signs of playing good rugby. It's an uphill battle whenever you're playing a man down, but we knew that if we could assert some control in the second half and stay accurate, we'd have a fighting chance.

That was basically what happened. We adjusted well. I came on in the 55th minute for Shannon Frizell and prepared to receive a kick-off after Aaron Smith appeared to have scored a try, but the TMO went back to a lineout and found an Ardie Savea knock-on. We got a penalty instead. Shortly after, Beaudy scored near the sideline, but Richie missed the conversion that would have edged us in front.

South Africa had already gone to their bench, and although they'd played with a man advantage for much of the match, they were deeper into the red zone than we were. I felt they were there for the taking. Deon Fourie had come on early for Bongi Mbonambi, and while Fourie was a very good utility player, we now had the advantage in scrums and were getting into their lineout in a big way. It felt like we had all the momentum and that any score would have landed like a knockout blow.

The big moment came with a little more than five minutes left, when we had a penalty on the angle near halfway and elected for a shot at goal. I'm not arguing with the decision we took, because if it had gone over we likely would have won. It was within Jordie's range, but complicating the matter was the fact that he was obviously gassed. He'd played brilliantly at second five-eighth – and, when required, on the side of the scrum – and was running on fumes. After Jordie's miss, we still had time to make something happen but we lacked field position and direction. I don't know why Richie wasn't on the field. He had consistently shown he could make something happen from nothing, but he was taken off in the 75th minute. I suppose, though, that when you lose by just one point, you can second-guess every decision.

With time up, it came down to a final scrum, and to our frustration the ball didn't go in when we probably had an edge.

Game over.

Silver medal.

'Gutted' doesn't quite cover it. The opposition had been on the ropes but we hadn't been able to square them up for the final blow.

So South Africa took from us what we thought we had, which was the unofficial title of the greatest rugby nation on Earth. They'd gone back to back, and won three tournaments away from home. They now had four titles to our three. The stats don't lie.

In the post-match huddle, I told our guys that there was no way anybody could fault our effort, urgency or desperation. I'm not sure if they took it in, but I hope so, because they weren't just empty words. I meant them.

Hannah brought the kids down to the ground. We walked slowly around the field, thanking the crowd. I was numb to the joy on the other side of the greatest rivalry in rugby's divide until I saw Damian de Allende, my old teammate at Panasonic, coming the other way. He knew the kids so we stopped for a chat. Two old friends who minutes ago were mortal enemies. Now one was feeling on top of the world, while the other was feeling like crap.

It was nice to chat. We said nothing particularly meaningful but it reinforced for me that I have nothing but respect for the Boks. They had a huge night of celebration ahead, while we had something different to contemplate. So we retired to the changing sheds and shed our second skins.

It took me a long time. There was a lot to digest. This wild trip, which had begun on a foul night in New Plymouth 13 years ago, was coming to an end.

Sharing a moment after the World Cup final with Damian de Allende.
(Michael Steel/World Rugby via Getty Images)

17

A CONVERSATION WITH MY FAMILY

OVER THE COURSE OF researching the details and recollections that make up my story, many conversations were had with family and others that played a big role in my development as a person and a player. The stirring up of old memories was a lot of fun. Here's a distillation of some of those conversations.

Cast: Caroline (Mum), Braeden (Dad), George (oldest brother), Adam (big brother), Luke (little brother), Darron Larsen (basketball coach), Rob Jones (school housemaster), Hannah (wife).

EARLY DAYS ON THE FARM

Caroline: Braeden was still playing club rugby for High School Old Boys when Samuel was born. He must have finished in 1989. I was in the stands in the club final against Varsity, I think, holding on to baby Sam, and George and Adam kept getting on the field.

Braeden: I thought to myself, 'Bloody hell! This is a final – who's that on the field?' I looked over and they were my kids.

I went to Flock House, the farm training centre near Bulls, when I left school, then went to Canterbury for a few years, where I met Caroline. When I came back to Manawatū, we had all these All Blacks playing for us. We had Gary Knight, Bruce Hemara, Frank Oliver, Mark Shaw, Geoff Old, Mark Donaldson, Doug Rollerson, Lachie Cameron, Mark Finlay, Craig Wickes. I was the youngest forward on that Manawatū team.

Caroline: You won that final. I think you got two tries that day and came off thinking, 'That'll do.' It was getting a bit busy with a big farm and three young boys (and Luke still to come), so Braeden made the call to finish playing.

I often get asked who my favourite son is. I don't know how they can ask me that. Cheeky buggers. I loved them all equally. The others always reckon Luke was the spoiled one, but I don't know if that's true. They were all spoiled.

Braeden: The boys did a TV show where Adam said Luke only stopped breastfeeding because he was going to be late for the school bus. Sam and Adam reckoned they only each got three weeks each, but Luke always got special treatment.

George: The old farmhouse had a grass tennis court. Mum and Dad used to put us in there to play because it had a high chain-link fence. It didn't take us long to learn how to climb up over it.

Adam: Rugby started early with us. We did play a bit on the tennis court, but our favourite 'pitch' was the trampoline. We played 'knee rugby', two on two, the two middle ones took on the oldest and youngest. George was always the strongest, so this was a way to even it out. It would just turn into a massive wrestle. It would normally end with someone crying – more often than not Luke, because he was the baby, but Samuel and I might have shed a few tears from time to time too.

George: Everyone had moments of getting shitty, but it was nothing we didn't get over.

Luke: There was a lot of competition growing up, and Sam – being just a couple of years older, and my roommate – was the obvious one for me to target. As a younger brother you're trying to prove yourself all the time, and taking on George – he was a teammate – and Adam probably seemed unrealistic, so Sam was my target. There were a few fights, a few tears from time to time, but a lot of laughs. That competition at home instilled a lot of the things we took into sport and life, really.

Adam: We always did things together, whether it was playing sport or setting off down the farm to do a bit of possum hunting or get up to mischief. We could be a bit rough on Luke. We'd jump on our bikes, but it took Luke ages to learn how to ride one so he'd set off on foot and always get to where we were ten minutes later, and by then we'd be ready to head off to the next place.

Because George and I roomed together and were a bit older, we'd sometimes decide on things we wanted to do without Samuel and Luke hanging around, and the easiest way to do that was to tell them we were going to a place on the farm where there were a lot of ferrets you had to fight your way past. Samuel wasn't keen on non-domesticated animals.

Luke: I'm grateful for my childhood growing up and all that space. I actually can't imagine growing up as four boys in town. Trouble follows boredom and we were never bored. We were also fortunate in that we weren't that far from Palmy, so it wasn't like we were totally isolated at the end of a road hundreds of kilometres from the nearest city.

GETTING FED

Caroline: Sam could never keep the fat on. His legs above the knee were skinnier than below – we always used to joke about that. He didn't get really tall until we sent him away to boarding school. In Year 10 he came home one weekend and I was like, 'Holy heck, what have they been feeding you?' He just sprouted. Mind you, his grandfathers were both six-three, six-four.

George: At home we'd go through a box of Weet-Bix between us for breakfast. We always had roasts for dinner, a two-litre tub of ice cream and a big tin of fruit salad for dessert. We were a big-eating family.

Caroline: Sam reckons he was skinnier than the rest because he always sat at the end of the table, and by the time the food was passed down to him there wasn't much left.

Luke: He probably missed the odd breakfast, because Samuel loved his sleep. I can still see his mop of long hair up one end of the bed and his feet hanging out the other. That and his Britney Spears music he insisted on listening to.

Braeden: He was always last out of bed.

George: He was so slow to eat. We'd all hoover up our food and he'd still be at the end of the table, just chewing away in his own time. We weren't allowed to get down from the table until he'd finished, so he wasn't always popular.

Adam: We never used to go out for dinner much when we were kids, but when we did I don't think it was that relaxing for Mum or Dad. As soon as we sat down they would order for all of us – four burgers or four plates of fish and chips – and tell the people running the place that it would be a good idea to get the food on the table quickly because they had four boys who were capable of wrecking the place.

INTRODUCTION TO FOOTY

George: My earliest memories of rugby are on the frosty fields of Ongley Park. Samuel tagged along with Adam and me. He might have been playing juniors for Old Boys, Dad's club, before he had started school. He would have been attracted by the fish and chips on the way home after practice on Thursday.

Adam: Mum and Dad were awesome supporters all the way through but they were low-key. It wasn't until we got to high school that Dad started to understand that he had some talent on his hands and we could play a bit of rugby. That's when he started to commit to coaching. Up until then he would be out on the farm on Saturday mornings, come in to take us to footy, watch our games, then we'd stop for a pie and a can of fizzy on the way home. Dad would be back into farm work until we got around the table that night and talked about our games. He obviously loved rugby, but I never felt like he was pushing us hard in that direction.

We'd have these VHS tapes, Super Rugby highlights or All Blacks top tries. I can't remember exactly what they were, but I know as kids we'd stick these tapes in the machine one after the other and watch them back to back for hours at a time.

Samuel would have picked up things from that, I certainly did, watching your heroes at that age.

Dad encouraged us to play in the backs because he probably knew with our size we'd eventually move into the forwards and he wanted us to grow our skill level. Samuel, being tall, was always a forward, but Luke and George definitely spent time in the backs as kids.

George: After school, Mum would pick us up from the bus stop, which was about three kilometres from here. Often she'd just pick our bags up and we'd run home. That was rugby training for us. We would have been between eight and 12, I guess.

SCHOOL DAYS

Caroline: When it came to high school, they were always going to go boarding.

Braeden: It was cheaper than keeping them at home and paying for food and petrol. If they were home, they would cut loose on the farm and we wouldn't see them for homework.

Caroline: Their dad and grandad had a history at Feilding High School, but the main thing for me was that it was co-ed.

George: Feilding High was renowned as a middle-of-the-road state school. Being the eldest, I led the way, so wherever I went, the others were always going to follow, so Mum and Dad sat me down to talk about which school I should go to. They just wanted us to grow up to be good people. They wanted us to be able to associate with women respectfully, and had some concerns that growing up in a house with four boys and then going to an all-boys school might have stunted that.

I was probably a bit upset, because most of my rugby friends were going from intermediate to Palmerston North Boys' High, but I look back on it now and we made the right choice. I have no qualms about it whatsoever. Going to Feilding made us work harder. We were playing First XV by Year 11. It was not easy. We were going out there and getting hidings. I remember Aaron Smith, who dripping wet was 50 kilograms, playing first-five as a Year 11 against these big Wesley College men. Future Wallaby Sekope Kepu was 130 kilograms as a No. 8 and lining him up.

Caroline: When we had all four of them there it was a bit embarrassing. We'd take them over and they'd have all their bikes and duvets and gear. I had to put a horse float on, and they were so embarrassed when we rocked up in that.

George: Roger Menzies came in as principal and suspended so many kids straightaway. He set the standard really high.

Braeden: George got in a bit of trouble, but he was never suspended. Samuel was the only one who was suspended.

Caroline: Didn't it involve throwing eels into the girls' showers?

Braeden: I'm not sure if that was the specific incident, but I do know the girls got their own back for that and put some old chooks in his drawers.

Caroline: I got the job of going over to pick him up. I got there and he was sitting on a bench seat with his head down. Got in the car and he never said a word the whole way home because he was so scared about what Braeden was going to say.

Braeden: He thought he had been expelled.

Caroline: Yes, he didn't know the difference between a suspension and an expulsion.

Luke: Samuel was sent away to boarding school, and it wasn't long before he was sent home for a cold shower and a bit of self-reflection. I think I quite enjoyed that.

George: The hostel manager was a guy named Rick Francis, who was the most instrumental single figure, outside our immediate family, in our careers.

He formed our habits. He was massive on goal setting. That's where the red book comes from, which Samuel lives by. He made a huge difference to our lives by making us reach for something and then holding us accountable to that. He was also big on the basics of life. We didn't take to the field in dirty boots. We didn't start our day with unmade beds.

Dad came on board with Rick to coach the colts, and we started from the bottom up, started tripping up a few big teams. We beat Kelston one year, which was an eye-opener for them.

Darron: Rick was walking me around the school when I joined the staff. George and Adam were in the pool and he introduced me. I was like, 'How long have you two been working here?' Turns out they were Year 11 and 12. They looked like fully grown men, shaving twice a day.

Rob: When I first came, I thought George was on the staff. Those boys would always look you in the eye and shake your hand – sometimes a bit harder than it actually needed to be.

Darron: Sam didn't play basketball in Year 9 but I had brought a whole lot of basketball-mad kids with me from North Street Intermediate to Feilding High, and he fell in with them as a friend group. At the end of Year 9 he asked me if he could play basketball. What was he then, 1.88 or 1.89 metres? I just said, 'Yes please.'

George: I knew Samuel was really talented from a young age. I don't think Adam will mind me saying that Samuel and Luke had a skills base that was higher than ours because Dad learned things along the way to help develop them earlier and faster. Adam and I were like guinea pigs, in a way. The other thing was that they played basketball. Looking back, that really helped with their coordination. It really balanced Samuel and Luke's skill sets, and they were both far more comfortable than me in particular with the aerial and ball-handling side of the game.

Braeden: When Sam and Luke used to come home for the weekends, they'd be constantly playing one-on-one with each other. When one of them scored they'd always say, 'Oh, baby!' We ended up naming one of our horses O Baby and she was the top three-year-old harness racing filly in New Zealand.

George and Adam weren't basketballers, but they were good athletes. George was a good runner, but Adam was elite. He never lost a race at Feilding High. Never. He always made the final of the 1500 metres and the 800 metres at the New Zealand Secondary Schools champs.

Caroline: Adam could run all day. He had the endurance.

Luke: I was a bit behind Sam in terms of what I offered in basketball. He had that extra height. I had a role to play in the team and provided that, but in terms of taking my game to the next level, rugby always collided, so high school was my level. I had a bloody good time, though.

Darron: In Year 12, Sam was invited by Basketball New Zealand to a camp for the top 30 school players in the country. It was at the same time he was picked for a national rugby squad, so he had to make a choice. His choice was this: pay

$560 and get yourself up to Auckland for a basketball camp, or show up to a flash hotel and get a big bag full of new kit for free to play rugby.

He liked basketball a lot, but, realistically, rugby was always going to be his path.

It would have been nice to see how far he could have gone because he had the physical attributes and he worked so hard. He did the grind work. Similar to rugby. When Sam was in Year 13, we finished third at regionals, having lost to the eventual national champions, St Pat's Town, in the semi-final. We qualified for nationals and would have done really well but we lost Sam, Mitchell Crosswell and Luke, who were playing for Hurricanes schools that same week. We lost three of our main six or seven players. We ended up pulling out of nationals because we would not have been competitive. I'd suggest with those three we would have been top eight definitely, and a real chance of top four.

His court vision, his passing, spatial awareness and above-the-rim skills he all transferred to rugby. Luke was a little more coordinated than Sam, but not as big. By Year 10, Sam was starting to dribble the ball. Yeah, a couple of attempts ended with the ball in the stands, but by Year 13 he could take the ball, run it up court a few steps and hit someone in the lanes in transition. You have to remember he started a year later than most, but worked that little bit harder than anyone else to catch up.

He could have made a career out of it, but not the same as rugby. Actually, I shouldn't say that, because Samuel worked so bloody hard, I don't really want to put a limit on what he could have achieved as a basketballer. He might have been a couple of centimetres short to make the NBA playing the type of game he did – but you know what, the way he worked at his game, he might have made it anyway.

He had a will to win and a doggedness. That group I had, I was tough on them in a way I probably couldn't get away with in this generation of kids. The amount of running I made them do at training, the water bottles that were thrown or kicked into the stands, the amount of pens and clipboards that were broken because I was so intense – they loved it, they didn't sulk, they soaked it up.

George: It was at school where we, as brothers, probably thought, 'Yeah, we could be okay at rugby.' We were all making Manawatū rep teams and Hurricanes schools. We had a lot of good guys around us – Nick and Mitch Crosswell, Chris Walker, Richie Tichborne, Daniel Smith – he was electric – but also a lot of players who never played again when they finished school.

Sam and Luke benefited from Adam and me going before them and accumulating this knowledge about what it took to stand out.

We'd be glued to the TV on Friday nights watching the Hurricanes. For whatever reason – call it the Rick Francis influence – we'd be pausing it, asking each other what we'd do in certain situations. All of us have been captains, and I reckon you can trace those leadership traits back to then. We just loved the game and quizzed each other all the time. 'If you were captain, what would you do here? If you were calling the lineout, would you go front, middle or back here?' We still do it now if we're together, but I tend to fall asleep during the night games, being a dairy farmer.

Adam: I was playing for Hurricanes schools and Samuel was skinny and rawboned. He was named in the New Zealand Schools team in Year 12 and I remember thinking, 'Wow, that's amazing. He's still got another whole year to go.' At the time he was still playing basketball and I think that was amazing for his skills. He played rugby above his head so much better than other tall kids his age. That was such a point of difference for him.

Darron: Luke was the most outgoing one, George was the most serious – he was head of the hostel in Year 12 and seemed to know what he wanted out of life. Adam was the most focused on his study and Sam was probably the rebellious one. Initially, schoolwork didn't seem that appealing to him, but I think a bit of Adam's diligence started to rub off on him.

Adam: Mr Francis was all about getting your shit in order. We did prep every night and I found that I really enjoyed it. I worked hard and before I knew it I was in the top academic bar for my year and was doing all the geeky subjects: chemistry, physics and calculus. I enjoyed learning, and I enjoyed getting good marks.

Caroline: All the boys were really good with talking to their elders. Senior citizens, old ladies. They get that from Grandad. If you were seated on a plane next to John and were counting on a bit of peace and quiet, you were out of luck because John loved meeting new people and finding out what made them tick.

They communicated well with their teachers and hostel masters.

Rob: Sam was in the middle of everything at school, but he wasn't necessarily a ringleader. He was a quieter type of leader.

People followed him, but not because he told them to or was a 'look at me' type of student.

We were a big goal-setting school under Rick. So in Sam's Year 13 group we had to come up with a training program, and had to state some short-term and long-term goals and say how this training program was going to help.

Sam's long-term goal, the one he wrote down, was to play at the 2011 Rugby World Cup. He asked me what my goal was. At the time I was doing a bit of ice climbing and I said, 'I love the thought of Mount Everest – I'd love to climb that.'

He said: 'I'll make the World Cup and you have to climb Everest.'

I'm like, 'Let's do it.'

I've still got that piece of paper somewhere. He typed it out.

Every time I see him, he'll ask, 'Have you done Everest yet?'

ON THEIR CHARACTER TRAITS AND HARD WORK

George: Adam is the joker of the family. Samuel's a bit quieter, a bit more like me in that he takes things pretty seriously, although he's probably a bit more relaxed than I am, and Luke, being the youngest, was just happy to go with the flow, but he possibly holds things in a bit more.

Luke: I was very lucky to have three older brothers. They set a really high standard at whatever they did, whether it was at home on the farm, at school or even just in how they dealt with people.

George: We were always told to stick together when we were growing up, and, being the oldest, I took that responsibility seriously. So yeah, I looked out for him, but we all looked out for each other, really. We could be problematic from time to time, like when we locked the babysitter out of the house and wouldn't let her in for an hour. There were a few tears that night when Mum and Dad got home, but all pretty harmless stuff.

As rugby players, I was the guy who grinded away. Adam, he had a massive engine. Huge. Probably the hardest-working back I've played with. Samuel had that natural height and skills to go with it, and Luke probably had the best pure skills out of the lot of us.

Caroline: In terms of personalities, the boys are all similar but different. I know that's not very insightful, but it's true.

Braeden: Adam has always been the most underestimated of the boys, probably because he played in George's teams and George was always captain, was always talking, and by default Adam was in his shadow.

Caroline: Adam is a deep thinker and a real people person. That's why he loves real estate, because he's always talking to people.

Braeden: George wouldn't have the patience for real estate because he's so cut and dried. He'd be like, 'This is what it's worth so either pay it or piss off.'

Caroline: They always fronted up and worked on Christmas Day.

Adam: It was the way we were brought up. You pitched in and helped out where you could, whether it was covering the silage stack a few hours after dark to get it done, or milking on Christmas Day. Even now, if we're home we'll get up at 4 am to go down to the shed and work. Two would go to one shed, two to the other and it was always a race to see who could get done quickest and get home for breakfast.

Those things Mum and Dad instilled into us, and they kept us humble. Dad didn't get School C. He got a lot of canings but he was smart. He started that business with 60 hectares and now he's got two and a half thousand cows. They have a massive asset and employ 15 people. Dad didn't go to uni and Mum worked at home, but they've been extremely successful, are good people and we're bloody lucky to have them as parents.

We were all so lucky to be able to play professional rugby but we'd still get a kick out of going home and working on the farm and being able to give the staff time off on Christmas. It was a way that Mum and Dad could make sure we never forgot our roots, and to be honest, they didn't have to ask.

ON LEAVING HOME FOR CANTERBURY

Braeden: People assume they all just followed George down to Canterbury, but that's not how it worked at all. They all went on different paths and George's actually started at Otago.

George: After a summer at my uncle's farm in Te Pōhue – I started to get fit and strong running all his hills – I went to Telford, the farm training school near Balclutha. I'd been there a few days when I had the New Zealand Under-19 trials in Taupō. I won the fitness test and got named as captain, and that was massive for me as I'd never made New Zealand Schools. I had envisaged a life on a farm with a bit of footy, but from that trial on, rugby took over.

Adam: George was smart in a really practical way, but I wanted to be the first from the family to go to university and get a degree. I took pride in that because I showed Samuel and Luke that it was possible for us farm boys to get decent marks and to go to university, and they both followed with scholarships.

They had to work on being studious, whereas I think I'm more that way by nature.

Luke: I was born in January so I was quite young for my year group, so I did a year abroad working at Loughborough Grammar School in the East Midlands. I was an extra staff member to help with school trips and in the sporting department. When I started, there were kids at the school older than me and I couldn't go to the pub with the other staff because I wasn't 18. I had a great time, though.

I didn't play rugby for a year. It gave me the opportunity to have a clean-up operation on my knee. Canterbury were really good. Like Sam before me, they basically let me give my body a rest before I tried to crack the professional game.

George: The others all ended up at university in Christchurch, which is pretty cool. I was flatting in Dunedin, playing club footy for Alhambra-Union and had just started making the Otago team when I got a call from Robbie Deans. He said that he thought I was a number seven and asked me if I wanted to give it a crack in Canterbury and the Crusaders.

Luke: I played for four or five years at Canterbury and had some opportunities with the Crusaders, but I was lacking a bit of identity. I don't mean this in a negative way at all, but I probably needed to break free of family. I had all that comfort and familiarity of having family around. The simple fact is that I felt like I had a lot more to give in terms of playing and leadership, but arguably wasn't playing to my potential, or just showed glimpses of it. Jamie Joseph flew me down to Dunedin, gave me a chance, and it was the best thing that happened for my rugby. I had four amazing seasons down there and have a lot to thank them for. Jamie and Tony Brown simplified what they wanted out of each player, what they wanted out of each position. Scott McLeod was a big influence, too. I started playing with a clarity I had been lacking.

LIFE AFTER RUGBY

Hannah: When Sam first made the All Blacks he was still finishing his degree at Lincoln, but even then he was worrying about what he was 'going to do'. It didn't matter how often I'd tell him to just enjoy being a professional rugby player, in the back of his mind he always knew his career could end at any time. I don't know if that makes any sense for people who don't know him, but that's how he was.

Buying the Hawke's Bay farm in 2017 not only gave Sam a bit of peace of mind for when his career finished, but it also gave him something else to keep his mind occupied. It wasn't rugby all the time.

George: I did a year in Japan at Panasonic in 2014 and promptly retired. I probably had a bit of good rugby left in me but I was over it, especially the demands of the game off the field. I was never that keen on that side. I still loved playing the game, but all the other stuff, I was sick of it, to be honest.

Kayla was playing hockey for New Zealand and there was an opportunity on the farm here. We didn't want to live our lives in different parts of the world for six months of the year, so while it was a massive call to retire, it was also an easy one.

Braeden: Half the farm is Braeside – mine and Caroline's side – and half is Galaxy. We've sold George and Kayla half the cows and he leases Galaxy.

George: I'm well established here now, and that was the other thing. I didn't want to play till my mid-30s and then take five years to get established on the farm, because I wanted to enjoy my kids from their ages five to 15. Those are golden years as far as I'm concerned, and I didn't want to spend every waking minute on the farm trying to establish myself when they were at that age.

Adam: Steve Hansen told one of the boys – I can't remember if it was George or Sam – that if I'd played number seven I would have been an All Black. Instead, I was a midfielder who often played on the wing. I wasn't an out-and-out speedster but I worked hard, chased every kick, got touches on the ball, won all the fitness tests and made a career out of that. I'm proud of my career and am stoked to have played for New Zealand Sevens. I had some bad injuries. I dislocated my elbow at Bayonne in my fourth game. I had it put in a sling and it locked at 90 degrees and I couldn't bend it. I had to have that operated on and fixed in New Zealand. I suffered a number of concussions, and the last one just wouldn't come right so I retired after 2017.

The first year or two after I retired was pretty tough. I was always angry at myself. I kept second-guessing myself as to whether I should have played on. I was still fit and there was part of me thinking I should have played on to 35 or 36. Yeah, that first year or two was not a good time in my life, but now I've found something I love doing in rural real estate. It's a job where I can really use all my skills: my accountancy degree, my networks, my people skills and my interest in farming all come together.

Luke: I learned from Adam having to retire early after head knocks that you don't always get to dictate how long you play for, and in the end I wanted to have an overseas experience before the game slipped away from me, which is why I left for Pau in 2019. The All Blacks were out of my control, to an extent. You're relying on a couple of opinions to fall your way. I wasn't like Sam, who was picked if he was available.

Braeden: Sometimes I think the Whitelock name might have been a positive and a negative for Luke.

Luke: I was probably viewed as the youngest Whitelock brother. I was overthinking things, trying to be perfect at everything, rather than nailing the things I was good at. I was identified as having some talent and got a taste of the All Blacks early on, so it was always a goal, but it wasn't until I actually let go of that goal and focused on what I could control that I got back in. I felt like I was playing well for a couple of years, but in 2019 I didn't make the team for Japan, and Claire and I decided it was time to enjoy a new experience.

Choosing to play overseas and what opportunity to take was in my control. There is no right or wrong, but ultimately it was the decision Claire and I made at the time rather than staying in New Zealand to chase another game for the All Blacks. The Highlanders had changed by then too, and it felt like time to hand the keys of that team over to the next generation.

That left Samuel as the last one standing in New Zealand.

ON SAM'S CAREER

Adam: There was one time that stood out for me in terms of realising Samuel had something special about him. It was his first year of Super Rugby. We were playing a semi-final against the Bulls. I was a non-playing reserve, sitting in the stands in a hostile environment in Soweto and watching Samuel steal a lineout ball off Victor Matfield and burst through the lineout on a 20-metre run. This was just going through the heart of the Bulls' biggest strength, and I recall watching it and thinking Samuel really had something about him – but he was my brother, so I couldn't get too excited.

I never got nervous watching Sam and Luke through the bulk of their careers, but I found myself getting nervous in 2023 because it was coming to an end and I honestly didn't want it to end for Samuel, because I got so proud watching him. I never took it for granted, sitting there on a Saturday night watching my brother run out to play for his country.

I watched all his games, but I didn't give him advice. I would send him a little text, though, telling him I liked his lineout steal or his hit on Brodie or something like that. I don't know why. I guess I wanted to let him know that I was not just watching the game, but I was keeping an eye out for him. It probably sounds a bit funny, but it was my way of telling him how proud I was of him without actually saying those words.

Braeden: Sam has a great temperament but he had to work on it big time. He used to get very nervous. He was tall and bony and was so anxious to get out there with his brothers that he used to get injured quite often in those first five minutes. We used to get him to rub his neck or shake his legs out just to get him less keyed up. So he had all these little twitches I could pick up on. I still know when he's going to jump at the lineout, every time. I can read his cues.

Hannah: The World Cup loss in Japan was the lowest I had seen him. Not getting the opportunity to play in the bronze-medal match. He tends to keep a lot to himself. He doesn't like to bring his 'rugby moods' home to me, but that was a time when it was obvious to me how much he was hurting.

The other time I noticed something was wrong was when we came back from Japan and went straight into Level Four lockdown. I was trying to engage in conversations and was getting nothing back. I was thinking to myself, 'What is happening here?' He finally told me that he'd just spoken to Fozzie and he'd been told Sam Cane was going to be captain. He was really gutted. He knew it was totally Fozzie's call to make, and that he'd do what he thought was best for the team, but a lot of the conversations they'd had were the types of conversations you'd think a coach would have with his incoming captain before they started a new era.

He'd never been promised anything, but he was second-guessing whether taking the sabbatical in Japan had hurt his captaincy chances. That, coming relatively soon after the World Cup disappointment, was the lowest I have seen him.

Caroline: Did I get nervous watching Sam play? Yes and no. You always want the best for your kids – you always want them to do well. You never want to see them hurt, so it's natural to feel a bit anxious. When the boys are playing I tend to watch them and no one else.

Hannah: I'm a naturally competitive person and I do get nervous in close games. When I watch, I watch to make sure Sam's up and moving, but I try to catch the wider game. I think Caroline pretty much exclusively watches him. I definitely check in after tackles and I touch base visually from time to time, but I'm not too obsessive.

Freddie is a pretty intense spectator when it comes to Dad. There was a game when we were at Panasonic, and Emma, David Pocock's wife, was trying to chat to Freddie, and he told her to shush because there was a scrum he wanted to concentrate on.

Caroline: Sam would give me a peck on the cheek when I went to his games. It was usually a bit grizzly and sweaty, but I took what I could get.

Hannah: Sometimes I would have liked him to show a bit more of his personality. People always say to me how serious Sam is, and that's not what he's like to be around. Absolutely, he takes his rugby and his leadership roles seriously, but at home he's always joking and stirring the pot. In public, he's more guarded and aware of how quickly something he says could be taken the wrong way.

He doesn't have a big social media profile, and when Silver Lake came in [the investment firm purchased a stake of the All Blacks in 2022], there were a lot more demands on the players for promotional stuff and I don't think Sam was big on that side of the game. His view was that it was their job to win games of rugby and all the other stuff would fall into place behind that.

I do ride the highs and lows with Sam because I see how much work goes into it, but there are times when I try to play, not so much the devil's advocate, but maybe try to offer a perspective that moves him out of that All Blacks bubble.

Caroline: Sam's very level-headed. I've only seen him have a real paddy twice. It takes a lot to get him rattled.

Luke: It's not until you step back and get an overview on it that you think, shit, to play one game for the All Blacks, the history and immense competition to make a squad and play a Test, is a hell of an effort. Then I think about Sam's career and I'm incredibly proud. The quality of rugby he's given to that black jersey is exceptional. He's played a lot of 80-minute Tests, he's played alongside some of the greatest All Blacks we've ever known, in some of the best All Blacks teams we've ever seen. When you step back and think of the two World Cups and trophies and milestones, it's hard to fathom.

He's a humble, head-down, work-hard guy. Yeah, I'm incredibly proud of what he's achieved and I hope he's as proud of it as I am. Sometimes it's hard to tell because he doesn't reflect that much. Now it's coming to the end. I hope he's thinking more about what he's managed to stack up.

Adam: My favourite photo is the one of us all in our black jerseys – Sam, George and Luke with their All Blacks jumpers and me in my Sevens one. It was Grandad's idea. We didn't really think anything of it, got it done and then probably went hunting. Now I look at it and it's one of my proudest moments.

I don't think we took it for granted then, but after you retire you certainly get more appreciation for the fact you got to play professional rugby with your brothers. The Barretts are getting to do it now, and you can see how much it means to them.

Luke: To have him come here to Pau and there being a full-circle element to it is really special.

Hannah: I know he's made his decision to retire, but he also told me he's going to keep a couple of pairs of boots aside just in case.

I probably haven't told him enough how proud I am of what he's done in rugby – but I am. We've grown up together and I've had a front-row seat to this unbelievable career and because it's been such a whirlwind, especially when you add children to the mix, we probably won't appreciate it fully until it's over and we can start to reflect.

George: Do I reflect on it? Yeah, it's pretty neat. The best thing about it, though, is all four of us are still as close now even if we live in different parts of the world. I take as much pride in that as I do in our rugby careers. We're bloody lucky.

My favourite thing to do in life these days is to watch the kids play sports – and it won't just be my kids, it will be Adam's, Samuel's and Luke's too. Let's face it, there's a good chance they're going to be sporty. We don't know where we're all going to end up, but I want to enjoy that, and I want Mum and Dad to enjoy watching the next generation too.

EPILOGUE

AS I WRITE THIS now, in February 2024, as the pit of a Pyrenees winter turns slowly to spring, I can smile about my ignorance. Remember what Andrew Hore had said to me and Owen Franks as we basked in the afterglow of the 2011 World Cup win? Never a truer word was spoken.

Right then, I had no f***ing idea what we'd just done.

Three World Cup campaigns later and with a stack of air miles, a bunch of records, plenty of mighty wins and too many crushing losses, I now have some idea, although I'd never claim to have figured it all out.

When I look back now, I see that my career has an unmistakable shape to it – that my club and international careers have worked on almost opposite trajectories. I had played more than 100 games for the Crusaders before we won anything, then it was bang, bang, bang, bang, bang – we couldn't stop winning. To an extent, with the All Blacks, it's been that journey in reverse. Back-to-back World Cup wins, going a whole year unbeaten, playing a style that nobody could live with, then a gradual diminishing of our status as the best team in the world.

If you drill down, 2017 was the year it started to change. That was when the Crusaders shed their 'dark days' as we won our first Super Rugby title since 2008. It was also the year the sense of inevitability and maybe even invincibility around the All Blacks started to slip. You can call it an aura if you like, but it's not a word we used.

I'm a terrible loser – just ask Hannah – but as much as losing grates, you learn to take the rough with the smooth. I'm not saying you necessarily want to embrace failure, but I have come to accept that it is part of who I am as a player and a person.

You'll know by now that I'm a huge basketball fan. If you'd asked me midway through high school what sport I thought would take me furthest, I reckon I would have said basketball. My height and wingspan gave me natural advantages over most schoolboys, but that wasn't the main reason I took to it. I loved the rhythm of the game, and also that it didn't matter what time of day or night it was – you could grab the key to the gym and shoot buckets with your mates. At that age I breathed the game. In particular, I loved doing the sort of unglamorous stuff on the court that others didn't – an attitude I would carry into rugby.

I've read books on many NBA greats, including Michael Jordan. There's a quote of his that accompanied an advertising campaign that became famous. It goes like this: 'I've missed more than 9000 shots in my career. I've lost almost 300 games. Twenty-six times I've been trusted to take the game-winning shot and missed. I've failed over and over and over again in my life. And that is why I succeed.'

I would never compare myself to Jordan, who is one of the most transcendent sports talents to ever lace them up, but there is something in his message I really relate to.

Yes, I'm the most capped All Black of all time, and I couldn't be more proud of that record. Even if I'm overtaken at some point, I will forever be the first All Black to have played 150 Tests. I've won two World Cups, 11 Tri Nations or Rugby Championships and a Grand Slam. I've taken home the Kelvin R. Tremain Memorial Trophy, seven Super Rugby titles, National Provincial Championships and the Ranfurly Shield. I've never played on a team that lost the Bledisloe Cup. Six times out of seven, teams I have played on have won the Hillary Shield; five times out of six the Dave Gallaher Cup. The last time New Zealand did not hold the Freedom Cup was the year before I made my debut.

But, equally, the past 14 years have not all been shiny trophies and personal accolades. At one time I held the record for the most yellow cards for an All Black (although I'm pretty sure Scooter Barrett has taken that dubious honour from me). I was a member of the first All Blacks team to lose a home series against Ireland. I was on the first All Blacks team to lose to Argentina, and the first to lose to them in New Zealand. I played in the All Blacks' heaviest loss to the Wallabies, at Perth in 2019. I was on the field for the All Blacks' heaviest ever Test loss, against South Africa at Twickenham in 2023.

I was the captain who handed the Dave Gallaher Cup back to France in 2021. I will never be part of a team to beat the Lions in a series.

And here is the stat that, for me, stands out the most: no All Black has experienced as many Test losses as me. Some 22 times I took the field, sang the anthem, performed the haka and went on to lose.

Twenty-two. If you look back in history, some very fine All Blacks did not get the chance to play 22 Tests, let alone lose that many.

As for the last of those losses … Yeah, that one still stings a lot.

*

I probably didn't appreciate just how different I'd find the French Top 14, especially culturally. Accepting a loss has never been my forte. My record with Section Paloise, as it stands at this very moment, is mixed. As I write this we have played 20, won 10 and lost 10. We're right in the mix for the playoffs and for a lot of people in the town and around the club that is a real sign of progress, but being the way I am, I instead tend to look at the games we could have and probably should have won and think we could be doing even better.

I'm getting a real kick out of watching the way Luke has developed as a player and a leader. Seeing him communicating with his teammates and referees in what, to my ears, sounds like perfect French blows me away. All bias aside, I've always rated him really highly as a player, and my respect for his ability has gone up another notch.

At Pau, we love to see ourselves as the underdog, which is a completely different mindset to the teams I've come from. At Canterbury, the Crusaders and the All Blacks, we embraced the pressure that comes from being favourites. It's a jarring shift to go into a team that sees every win as an overachievement. If there's one thing I'd like to impress upon my teammates, it is not to shrink from pressure – instead, we must always remember that if we play to our potential and play to our plans, we will win.

It's been a challenge coming to a new environment, but Hannah and I knew it would be. Communication is the key. My French is very average. Hannah's is much better than mine, and while rugby is a game you can, to an extent, play on natural instincts, it helps when your tongue works as fast as your brain does. I'm still searching for, and not finding, the right word or two at critical junctures.

The kids have adjusted well. Within a couple of days, they had made friends at their new school, and they've enjoyed having their dad around a bit more than they're used to. Every now and then they admit to missing friends and family back home, but it's nothing that a bit of distraction – like a trip to the snow – can't fix.

It was a disorienting feeling being in the middle of a European winter when preseason prep for a New Zealand season was getting into full swing. In the middle of Razor's first All Blacks camp, my phone started pinging. Players were messaging me their fitness test scores. I was hearing about PBs and what life was like in the All Blacks under the new regime.

I'm not going to lie: getting those messages was strange. I felt something similar to, but not exactly the same as, FOMO (fear of missing out). Seeing my old mates Owen Franks and Ryan Crotty back at the Crusaders has added to that sense. They're the same age as me but had left New Zealand after the 2019 World Cup.

The last Test I played for the All Blacks still haunts me. I texted Fozzie a couple of months after, saying, 'It's a bit of a weird feeling, eh?' He replied that there hadn't been a night that had passed when he hadn't tried to find an extra point or two. That made two of us. That result crushed me in ways other losses haven't. I know there's nothing I can do to change it, but I replay the final stages at Stade de France over and over again in my mind. Was there something else I could have done in my 25 minutes on the field? Was there something I should have seen from my position on the bench? Was there some tool I had learned in my 13 years as an All Black that I could have utilised better? It's literally a pointless exercise, but there you go.

Others are built differently. Take Sonny Bill Williams. The day after our defeat to England in Yokohama at the 2019 World Cup, somebody asked him how he was feeling, and without hesitation he said he was over it already. I couldn't believe it at the time, but a part of me envies him. Sonny Bill was the type of guy who was always looking forward, always focused on the next thing. He knew he couldn't do anything about the past, so why waste a thought on it? As I said, we're all different.

In 2023, I wanted it all. I wanted the caps record, the 150 Tests, the start in another World Cup final. The tickertape parade. It didn't happen the way I drew it up.

*

Epilogue

Will there be another chapter in my rugby story? A coaching story? That I honestly don't know. By the time you read this, maybe things will be clearer, but for now I want to finish by telling the story of a black jersey.

Most, if not all, of my grandad Nelson Dalzell's jerseys were worn and then thrown out, much to the eternal regret of the wider Dalzell/Whitelock clan. If they're still in circulation somewhere, we don't know about it. Mum and her siblings have a couple of little mementos from his 22 matches, including programs and that player-of-the-match cigar, but nothing major. There's no jersey we can display. Incredibly, we met a guy in France who was wearing one of Grandad's All Blacks ties. Mum was pretty keen to get that back in the family, so we made an arrangement that he could have some stuff from me in return for the tie. It was great to have that, but it's not the same.

Then there was Hubert Turtill, known to all as 'Jum', Hannah's great-great-grandfather. None of his New Zealand–based ancestors seemed to have any of his stuff. Certainly Genevieve, my mother-in-law, didn't. Her mother, Hannah's grandmother, had a few items of interest, but gave them away in good faith to somebody who claimed to be writing a history book and never received them back. The 'author' just disappeared.

By coincidence, soon after I'd asked Hannah and her grandmother whether they had any of Jum's memorabilia, an item appeared in *The New Zealand Herald* about an All Blacks jersey that belonged to him that was being put up for auction in Wales. The article was shared on our family group chat, and Hannah looked at me and said: 'I'd love to get that back in the family.'

We contacted the sellers, who were distant relatives of Hannah, and explained who we were and why we wanted it. They were perfectly civil but we couldn't strike a deal to buy it before it went to auction. The auction fell on a day when neither of us could participate, so I must give massive credit here to my manager, Greg Dyer, who not only manned the phones but placed the winning bid. We couldn't follow the auction live, so we had to wait for him to phone through with the good news. The jersey is an extremely valuable piece of clothing, and not just from a sentimental standpoint.

That left me with the problem of how to get it back to New Zealand. Steve Tew was in the United Kingdom at the time, and after I explained what Hannah and I had done, he travelled from London to Wales to pick it up. When he arrived back in New Zealand, Mum and Dad drove from home to Wellington airport to meet him off the plane. It was quite the operation, with the sort of care taken that you might expect of a drug trafficker – which is an apt comparison in a way, as the jersey was wrapped and bundled up like it was a piece of contraband.

The package was taken to the curators at the New Zealand Rugby Museum. They were amazing with the restoration, and now it's on display there. The ownership remains with us, but for now everyone can go and see what we believe is the oldest All Blacks jersey in New Zealand.

There are things in my life I believe strongly in, and one of those is that it doesn't matter when or how many games someone played for the All Blacks – we are all temporary guardians of this magnificent garment we call 'the Jersey'. I got to play in it more than 150 times, Jum Turtill just once.

Epilogue

You don't get to choose your own legacy. That's for others to decide. But I will say this: I hope that in 120 years' time, a distant relative of mine, perhaps someone with All Blacks dreams and aspirations themselves, might find value in the first black jersey I wore.

We fought hard to get Jum's jersey because I know how hard I fought to get mine.

CAREER RECORDS

OF THE

WHITELOCK FAMILY

COMPILED BY CHRIS 'SARGE' JANSEN AND
THE NEW ZEALAND RUGBY MUSEUM

Whitelock family first-class appearances

As of 28 October 2023

	All Blacks		Junior All Blacks	NZ U21 (Colts)	NZ U20	NZ Universities	NZ Baa-baas	Super Rugby	Provincial	Franchise Games	UK Baa-baas	First Class Games	Total Games	Total Points
	Tests	Games	Games											
Alex Dalzell									2				2	
Anthony Dalzell						2			5			16	23	7 Tries
Hamish Dalzell					10	1		2	55				68	3 Tries
Nelson Dalzell	5	17							56			9	87	12 Tries
Allan Elsom	6	15							85			16	122	68 Tries, 1 Dg
Ben Funnell								92	93	1		3	189	27 Tries
Hayden Hazlitt									4				4	
Graeme Higginson	6	14							89			22	131	11 Tries
Will Jordan	33				7			52	34			1	127	104 Tries
Hubert Turtill	1								18			4	23	2 Tries, 4 Cons
Braeden Whitelock				5					35			2	42	
Adam Whitelock								55	55	1		1	112	21 Tries
George Whitelock	1		1	1				85	80	1	1		170	24 Tries
Luke Whitelock	7	1			9		1	102	75	1	5	4	205	21 Tries
Samuel Whitelock	153				5			181	22	1		1	363	20 Tries
FAMILY TOTALS	210	47	1	6	31	3	1	569	700	5	6	79	1658	316 Tries, 4 Cons, 1 Dg

Whitelock family non-first-class appearances

As of 19 May 2024

	NZ Schools	NZ U17	NZ U19	NZ Universities	NZ Sevens	Non-NZ Super Team	Panasonic Wild Knights	Ricoh Black Rams	Kamaishi Seawaves	Section Paloise	Bayonne	Rugby New York	Total Games	Total Tries
Hamish Dalzell							1		9			17	27	1
Ben Funnell	3					5		9					17	25
Adam Whitelock		1			2						16		19	5
George Whitelock			5				9						14	2
Luke Whitelock	3									77			80	2
Samuel Whitelock	4		4	4			5			12			29	1
FAMILY TOTALS	10	1	9	4	2	5	15	9	9	89	16	17	186	39

ABBREVIATIONS USED IN THE TABLES

Dg   Drop goal
Cons   Conversions
Pen   Penalty goals

250+ first-class games

As of 14 April 2024

Player	Years	Games	Player	Years	Games
K.F. Mealamu	1999–2014	384	T.T.R. Perenara	2010–2024	280
W.W.V. Crockett	2005–2019	375	A.J. Wyllie	1964–1980	279
A.L. Smith	2008–2023	366	C.J. Spencer	1992–2005	277
S.L. Whitelock	2008–2023	363	J.A. Collins	1994–2010	275
C.E. Meads	1955–1974	361	S.J. Savea	2010–2023	275
L.J. Messam	2003–2022	351	A.M. Stone	1980–1994	275
S.B.T. Fitzpatrick	1983–1997	348	S.J. Cane	2010–2023	274
M.A. Nonu	2000–2021	348	A.L. Dixon	2008–2021	274
K.J. Read	2004–2020	341	L. Romano	2009–2023	271
R.H. McCaw	2000–2015	334	M.J.A. Cooper	1985–1999	270
T.D. Woodcock	2000–2015	330	D.E. Holwell	1995–2010	270
J.F. Umaga	1994–2011	329	J.M. Muliaina	1999–2014	270
A.M. Haden	1971–1986	328	B.G. Williams	1968–1984	269
Q.J. Cowan	2000–2016	326	J.J. Kirwan	1983–1994	268
R.W. Loe	1980–1997	321	K.R. Tremain	1957–1972	268
O.T. Franks	2007–2024	317	A.M. Ellis	2004–2016	267
B.J. Barrett	2010–2023	315	L.R. MacDonald	1994–2009	266
G.W. Whetton	1979–1995	314	C.G. Smith	2003–2015	266
Z.V. Brooke	1985–1997	311	C.C. King	2002–2018	265
A.K. Hore	1999–2014	311	G.L. Slater	1991–2005	263
W.F. McCormick	1958–1978	310	R.D. Thorne	1996–2011	263
D.S. Coles	2007–2023	308	H.T.P. Elliot	2005–2017	261
C.S. Ralph	1996–2008	306	T.J. Blackadder	1990–2001	260
G.J. Fox	1982–1995	303	K.J. Crowley	1980–1994	260
A.D. Oliver	1993–2007	300	C.H. Hoeft	1993–2005	260
N.J. Hewitt	1988–2001	296	A.S. Savea	2012–2023	260
J. Kaino	2004–2018	296	I.A. Eliason	1964–1982	259
S.C. McDowall	1982–1998	294	C.S. Jane	2004–2017	259
R.M. Brooke	1987–2001	292	B. May	2004–2022	259
R.S. Crotty	2008–2024	290	E. Clarke	1990–2005	258
C.R. Flynn	2001–2017	289	S.J. Bachop	1986–1999	257
D.W. Carter	2002–2015	287	G.A. Knight	1972–1986	255
I.D. Jones	1988–2000	286	G.M. Somerville	1997–2008	255
I.A. Kirkpatrick	1966–1979	286	Tu'ungafasi A.O.H.H.	2012–2024	255
W.K. Little	1988–2000	285	B.A. Retallick	2010–2023	254
J.W. Marshall	1992–2005	284	I.J. Clarke	1951–1963	252
B.R. Smith	2007–2019	284	S.M. Going	1962–1978	252
P.A.T. Weepu	2003–2017	284	B.J. Robertson	1971–1984	250
A.P. Mehrtens	1993–2005	282	C.J.D. Taylor	2012–2023	250

Samuel Whitelock All Blacks statistics

All Black debut	Saturday, 12 June 2010
	vs Ireland at New Plymouth
	aged 21 years, 243 days
All Black last Test	Saturday, 28 October 2023
	vs South Africa at Paris
	aged 35 years, 16 days
Total All Black Tests	153 (26 as a substitute)
Starting positions	Jersey Number 4 : 24
	Jersey Number 5 : 103
	Jersey Number 18 : 13
	Jersey Number 19 : 13
All Black captaincy	18 games as captain
All Black Test points	35pts (7t, 0c, 0p, 0dg, 0m)
All Black number	1104

Most appearances in All Blacks matches

As of 28 October 2023

S.L. Whitelock	153	G.J. Fox	78	C.M. Cullen	60
R.H. McCaw	149	R.W. Loe	78	B.C. Thorn	60
C.E. Meads	133	W.J. Whineray	77	A.O.H.M. Tu'ungafasi	59
K.F. Mealamu	133	A.J. Williams	77	A.G. Dalton	58
S.B.T. Fitzpatrick	128	W.K. Little	75	B.T. Kelleher	58
K.J. Read	128	M.N. Jones	74	S.W. Williams	58
A.L. Smith	125	J.T. Lomu	73	J.M. Barrett	57
B.J. Barrett	124	P.A.T. Weepu	73	C.R. Laidlaw	57
T.D. Woodcock	118	W.W.V. Crockett	72	J.P.T. Moody	57
A.M. Haden	117	A.P. Mehrtens	72	R.F. Mo'unga	57
I.A. Kirkpatrick	113	M.G. Mexted	72	G.B. Batty	56
B.G. Williams	113	S.K. Barrett	71	J.A. Kronfeld	56
D.W. Carter	112	A.R. Lienert-Brown	71	L.R. MacDonald	56
B.A. Retallick	109	J.W. Wilson	71	M.J. Dick	55
O.T. Franks	108	R.M. Brooke	69	B.G. Fraser	55
I.D. Jones	105	O.M. Brown	69	C.S. Jane	55
M.A. Nonu	104	F.E. Bunce	69	K.W. Stewart	55
J.M. Muliaina	102	R.E. Ioane	69	R.A. White	55
B.J. Robertson	102	J.T. Rokocoko	69	P.J. Whiting	55
G.W. Whetton	101	M.W. Shaw	69	G.T.M. Bachop	54
M.Z.V. Brooke	100	B.J. Lochore	68	D.S. Loveridge	54
S.J. Cane	96	C.W. Dowd	67	M.J. Pierce	54
J.J. Kirwan	96	C.R. Jack	67	S.J. Savea	54
C.G. Smith	94	A.D. Oliver	67	Q.J. Cowan	53
D.S. Coles	90	G.M. Somerville	67	W.L. Davis	53
D.B. Clarke	89	I.J.A. Dagg	66	D.J. Graham	53
J.W. Marshall	88	G.A. Knight	66	N.E. Laulala	53
S.M. Going	86	A.R. Sutherland	65	J.C. Ashworth	52
K.R. Tremain	86	A.J. Whetton	65	I.N. McEwan	52
B.R. Smith	85	T.J. Wright	64	F. Roberts	52
C.J.D. Taylor	85	D.C. Howlett	63	R.W.H. Scott	52
S.S. Wilson	85	K.L. Skinner	63	D.C. Howlett	51
I.J. Clarke	83	R. So'oialo	63	M.F. Nicholls	51
A.K. Hore	83	M.R. Brewer	61	R.D. Thorne	51
J. Kaino	83	M.J. Brownlie	61	W.J. Wallace	51
A.S. Savea	83	G.N.K. Mourie	61	R.W. Caulton	50
S.C. McDowall	81	R.W. Norton	61	A.W. Cruden	50
T.T.R. Perenara	81	T.C. Randell	61	C.C. Faumuina	50
J.F. Umaga	79	D.Young	61	J.K.R. Timu	50

All Blacks games played by Samuel Whitelock

(+) = substitute; (-) = replaced

2010
12 Jun vs Ireland at New Plymouth 66–28 (+)
19 Jun vs Wales at Dunedin 42–9 (+)
26 Jun vs Wales at Hamilton 29–10 (+)
10 Jul vs South Africa at Auckland 32–12 (+)
17 Jul vs South Africa at Wellington 31–17 (+)
31 Jul vs Australia at Melbourne 49–28 (+)
7 Aug vs Australia at Christchurch 20–10 (+)
21 Aug vs South Africa at Johannesburg
   29–22 (+)
30 Oct vs Australia at Hong Kong 24–26 (+)
6 Nov vs England at London 26–16 (-)
13 Nov vs Scotland at Edinburgh 49–3
20 Nov vs Ireland at Dublin 38–18 (+)
27 Nov vs Wales at Cardiff 37–25 (-)

2011
22 Jul vs Fiji at Dunedin 60–14 (+)
30 Jul vs South Africa at Wellington 40–7 (-)
6 Aug vs Australia at Auckland 30–14 (+)
20 Aug vs South Africa at Port Elizabeth 5–18
27 Aug vs Australia at Brisbane 20–25
9 Sep vs Tonga at Auckland 41–10 (+)
16 Sep vs Japan at Hamilton 83–7
24 Sep vs France at Auckland 37–17 (-)
2 Oct vs Canada at Wellington 79–15
9 Oct vs Argentina at Auckland 33–10 (-)
16 Oct vs Australia at Auckland 20–6 (-)
23 Oct vs France at Auckland 8–7 (-)

2012
9 Jun vs Ireland at Auckland 42–10
16 Jun vs Ireland at Christchurch 22–19
23 Jun vs Ireland at Hamilton 60–0 (-)
18 Aug vs Australia at Sydney 27–19
25 Aug vs Australia at Auckland 22–0
8 Sep vs Argentina at Wellington 21–5 (+)
15 Sep vs South Africa at Dunedin 21–11
29 Sep vs Argentina at La Plata 54–15
6 Oct vs South Africa at Johannesburg 32–16
20 Oct vs Australia at Brisbane 18–18
11 Nov vs Scotland at Edinburgh 51–22 (-)
17 Nov vs Italy at Rome 42–10 (+)
24 Nov vs Wales at Cardiff 33–10
1 Dec vs England at London 21–38

2013
15 Jun vs France at Christchurch 30–0 (-)
22 Jun vs France at New Plymouth 24–9
17 Aug vs Australia at Sydney 47–29

24 Aug vs Australia at Wellington 27–16 (-)
7 Sep vs Argentina at Hamilton 28–13 (-)
14 Sep vs South Africa at Auckland 29–15
28 Sep vs Argentina at La Plata 33–15
5 Oct vs South Africa at Johannesburg 38–27
19 Oct vs Australia at Dunedin 41–33
9 Nov vs France at Paris 26–19
16 Nov vs England at London 30–22
24 Nov vs Ireland at Dublin 24–22

2014
7 Jun vs England at Auckland 20–15
14 Jun vs England at Dunedin 28–27
21 Jun vs England at Hamilton 36–13
16 Aug vs Australia at Sydney 12–12
23 Aug vs Australia at Auckland 51–20
6 Sep vs Argentina at Napier 28–9 (-)
27 Sep vs Argentina at La Plata 34–13
4 Oct vs South Africa at Johannesburg 25–27
18 Oct vs Australia at Brisbane 29–28 (-)
8 Nov vs England at London 24–21
22 Nov vs Wales at Cardiff 34–16 (-)

2015
8 Jul vs Samoa at Apia 25–16 (-)
25 Jul vs South Africa at Johannesburg
   27–20 (+)
8 Aug vs Australia at Sydney 19–27 (+)
15 Aug vs Australia at Auckland 41–13
20 Sep vs Argentina at London 26–16
24 Sep vs Namibia at London 58–14 (-)
2 Oct vs Georgia at Cardiff 43–10
9 Oct vs Tonga at Newcastle upon Tyne 47–9 (-)
17 Oct vs France at Cardiff 62–13
24 Oct vs South Africa at London 20–18
31 Oct vs Australia at London 34–17

2016
18 Jun vs Wales at Wellington 36–22
25 Jun vs Wales at Dunedin 46–6
20 Aug vs Australia at Sydney 42–8
27 Aug vs Australia at Wellington 29–9
10 Sep vs Argentina at Hamilton 57–22
17 Sep vs South Africa at Christchurch 41–13
1 Oct vs Argentina at Buenos Aires 36–17 (+)
8 Oct vs South Africa at Durban 57–15
22 Oct vs Australia at Auckland 37–10
19 Nov vs Ireland at Dublin 21–9
26 Nov vs France at Paris 24–19

2017

16 Jun vs Samoa at Auckland 78–0 (-)
24 Jun vs British & Irish Lions at Auckland 30–15
1 Jul vs British & Irish Lions at Wellington 21–24 (-)
8 Jul vs British & Irish Lions at Auckland 15–15 (-)
19 Aug vs Australia at Sydney 54–34 (-)
26 Aug vs Australia at Dunedin 35–29
16 Sep vs South Africa at Albany 57–0
7 Oct vs South Africa at Cape Town 25–24
21 Oct vs Australia at Brisbane 18–23
11 Nov vs France at Paris 38–18
18 Nov vs Scotland at Edinburgh 22–17
25 Nov vs Wales at Cardiff 33–18 (Captain)

2018

9 Jun vs France at Auckland 52–11 (Captain)
16 Jun vs France at Wellington 26–13 (Captain)
23 Jun vs France at Dunedin 49–14 (-) (Captain)
18 Aug vs Australia at Sydney 38–13
25 Aug vs Australia at Auckland 40–12
8 Sep vs Argentina at Nelson 46–24 (+)
15 Sep vs South Africa at Wellington 34–36
29 Sep vs Argentina at Buenos Aires 35–17 (-) (Captain)
6 Oct vs South Africa at Pretoria 32–30
27 Oct vs Australia at Yokohama 37–20 (-)
10 Nov vs England at London 16–15
17 Nov vs Ireland at Dublin 9–16

2019

27 Jul vs South Africa at Wellington 16–16
10 Aug vs Australia at Perth 26–47 (-)
17 Aug vs Australia at Auckland 36–0
7 Sep vs Tonga at Hamilton 92–7 (-)
21 Sep vs South Africa at Yokohama 23–13
2 Oct vs Canada at Oita 63–0 (+)
6 Oct vs Namibia at Tokyo 71–9 (Captain)
19 Oct vs Ireland at Yokohama 46–14
26 Oct vs England at Yokohama 7–19 (-)

2020

11 Oct vs Australia at Wellington 16–16
31 Oct vs Australia at Sydney 43–5
7 Nov vs Australia at Brisbane 22–24
14 Nov vs Argentina at Sydney 15–25
28 Nov vs Argentina at Newcastle 38–0 (-)

2021

3 Jul vs Tonga at Auckland 102–0 (Captain)
10 Jul vs Fiji at Dunedin 57–23 (+)
17 Jul vs Fiji at Hamilton 60–13 (Captain)
7 Aug vs Australia at Auckland 33–25 (Captain)
14 Aug vs Australia at Auckland 57–22 (Captain)
23 Oct vs USA at Washington DC 104–14 (-) (Captain)
30 Oct vs Wales at Cardiff 54–16 (Captain)
6 Nov vs Italy at Rome 47–9 (+)
13 Nov vs Ireland at Dublin 20–29 (Captain)
20 Nov vs France at Paris 25–40 (-) (Captain)

2022

2 Jul vs Ireland at Auckland 42–19
16 Jul vs Ireland at Wellington 22–32
6 Aug vs South Africa at Mbombela 10–26
13 Aug vs South Africa at Johannesburg 35–23
27 Aug vs Argentina at Christchurch 18–25
3 Sep vs Argentina at Hamilton 53–3
15 Sep vs Australia at Melbourne 39–37
24 Sep vs Australia at Auckland 40–14 (Captain)
5 Nov vs Wales at Cardiff 55–23 (Captain)
13 Nov vs Scotland at Edinburgh 31–23 (Captain)
19 Nov vs England at London 25–25 (Captain)

2023

29 Jul vs Australia at Melbourne 38–7 (+)
5 Aug vs Australia at Dunedin 23–20
25 Aug vs South Africa at London 7–35 (-)
8 Sep vs France at Paris 13–27 (-)
15 Sep vs Namibia at Toulouse 71–3
29 Sep vs Italy at Lyon 96–17 (+)
5 Oct vs Uruguay at Lyon 73–0 (-)
14 Oct vs Ireland at Paris 28–24 (+)
20 Oct vs Argentina at Paris 44–6 (-)
28 Oct vs South Africa at Paris 11–12 (+)

Samuel Whitelock points scored for the All Blacks

Versus	Tries	Cons	Pen	Dgs	Points
Ireland, 12 Jun 2010	2	-	-	-	10
Ireland, 20 Nov 2010	1	-	-	-	5
South Africa, 6 Oct 2012	1	-	-	-	5
South Africa, 17 Sep 2016	1	-	-	-	5
Namibia, 6 Oct 2019	1	-	-	-	5
Australia, 24 Sep 2022	1	-	-	-	5
Totals	7	0	0	0	35

Samuel Whitelock Test record by nation

Test Record by Nation	Played	Win	Draw	Loss	Tries	Cons	Pen	Dgs	Points
Argentina	17	15	-	2	-	-	-	-	-
Australia	38	29	3	6	1	-	-	-	5
British & Irish Lions	3	1	1	1	-	-	-	-	-
Canada	2	2	-	-	-	-	-	-	-
England	10	7	1	2	-	-	-	-	-
Fiji	3	3	-	-	-	-	-	-	-
France	13	11	-	2	-	-	-	-	-
Georgia	1	1	-	-	-	-	-	-	-
Ireland	13	10	-	3	3	-	-	-	15
Italy	3	3	-	-	-	-	-	-	-
Japan	1	1	-	-	-	-	-	-	-
Namibia	3	3	-	-	1	-	-	-	5
Samoa	2	2	-	-	-	-	-	-	-
Scotland	4	4	-	-	-	-	-	-	-
South Africa	24	17	1	6	2	-	-	-	10
Tonga	4	4	-	-	-	-	-	-	-
Uruguay	1	1	-	-	-	-	-	-	-
USA	1	1	-	-	-	-	-	-	-
Wales	10	10	-	-	-	-	-	-	-
Totals	153	125	6	22	7	0	0	0	35

Samuel Whitelock Rugby World Cup Tests

Test	Date	Home	For	Against	Away	City	Tournament
1	Sep 9 2011	New Zealand	41	10	Tonga	Auckland	RWC Pool Match
2	Sep 16 2011	New Zealand	83	7	Japan	Hamilton	RWC Pool Match
3	Sep 24 2011	New Zealand	37	17	France	Auckland	RWC Pool Match
4	Oct 2 2011	New Zealand	79	15	Canada	Wellington	RWC Pool Match
5	Oct 9 2011	New Zealand	22	10	Argentina	Auckland	RWC Quarter Final
6	Oct 16 2011	New Zealand	20	6	Australia	Auckland	RWC Semi Final
7	Oct 23 2011	New Zealand	8	7	France	Auckland	RWC Final
8	Sep 20 2015	New Zealand	26	16	Argentina	London	RWC Pool Match
9	Sep 24 2015	New Zealand	58	14	Namibia	London	RWC Pool Match
10	Oct 2 2015	New Zealand	43	10	Georgia	Cardiff	RWC Pool Match
11	Oct 9 2015	New Zealand	47	9	Tonga	Newcastle	RWC Pool Match
12	Oct 17 2015	New Zealand	62	13	France	Cardiff	RWC Quarter Final
13	Oct 24 2015	New Zealand	20	18	South Africa	London	RWC Semi Final
14	Oct 31 2015	New Zealand	34	17	Australia	London	RWC Final
15	Sep 21 2019	New Zealand	23	13	South Africa	Yokohama	RWC Pool Match
16	Oct 2 2019	New Zealand	63	0	Canada	Oita	RWC Pool Match
17	Oct 6 2019	New Zealand	71	0	Namibia	Tokyo	RWC Pool Match
18	Oct 19 2019	New Zealand	46	14	Ireland	Yokohama	RWC Quarter Final
19*	Oct 26 2019	New Zealand	7	19	England	Yokohama	RWC Semi Final
20*	Sep 8 2023	New Zealand	13	27	France	Paris	RWC Pool Match
21	Sep 15 2023	New Zealand	71	3	Namibia	Toulouse	RWC Pool Match
22	Sep 29 2023	New Zealand	96	17	Italy	Lyon	RWC Pool Match
23	Oct 5 2023	New Zealand	73	0	Uruguay	Lyon	Rugby World Cup
24	Oct 14 2023	New Zealand	28	24	Ireland	Paris	RWC Quarter Final
25	Oct 20 2023	New Zealand	44	6	Argentina	Paris	RWC Semi Final
26*	Oct 28 2023	New Zealand	11	12	South Africa	Paris	RWC Final

* All Blacks loss

ACKNOWLEDGEMENTS

WHEN I WAS FIRST approached about the idea of putting my life and career on the record, I didn't want to write a memoir. Who would be interested in reading a book about me, a kid from the country who never seriously thought he would play a professional game of rugby, let alone have a record-breaking career?

So first I would like to thank the people who convinced me that mine was a story worth telling; that the true value of this book may lie with my children or any grandchildren that may come, when they are old enough and interested enough to read about their dad or grandad.

While I was deciding, I thought about my grandad Nelly, Nelson Dalzell, and how amazing it would have been to have had a written record of his time as an All Black and how much I would have enjoyed reading about it. My late grandad John was a hobbyist author, and his two books are precious family records to look back on.

So to Dylan Cleaver, thank you for the many hours on Zoom, the countless phone calls and back-and-forth emails to put my story down on paper. You have a knack for asking the right questions in the right way – it allowed me to open up so much more than I have ever done during any media interviews.

Thanks to Alex Hedley at HarperCollins Publishers New Zealand for understanding all my emails and for getting all the small details right with the book, the cover and the launch.

Thank you to all the different clubs, unions and teams I have played for: Palmerston North High School Old Boys; Palmerston North Intermediate Normal; Manawatū under-11s, -13s, -16s, -18s; Manawatū Evergreens; Feilding High School under-14s, Colts, 1st XV and Hostel; Merlins; Lincoln University; New Zealand Universities; Canterbury Colts; Canterbury; Crusader Development; Crusaders; South Island; Panasonic Wild Knights; Section Paloise (Pau); NZ Secondary Schools, Under-19s and Under-20s; and last but not least the All Blacks. No matter what jersey I was pulling on I was always 100 per cent committed to that game and that team. It has been an absolute privilege every time.

One team I would love to add to the list before it's all done is Barbarian F.C., the Baa-baas. Time will tell.

I have had some amazing people that have helped me along in my career including coaches, managers, trainers, physios, doctors, massage therapists, player development managers, mental skills coaches, logistics managers, security guards, Adidas reps and all the other sponsors. Thank you for the chats, the laughs and the work. You have all had an impact on my career, some for longer than others. Even if it seemed at times like I wasn't listening, in my own way I did always try to take on board what was being said. It has been impossible to mention and thank everyone in this book individually but know that I have valued you and your expertise. I hope to coach in some form in the future and pass on your knowledge that I have been lucky enough to have collected over the years.

Acknowledgements

I have had some incredible teammates and, as we say, there are many that I would go to war with. I hope you have enjoyed your rugby and the teams we played in together as much as I have. I hope I allowed you to be the best player you could be because I was on your team. The teammates that helped me be a better player simply by doing their job to the highest level were those I enjoyed playing with the most.

While writing this book I was conscious not to pump current players up too much as I know there is already a lot of pressure on players to perform week in and week out. In this regard, I have talked more about people that have already finished their careers, rather than those that are still playing. For the boys still out there, enjoy the journey – it goes so fast.

I have had, and still have, huge family support. Parents, siblings, grandparents, uncles, aunts, cousins, in-laws, nieces and nephews. Whether that's a message of congratulations or encouragement on one of the many family group chats, or being able to see family in the stands after a game, you have been there from the very start, for all the ups and the downs, and regardless of all the outside noise, have always treated me as the same old Samuel – the tall, skinny beanpole.

This book doesn't come together without my brothers, George, Adam and Luke and their families. Like me, you find it hard to talk about yourselves, so thanks for the time you each gave to Dylan during the writing of the book. We love to challenge each other every step of the way. We did it as we were growing up and we still do it now. That has, I think, made us strive to be better in every aspect of life, so thank you. I can now see some of those same competitive family traits coming out in our children. And, just so you know, I haven't changed any of the stories you told and I'm sure you've all added a small amount of GST to those tales!

Mum and Dad, I don't know quite what to say or how to say it. The opportunities that you have given four boys is nothing short of amazing. From brainwashing us as kids to 'never give in' and instilling a strong work ethic, you not only set us up to succeed as best we can, but have given the next generation a head start too. We have had outstanding role models to follow, as you did with your parents. I know you have watched an almost countless amount of games and I know you found it tough on occasion having to choose who to watch when we were playing in different parts of the world. Even now I know you hate missing games and I want you to know it gave us all a lift knowing that you were there watching us having fun over the years.

To Fred, Iris and Penelope: thanks for understanding as best you can why your dad is away so much and misses out on things at kindy and school. One of my best memories (despite the score) is immediately after the 2023 World Cup final. I walked around the stadium with the three of you and watched each of you taking it all in. I'll always remember watching your little faces, watching you smile and wave to the crowd. In that moment you were able to take the hurt of the result away just by being kids. You don't have to play rugby because Dad did, but if you want to, then that's okay as well.

Hannah, we have come a long way since sitting next to each other on that first day at Lincoln University. Best unplanned seating arrangement ever. From that first game for Canterbury, right up until my last, you have been there with me, even if not at the ground, for every single professional game of rugby

I have played. Your understanding of the game is amazing. Thank you for all the times you have given me encouragement, allowed me to vent my frustration or squared me up when I needed it. Thank you for filling up the ice pack, for removing stitches and washing dirty rugby gear. Thank you for being a solo parent to our three children when I have been away – sometimes for weeks on end. And thanks for allowing the end-of-season do to be held in the back paddock! As I have been told countless times, 'The most important selection you will make is your partner.' I made a good one! There is no way any of this would have been possible without you. Thank you, I love you.

To all the fans, thank you for all your support and for loving the game of rugby. Without you, there is no such thing as a professional rugby player. Keep turning up and filling those stadiums. It makes a difference.